Prayer Book Studies Volume Two

Initial Daily Office Efforts, Issues V-IX

Edited by
Derek A. Olsen

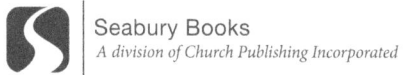

Seabury Books
A division of Church Publishing Incorporated

Copyright © 2026 The Domestic and Foreign Missionary Society of the Protestant Episcopal Church in the United States of America

The English text of the liturgies presented in this book is in the public domain and is freely available for quotation without restriction.

Unless otherwise noted, Scripture quotations are from The New Revised Standard Version Bible, copyright © 1989 National Council of the Churches of Christ in the United States of America. Used by permission. All rights reserved worldwide.

Seabury Books
19 East 34th Street
New York, NY 10016
www.churchpublishing.org

Seabury Books is an imprint of Church Publishing Incorporated.

Cover design by Newgen
Typeset by Integra Software Services Pvt. Ltd.

ISBN 978-1-64065-924-7 (paperback)
ISBN 978-1-64065-925-4 (hardback)
ISBN 978-1-64065-926-1 (eBook)

Library of Congress Control Number: 2025945258

CONTENTS

Introduction vii

Prayer Book Studies V: The Litany

Preface 3

History 5
  1. Source 5
  2. The Problem of 'Leading in Prayer' 5
  3. The Eastern Litany-Form 6
  4. Early Western Litanies 9
  5. The Litany of the Saints 10
  6. Cranmer's English Litany 12
  7. Revisions of the Litany 13
  8. The Use of the Litany 16

Proposed Text 21
  1. Title 21
  2. Initial Rubric 22
  3. Arrangement 24
  4. Alterations 25
  5. Additions 27
  6. Conjunction with the Liturgy 28
  7. The Supplication 28

'The Litany of Saint Chrysostom' 30

The Revised Version 32
  The Great Litany 32
  The Supplication 36
  The Litany of Saint Chrysostom 37

Prayer Book Studies VI: Morning And Evening Prayer

Preface 41

History of Revision 44

Proposed Revisions 47

Outline and Arrangement............................... 49

Recommended Changes 51
   The Introduction................................... 51
   The Opening Sentences............................. 51
   The Exhortations 52
   The Confession and Absolution..................... 53
   Psalms and Canticles............................... 55
   The Creed and Prayers.............................. 58
   Evening Prayer 59

The Order for Daily Morning Prayer................... 61
   The Introduction................................... 61
   The Psalter 65
   The Word of God 67
   The Apostles' Creed 70
   The Prayers.. 71

The Order for Daily Evening Prayer.................... 74
   The Introduction................................... 74
   The Psalter 75
   The Word of God 76
   The Apostles' Creed 78
   The Prayers.. 78

Prayer Book Studies VII: The Penitential Office

Preface 83

Introduction... 86

Proposed New Office.................................. 87

The Penitential Office................................. 88
   Contrition 88
   Self-Examination................................... 89
   Confession and Absolution 90

Prayer Book Studies VIII: The Ordinal

Preface 95

The Ordinal 98

Contents v

The Development of the Ordinal 98
Early Sacramentaries 98
English Ordinals 101
American Ordinals 104

Proposed Revision 105
Changes Common to the Three Rites 106
Changes in Each Rite 109

The Ordinal 112
The Preface 112
The Litany and Suffrages for Ordinations 112
The Form and Manner of Ordaining Deacons 114
The Form and Manner of Ordaining Priests 118
The Form of Ordaining or Consecrating a Bishop 125

Prayer Book Studies IX: The Calendar

Preface 135

The Proposed Calendar 138

Part One
The History of Prayer Book Calendar Revision

The Reformation 150

Red and Black Letter Days 153

Recent Anglican Revisions 156

Part Two
Principles of Calendar Construction

The Development of Saints' Days 159

The Problem of Modern Reconstruction 164

Recent Anglican Calendars 167

Part Three
Proposals for Revision

Principles of the Present Proposals 171

Changes Proposed in the Red Letter Days 174

Notes on the Black Letter Days 176
January 177
February 181
March 184
April 188
May 192
June 196
July 200
August 203
September 208
October 212
November 215
December 218

Appendix 1: Comparative Tables of Anglican Calendars 220

Appendix 2: The Proposed Calendar in Chronological
and Topical Order 245

Appendix 3: Notes on Certain Rejected Commemorations . . 250

Appendix 4: General Bibliography 252

Appendix 5: Alphabetical Index of Commemorations,
with Special Bibliographies 253

INTRODUCTION

The Series as a Whole

The *Prayer Book Studies* (PBS) series documents the 26-year process of study and conversation that led to the adoption of the American 1979 Book of Common Prayer. It falls broadly into two parts, distinguished by the use of Roman numerals and Arabic numerals. PBS I-XVII were published by the members of the Standing Liturgical Commission between 1950 and 1966 to communicate research and draft liturgies leading toward a revision process; PBS 18-29 were published by the various drafting committees between 1970 and 1976 once the revision process was formally begun and the earlier drafts were being transformed into new usable liturgies, leading up to the adoption of the new prayer book in 1979. Finally, PBS 30 and its commentary were added in 1989 to discuss inclusive and expansive language for God for further liturgical efforts.

Context of these Studies

The studies contained in this volume, PBS V-IX, should be seen within the broader context of PBS I-XIV. These fourteen studies that appeared in ten publications (four volumes contain two studies) systematically explore all of the liturgical materials within the 1928 Book of Common Prayer, incorporating scholarly research alongside input from clergy and congregations, concluding each study with a sample liturgy based on the study and reflection of the Commission.

Each of these fourteen studies begin with an identical preface laying out the guiding principles: to objectively and impartially inform the broader church on the principles and issues involved in the revision of each portion, not for the benefit of one theological party but to the education of all.

The overwhelming impression of these documents is of a committee, anchored by Bayard Jones, Morton Stone, and Massey Shepherd Jr.—the professors of the leading Episcopal seminaries of the day—that accomplished its work in a careful and thorough fashion. A great deal of thought, discussion, and argument has gone into these materials. The results are careful and fairly conservative modifications, assuming a retention of the "traditional" Elizabethan/Jacobean idiom of the English Prayer Book and the King James Bible.

These Studies

PBS V

This first study on the Litany follows the typical pattern with a historical survey, principles of revision, and a revised rite. The version of the Great Litany here contains some minor tweaks in terms of phrases and individual words and is substantially found in the revised prayer book. It also includes a Byzantine-derived "Litany of St. Chrysostom" not included in the revised book.

PBS VI/VII

This second study on the Morning and Evening Prayer betrays by its brevity that it is a very modest revision of the 1928 rites. A few new canticles have been added, but psalms are still offered as alternates in Evening Prayer, and the concluding collects are largely those of former editions. The lectionary is not addressed at all.

The third study on the Penitential Office is a revision of the old Commination, a liturgy of repentance originally derived from the Sarum Ash Wednesday liturgy. While bound with the previous study, it does not pertain to the Daily Office. Here, the commission is thinking through sin and repentance from a mid-century psychological perspective. While little, if any, of this material ultimately appears in the revised prayer book, this study is helpful in illuminating their initial thinking around a modern approach to penitence.

PBS VIII

The other study not pertaining to the Daily Office in this volume, the fourth study, contains initial work on the Ordinal: the making of deacons, priests, and bishops. Another conservative revision, it takes great pains to point out that the essential structure and intent of the rite are in no way changed. Thus, the shadow of Roman concerns regarding the efficacy of Anglican orders still lies upon this effort, as well as implications for relations with other Anglican churches.

PBS IX

By far the largest study in this volume (although only half the size of PBS IV on the Eucharist), the fifth and final study tackles the calendar and, in particular, the question of the liturgical celebration of sanctity. While there is the usual survey of historical materials and recent efforts across the Anglican Communion, it is noteworthy that in exploring historical and contemporary sanctoral calendars, there is very little theological discussion of sanctity and how the notion of sanctity connects to Anglican theology as a whole. Thus—in my subjective opinion—the seeds for the ongoing controversy around the prayer book's sanctoral calendar were sown here with the recommendation of such a calendar, but with no clear theology of sanctity to underpin it.

PRAYER BOOK STUDIES V: THE LITANY

The Standing Liturgical Commission
of the Protestant Episcopal Church in the
United States of America

1953

PREFACE

The last revision of our Prayer Book was brought to a rather abrupt conclusion in 1928. Consideration of it had preoccupied the time of General Convention ever since 1913. Everyone was weary of the long and ponderous legislative process, and desired to make the new Prayer Book available as soon as possible for the use of the Church.

But the work of revision, which sometimes has seemed difficult to start, in this case proved hard to stop. The years of debate had aroused widespread interest in the whole subject: and the mind of the Church was more receptive of suggestions for revision when the work was brought to an end than when it began. Moreover, the revision was actually closed to new action in 1925, in order that it might receive final adoption in 1928: so that it was not possible to give due consideration to a number of very desirable features in the English and Scottish revisions, which appeared simultaneously with our own. It was further realized that there were some rough edges in what had been done, as well as an unsatisfied demand for still further alterations.

The problem of defects in detail was met by continuing the Revision Commission, and giving it rather large 'editorial' powers (subject only to review by General Convention) to correct obvious errors in the text as adopted, in the publication of the new Prayer Book. Then, to deal with the constructive proposals for other changes which continued to be brought up in every General Convention, the Revision Commission was reconstituted as a Standing Liturgical Commission. To this body all matters concerning the Prayer Book were to be referred, for preservation in permanent files, and for continuing consideration, until such time as the accumulated matter was sufficient in amount and importance to justify proposing another Revision.

The number of such referrals by General Convention, of Memorials from Dioceses, and of suggestions made directly to the Commission from all regions and schools and parties in the Church, has now reached such a total that it is evident that there is a widespread and insistent demand for a general revision of the Prayer Book.

The Standing Liturgical Commission is not, however, proposing any immediate revision. On the contrary, we believe that there ought to be a period of study and discussion, to acquaint the Church at large with the principles and issues involved, in order that the eventual action may be taken intelligently, and if possible without consuming so much of the time of our supreme legislative synod.

Accordingly, the General Convention of 1949 signalized the Fourth Centennial Year of the First Book of Common Prayer in English by authorizing the Liturgical Commission to publish its findings, in the form of a series of *Prayer Book Studies*.

It must be emphasized that the liturgical forms presented in these *Studies* are not — and under our Constitution, cannot be — sanctioned for public use. They are submitted for free discussion. The Commission will be grateful for copies or articles, resolutions, and direct comment, for its consideration, that the mind of the Church may be fully known to the body charged with reporting it.

In this undertaking, we have endeavored to be objective and impartial. It is not possible to avoid every matter which may be thought by some to be controversial. Ideas which seem to be constructively valuable will be brought to the attention of the Church, without too much regard as to whether they may ultimately be judged to be expedient. We cannot undertake to eliminate every proposal to which anyone might conceivably object: to do so would be to admit that any constructive progress is impossible. What we can do is to be alert not to alter the present *balance* of expressed or implied doctrine of the Church. We can seek to counterbalance every proposal which might seem to favor some one party of opinion by some other change in the opposite direction. The goal we have constantly had in mind — however imperfectly we may have succeeded in attaining it — is the shaping of a future Prayer Book which *every* party might embrace with the well-founded conviction that therein its own position had been strengthened, its witness enhanced, and its devotions enriched.

The objective we have pursued is the same as that expressed by the Commission for the Revision of 1892: "*Resolved*, That this Committee, in all its suggestions and acts, be guided by those principles of liturgical construction and ritual use which have guided the compilation and amendments of the Book of Common Prayer, and have made it what it is."

THE STANDING LITURGICAL COMMISSION:

GOODRICH R. FENNER, *Chairman*
ARTHUR C. LICHTENBERGER
BAYARD H. JONES, *Vice Chairman*
MORTON C. STONE, *Secretary*
JOHN W. SUTER, *Custodian*
MASSEY H. SHEPHERD, JR.
CHURCHILL J. GIBSON
WALTER WILLIAMS
SPENCER ERVIN
JOHN ASHTON

History

1. Source

The Litany-form arose as a special development of the General Intercession in the eucharistic Liturgy.

A universal supplication for all estates of men in the whole Church is explicitly indicated in 1 Timothy 2:

> I exhort therefore, that, first of all, supplications, prayers, intercessions, and giving of thanks, be made for all men: for kings, and for all that are in authority, that we may lead a quiet and peaceable life in all godliness and devotion. For this is acceptable in the sight of God our Saviour, who will have all men to be saved, and to come unto the knowledge of the truth. . . . I will therefore that men pray everywhere, lifting up holy hands, without anger and disputation.[1]

Accordingly, in the first written description of the Liturgy in Justin Martyr, about the year 150, we read that the newly baptized person was brought to 'where the "brethren," as we call them, are gathered together to make common prayers earnestly for themselves, and the newly "enlightened" one, and all others everywhere.' The Kiss of Peace and the Offertory of the Baptismal Eucharist followed immediately.[2] Likewise, these 'earnest common prayers' were also a feature of the corresponding place in the normal Sunday Eucharist, where they followed the Lessons and Sermon, and preceded the *Pax* and Offertory.[3]

2. The Problem of 'Leading in Prayer'

The way in which the specialized structure of the Litany was evolved from the primordial Intercession of the Liturgy is very interesting, and most illuminative as to the character and functioning of the several forms and methods of prayer employed by the Church.

It seems to have been realized from the first that there is a real problem in the effectual rendering of public prayer, to insure that the supplication should be offered by all as well as on behalf of all, and to secure the wholehearted singleness of mind set forth as its goal in 1 Timothy, and the earnestness mentioned by Justin. In terms of the significant phrase of our day, there is no real leading in prayer when the officiating minister voices a general supplication in however telling terms, if the congregation is paying little attention to what he is saying.

---

1. 1 Tim. 2:1-4, 8.

2. *I Apology*, c. 65.

3. *I Apology*, c. 67.

They must bear their part in appropriating his petitions, and in offering them from their own hearts along with their spokesman. And a very practical solution of this problem was found in the use of some form of 'bidding,' to tell the people the subject for which their prayers were desired, and then to provide for some sort of spoken response from them.

This sound general formula was applied by two quite different methods. In Egypt, and throughout the West, the mechanism employed might be called that of *parallelism*. The constituent subjects of a long prayer were taken one at a time. Each one was prefaced by an explicit Bidding addressed to the people. Then there was a pause for each one to make silentprayer in his own heart, with his particular application of the theme. Then the officiant *gathered up* all those unspoken petitions in a summary *Collect*: to which the people replied with the ancient Hebrew response, *Amen*. And so the chain of supplications went on, in the form of paired Biddings and Collects, to the conclusion of the whole pattern.

This procedure was especially characteristic of the Gallican Rite, where it affected virtually every constituent of the Liturgy. The word 'Collect,' indeed, is peculiar to the Gallican sphere of influence. It was unknown to the old Roman Rite, and Rome does not use it now. They always say *Oratio* ('Prayer') for this sort of short summary petition. The temporary use of the term *Oratio ad collectam* in the time of Innocent III at the beginning of the thirteenth century to indicate a 'Prayer over the congregation assembled' to go in procession to the church of a papal 'Station' was never the source of this Gallican expression.[4] Nor did it get its name from the idea of 'collecting' the teaching of the day in the Epistle and Gospel, though that rationalization was also current for a time, and some of our Reformation Collects were written to do so.

But though the term was never understood at Rome, the function of this method was native there. The best of all examples of this form is to be found in the chain of intercessory Biddings and Collects in the special order of service for Good Friday in the Roman Missal. And the original procedure has left its mark upon all the Western Collects, where the initial 'Let us pray' survives from a former Bidding which once mentioned the subject of the prayer, in the brief and summary character of the Collects, and of course in the final *Amen*.

3. The Eastern Litany-Form

A distinctly different application of these same fundamental principles originated in Syria, whence it radiated to all the Eastern Churches in the great domain of Antioch, and eventually throughout the world. Instead of the rhyming couplets of paired Biddings and Collects, this Syrian form followed the pattern of a 'periodic' sentence, which does not pause until the whole of its elaborate course of thought

---

4. Innocent III, *De sacro altaris mysterio* II. xxvii.

has been completed, and presented all the heads of a General Intercession in a single unbroken series, and only then concluded by gathering up the intentions in the minds of all by a final summary Collect.

If this were all, we would have found a Bidding Prayer, like the one on pp. 47-48 of our Prayer Book.[5] The thing that created the characteristic Litany form was the bringing in after each suffrage of the fixed response of 'Lord, have mercy!' by the people. It is of course possible that the Litany may have originated as a Bidding Prayer, to which the people made spontaneous response. If so, we would have expected that the acclamations of the people would have been

---

5. A Bidding Prayer

¶ *To be used before Sermons, or on Special Occasions.*

¶ *And* NOTE, *That the Minister, in his discretion, may omit any of the clauses in this Prayer, or may add others, as occasion may require.*

GOOD Christian People, I bid your prayers for Christ's holy Catholic Church, the blessed company of all faithful people; that it may please God to confirm and strengthen it in purity of faith, in holiness of life, and in perfectness of love, and to restore to it the witness of visible unity; and more especially for that branch of the same planted by God in this land, whereof we are members; that in all things it may work according to God's will, serve him faithfully, and worship him acceptably.

Ye shall pray for the President of these United States, and for the Governor of this State, and for all that are in authority; that all, and every one of them, may serve truly in their several callings to the glory of God, and the edifying and well-governing of the people, remembering the account they shall be called upon to give at the last great day.

Ye shall also pray for the ministers of God's Holy Word and Sacraments; for Bishops (and herein more especially for the Bishop of this Diocese), that they may minister faithfully and wisely the discipline of Christ; likewise for all Priests and Deacons (and herein more especially for the Clergy here residing), that they may shine as lights in the world, and in all things may adorn the doctrine of God our Saviour.

And ye shall pray for a due supply of persons fitted to serve God in the Ministry and in the State; and to that end, as well as for the good education of all the youth of this land, ye shall pray for all schools, colleges, and seminaries of sound and godly learning, and for all whose hands are open for their maintenance; that whatsoever tends to the advancement of true religion and useful learning may for ever flourish and abound.

Ye shall pray for all the people of these United States, that they may live in the true faith and fear of God, and in brotherly charity one towards another.

Ye shall pray also for all who travel by land or sea; for all prisoners and captives; for all who are in sickness or in sorrow; for all who have fallen into grievous sin; for all who, through temptation, ignorance, helplessness, grief, trouble, dread, or the near approach of death, especially need our prayers.

Ye shall also praise God for rain and sunshine; for the fruits of the earth; for the products of all honest industry; and for all his good gifts, temporal and spiritual, to us and to all men.

Finally, ye shall yield unto God most high praise and hearty thanks for the wonderful grace and virtue declared in all his saints, who have been the choice vessels of his grace and the lights of the world in their several generations; and pray unto God, that we may have grace to direct our lives after their good examples; that, this life ended, we may be made partakers with them of the glorious resurrection, and the life everlasting.

And now, brethren, summing up all our petitions, and all our thanksgivings, in the words which Christ hath taught us, we make bold to say, [[the Lord's Prayer follows.]]

somewhat varied. This is a characteristic which the later Litanies do indeed display; but the earliest ones do not.

There are traces of this kind of responsive prayer in pagan and Jewish use.[6] It is certainly pre-Christian: our first record of its ritual use is in a pagan context.[7] And on the whole it seems probable that the Litany form may have been borrowed from pagan devotions.

As to the date of this development, we do not have any certain indications. The first written Litanies are found in the *Apostolic Constitutions* of the fourth century. But there they are already fully developed, and differentiated into a number of forms. Manifestly they are of long standing in the Church. St. Basil the Great, who was born about 330, and Archbishop of Caesarea 370-379, observed that the litanies which were in use in his day had not been known in the reign of his predecessor St. Gregory 'Thaumaturgus,' who died in 254.[8] If the rise of the Litany form had taken place in his own lifetime, he would hardly have gone back so far as the year 254 for a point of reference. It therefore seems entirely possible that the Syrian litanies may have originated in the third century; at the latest, early in the fourth.

It may be noted that the Antiochene device of a Litany structure had some distinctive qualities of its own. The Egyptian and Western arrangement of repeated pairs of Bidding and Collect, Bidding and Collect, kept all the constituent supplications pretty much on the same emotional level. The 'periodic' character of the Litany had cumulative force, and was capable of building up to great climaxes of really remarkable power.

Another characteristic of this kind of a dramatization of the Great Intercession in dialogue form was that it made the Litany into a sort of action, complete in itself: and thereby it became, as it were, *portable*. The original Offertory Litany was so effective in uniting the congregation with the officiant in a really cooperative act of prayer, that this form was freely utilized at other portions of the Liturgy, where it was desired to engage the attention of the people in what the Byzantine Rite calls a '*fervent* supplication'[9] - *cf.* Justin's expression of '*earnest* common prayers.'

Some of these diaconal Biddings were very brief, consisting of little more than the opening and concluding clauses of a normal Litany, and of little more significance than the Salutation, 'The Lord be with you,' which the Western rites employ to call the congregation to attention at a significant prayer. Sometimes they were specialized in content, such as the Litanies for the Dismissal of the Catechumens, or as an introduction to the Lord's Prayer or the Post-Communion

---

6. Eisenhofer, *Handbuch der katholischen Liturgik* (Freiburg: Herder, 1932), I. 198.

7. Epictetus (c. 60-140 A.D.), *Dissertations* II. 7.

8. Basil, *Ep.* 207.

9. Brightman, *Liturgies Eastern and Western* (Oxford: Clarendon, 1896), 373b.4.

Thanksgiving: *cf.* the suffrages 'for the newly enlightened one' which Justin indicates at a Baptismal Eucharist. But in one guise or another, the present Byzantine Liturgy contains no less than ten Litanies, or shreds of Litanies. Each Litany is accompanied by a Collect; though nowadays time is saved in an overlong service by having the Celebrant say the Collect silently within the closed sanctuary, while the Deacon is proclaiming the Litany aloud outside.

As early as the time of the *Apostolic Constitutions*,[10] the Litany form was used also in the general services of Morning and Evening Prayers; and now it is a prominent constituent of all the offices of the Eastern Church. The next step was for this self-contained and self-complete form to free itself entirely of its original liturgical context, and to be carried about from one Church to another, and eventually to be used as an Office by itself.

4. Early Western Litanies

Accordingly, from the fifth century on, we find that Litanies of obviously Syrian provenance and content were imported into the Egyptian and the Western rites, which originally did not contain them, and where they were freely employed, both as constituents of the Liturgy, and as supplications during solemn processions.

Until the end of the seventh century, the only form of the Litany used in the West was one derived directly from the Byzantine Litany after the Gospel.[11] It did not have the varied structure of the later 'Litany of the Saints,' since it was composed of Intercessions alone. We have almost identical texts of this form preserved in the *Stowe Missal* from Ireland, and from an old codex from Fulda in Germany; and a closely allied version remains in use to the present day in the Ambrosian Rite at Milan on the Sundays in Lent.[12]

This form seems to have been introduced into France in the first part of the fifth century — early enough for it to have come into use, fallen into neglect, and been vigorously revived by Mamertus of Vienne about the year 468 for use in the processions on the Rogation Days, which he then instituted.[13] Pope Gelasius (492-6) adopted it at Rome at the beginning of the Mass. In the following century, however, the introduction of the joyful chant of *Gloria in Excelsis* to this same part of the service brought a certain conflict of mood with the more somber tone of the Litany. It was probably a realization of this situation which caused Gregory the Great (590-604) to reduce the Liturgical Litany to its final

---

10. *A. C.* VIII. xxxvi-xxxix.

11. Brightman, *LEW.*, 373.

12. Texts of these forms are conveniently printed in F. E. Warren, *The Liturgy and Ritual of the Celtic Church* (Oxford: Clarendon, 1880, 229 f., 252, 254; summarized in English in Parsons and Jones, *The American Prayer Book* (N. Y.: Scribners, 1937), 127 ff.

13. *Cf.* the interesting account in J. H. Blunt, *Annotated Book of Common Prayer* (London: Rivingtons, 1866), 46.

triple *Kyrie eleison*, which the Roman form had retained in untranslated Greek; and which Gregory modified by altering the middle repetition to *Christe eleison*. Hence the term 'Lesser Litany,' which ever since has designated the *Kyries*.

The use of this 'Gelasian' Litany at the Mass has left behind it the legacy of the use of a Litany, which nowadays of course is a version of the 'Litany of the Saints,' at the Liturgy upon such occasions as the Vigil services of Easter and Pentecost, and at Ordinations and the Consecration of Churches.

Another inheritance of this Litany is that during the period when it was generally employed, it assimilated to its own purposes a feature of the service which was older than itself. This was the initial prayer of the Liturgy, which we find in the middle of the fourth century in the Sacramentary of Serapion under the title, 'The First Prayer of the Lord's Day,' and which still survives in the Coptic Rite in Egypt as 'The First Prayer of the Morning.'[14] Like most other constituents of the service, in the West this became a variable prayer, changing with the occasion: and we call it 'The Collect of the Day.' It is because the Liturgical Litany appropriated this prayer to be its Litany-Collect, to gather up its devotional thoughts in a round and comprehensive expression, that so many of our Collects in the course of the year are in such very general terms. Most of those in Epiphany- and Trinity-tides display no particular appropriateness to the occasions to which they are assigned, and could be freely exchanged with each other in any order.

5. The Litany of the Saints

In the years 687-701 the Roman Church was presided over by Sergius I, a Greek-speaking Pope from the region of Antioch. He is remembered for having advocated two cults at Rome, that of the Holy Cross, and that of Christ as the 'Lamb of God': he introduced the singing of the *Agnus Dei* in the Mass. Now both of these originated at Jerusalem, and were features of the 'Liturgy of St. James,' which by this time had supplanted the older Liturgy as found in the *Apostolic Constitutions* throughout the Antiochene Patriarchate.

Modern investigation attributes to Sergius the introduction of the new form of the 'Litany of the Saints,' which from the eighth century on enriched, absorbed, and eventually supplanted the relatively simple Byzantine form hitherto used throughout the West.

We are so fortunate as to have preserved for us two versions of this Sergian Litany, which present it virtually *in statu nascendi*, in the *Stowe Missal*, and in Alcuin's *Officia per ferias*.[15] These primordial texts are in the barest possible outline; but the essentials of the present varied and highly organized structure are all there.

---

14. Brightman, *LEW.*, 147.3.

15. Warren, *op. cit.*, 226 and 228 f.; P.L. 101. 522 ff.; given in a conflated translation in Parsons and Jones, *op. cit.*, 129 f.

This Litany begins with the penitential Antiphon 'Spare us'; it continues with the Invocation of the Saints, which comprise the great bulk of this form; it includes representations of each of the major structural divisions of the present developed text, although there is only a single Deprecation ('From all evil'), a single Obsecration ('By thy Cross'), and a single Intercession ('That thou wilt grant us peace') ; and it concludes with the Invocations of Christ as the Son of God and the Lamb of God, triple Kyries, Lord's Prayer, suffrages, and Collect.

The arrangement of this material is Sergius' own. So is the idea of an 'Obsecration,' calling upon our Lord to deliver his people by a kind of *Anamnesis* of the mighty acts of his Redemption. And so is the importation of the *Agnus Dei* into the Litany form. 'By thy Cross,' and 'O Lamb of God,' are, indeed, as it were, Sergius' thumb-prints upon this composition.

Yet all these features had their roots in the rite of Jerusalem-Antioch. The *Agnus Dei* was drawn from the communion devotions;[16] but the pleading of the power of the Holy Cross is found in one of the litanies in 'St. James.'[17] So are the 'Deprecations' or petitions for deliverance from evil, which have sometimes been thought to be peculiar to the Western Litany.[18] And like all Eastern litanies, Sergius' supplication is distinctively *a prayer to Christ*.[19] (This is still true of our Litany to the present day, between the initial Invocations of the Holy Trinity and the appended Collects addressed to the Father.)

It seems probable that another characteristic feature of Sergius' Litany of the Saints may have been derived from a constituent of an Eastern Liturgy, though this time it is that of Constantinople. The long lists of the Saints invoked by classes and by name with which the Western Litany opens, correspond with the commemoration of the Saints by categories with which every Eastern Litany concludes. Now in the Byzantine Liturgy, the 'Great Litany' of General Intercession no longer occurs after the Gospel, as it certainly did in the early fifth century, when the West borrowed that form[20] but most of its content has been transferred to a new Litany at the very beginning of the Liturgy proper.[21] And this in turn has been prefaced by an 'Office of Prothesis,' in which the Elements are prepared with a very elaborate ritual which makes commemoration of the Saints by category and by name.[22] Sergius could not have been ignorant of this arrangement in

---

16. Brightman, *LEW.*, 62b.24.

17. Brightman, *LEW.*, 37.21.

18. Brightman, *LEW.*, 34a.27.

19. Brightman, *LEW.*, 40.6.

20. Verbal identities make it unmistakable that the 'Gelasian' Litany was derived from the Byzantine Litany after the Gospel, but its content covers the later Enarxis Litany as well. The Western version is valuable evidence for the original text of the Byzantine before the initial Litany came into existence.

21. Brightman, *LEW*, 362 f.

22. Brightman, *LEW.*, 357.27-359.3.

what even then was the dominant Eastern Rite: and it is presumable that it was this knowledge which inspired him to open his Litany with the Invocations of the Saints.

The new format of the Sergian Litany proved extremely popular, and proliferated in innumerable local forms throughout Europe. It absorbed the content of the previous 'Gelasian' litanies of Byzantine type; it continued to assimilate ingredients from Eastern sources; and it freely added new phrases, and elaborations of existing expressions. The Roman Liturgical Litany (which we find in the service for Easter Even in the Missal) was rather conservative about such additions, and the Processional Litany (in the Breviary) only less so; but the North European tradition is very rich.[23]

6. Cranmer's English Litany

The Processional Litany was a favorite service in England. It had been familiar to the people in the English versions of the Primers since about the year 1400. Cranmer put forth his official rendering in 1544, five years before the First Prayer Book. Thus the Litany was the first service in the Book of Common Prayer to appear: as it was likewise the only service to continue in use in the reign of Mary, when the Prayer Book was suppressed in favor of a revival of the Sarum books.

Cranmer's work was based primarily upon the Processional Litany of the Sarum Breviary: but he freely enriched this with congruous material from quite a variety of other sources, some of them rather remote.

One main source of contributions was Martin Luther's Latin Litany of 1529 — much the best liturgical work Luther ever achieved, entirely orthodox in every respect, and especially valuable for gathering up many details in the uses of Northern Europe. Luther's work included also some distinctive Roman phrases which were not in the Sarum form, and which were incorporated by Cranmer. Other such Roman expressions seem to have infiltrated into the English text from the Litany in the reformed Breviary of Cardinal Quiñones which appeared in 1535-7, and which furnished the starting-point for Cranmer's revision of the Daily Offices.

Other constituents were adopted from other English Uses besides that of Sarum, such as York, Westminster, and even Brixen. And Cranmer levied upon other forms, such as the Sarum Litany for the Dying, the special supplications In Time of War, and the Office for the Unction of the Sick.

---

23. Yet this tradition is seldom if ever extravagant. An obviously manufactured pleasantry, instancing a supposed Deprecation 'From ghoulies, and ghostes, and things that go *boomp* in the night,' mendaciously alleged to hail from 'an old Scottish Litany,' periodically makes the rounds of newspaper miscellany. It ought to be superfluous to point out that this was made up out of whole cloth. Yet the clergy are continually pestered with inquiries on this subject; and even some of them are taken in.

Still farther afield, Cranmer recurred to the Byzantine Liturgical litanies for two phrases, and for the so-called 'Prayer of St. Chrysostom.' Dowden has identified the precise source of this matter in the 1528 Venice edition of the Byzantine Liturgy which printed the 'Anaphora of St. Chrysostom' in its place in the framework of the service *without* giving the alternative 'Anaphora of St. Basil.' This induced Cranmer to attribute the Prayer to 'St. Chrysostom,' whereas it really is part of the general framework, not of either of the Anaphoras. Likewise the English version of the Prayer is from the parallel Latin translation in that edition, not from the Greek.[24]

But it may justly be said that the Greek rites had a much more extensive effect upon the English Litany than these few details, for Cranmer followed the Greek method of grouping congruous clauses together in one suffrage, instead of taking them singly as the Latin does. This resulted in greatly enhancing the grandeur of the style of the Litany, which continually builds itself up to noble climaxes.

All this material from these divers and sometimes distant sources is by no means a magpie collection, but a real integration by a master hand. As Dr. Brightman remarked, 'Cranmer was not original, but, as the Litany is enough to prove, he had an extraordinary power of absorbing and improving upon other people's work.'[25]

7. Revisions of the Litany

The comprehensive scope of the Intercessions of the Litany, their remarkable incisiveness and moving power, and the balanced perfection of their organizing form, have had their effect in the fact that the Litany has undergone fewer revisions than any other office in the Prayer Book.

In his first draft of 1544, Cranmer reduced the number of the Invocations of the Saints (which in some medieval examples ran to as many as 200 names) to three suffrages, embracing the same summary classes as in the origin of this feature in the Syrian Litanies.[26] Even these three were eliminated in 1549.

---

24. John Dowden, *The Workmanship of the Book of Common Prayer* (London: Methuen, 1899), 227-9.

25. F. E. Brightman, *The English Rite* (London: Rivingtons, 1915), I. lxvii.

26. Ed. Note: The three invocations are these: Saint Mary, mother of God our Savior, Jesus Christ,
Pray for us
All ye holy angels and archangels, and all ye holy orders of blessed spirits,
Pray for us
All ye holy patriarchs and prophets, apostles, martyrs, confessors, virgins, and all the blessed company of heaven,
Pray for us

The Elizabethan Litany of 1559 dropped the uncharitable and undignified Deprecation against 'the tyrannye of the bisshoppe of Rome and all his detestable enormities.'

The Restoration Prayer Book of 1662, amended the Lutheran phrase for 'all Bysshoppes, pastours, and ministers of the Churche' to the more accurate and traditional form of 'Bishops, Priests, and Deacons.' This was a corrective of the 'Presbyterian' theories which had sought to extinguish the Church's essential threefold ministry during the fifteen years of the Commonwealth. The addition of the mention of 'rebellion' and 'schism' to the Deprecation beginning 'From all sedition' was no doubt also in retrospect upon those days.

The first American Prayer Book of 1789 made a number of verbal changes, such as 'those who' for 'them that'; 'from all inordinate and sinful affections' for 'from fornication, and all other deadly sin'; 'in all time of our prosperity' (as in the Scottish Book of 1637) to restore the obsolete sense of the word 'wealth' in this context; 'to love and fear thee' for 'to love and dread thee'; and 'all women in childbirth' (as in the American 'Proposed Book' of 1785) instead of 'all women labouring of child.'

The only major change of the text of the Litany in 1789 consisted of substituting for four suffrages for the King and the Royal Family the single petition 'That it may please thee to bless and preserve all Christian Rulers and Magistrates, giving them grace to execute justice, and to maintain truth.' This is a condensed paraphrase of the passage from the Prayer for the Church in the Liturgy, 'to direct and dispose the hearts of all Christian Rulers, that they may truly and impartially administer justice, . . . to the maintenance of thy true religion, and virtue.'

This book also provided for shortening the Litany by omitting at discretion the old Sarum Supplication In Time of War. Cranmer had incorporated this into the Processional Litany of 1544 which was issued by Royal Authority on the specific occasion of the war with Scotland and France; and it had been retained ever since, more by conservative inertia than because this Supplication was ever really a part of the normal Litany, or made any actual contribution to it. This matter, to be sure, is entirely congruous in style, and even displays the same artless combination of 'responsive' portions addressed to Christ, with prayers directed to God the Father, which characterizes the Litany proper. In such troubled times as gave it birth, the Supplication has a particular poignancy. But under more tranquil conditions and upon all ordinary occasions, it serves only to underscore the note of 'Deprecation,' of prostrate petition for delivery from calamities beyond our control. This theme exists in the normal Litany, but there it has been dealt with, and done with. It is actually a structural fault that it should be renewed here, when the cycle of Intercessions has been brought to a triumphant completion, and its symphonic form is obviously demanding the final major chords of its concluding Collect.

However, the manner of the shortening in 1789 was not happy. It allowed the omission of everything from 'O Christ, hear us,' through the *Preces* ending 'As we do put our trust in thee.' This eliminated the *Kyries* and the Lord's Prayer from the Litany. This was very well when the Litany was used with Morning Prayer and the Liturgy, as it always was in those days, since the Lord's Prayer occurred in both the other services, and the *Kyries* in the Decalogue in the Liturgy. But the Litany could not be used by itself in the shortened form without mutilating the service.

The one change in the Litany made in the Revision of 1892 met an old criticism that this form of General Intercession contained no petition for the extension of the Church, or the increase of the ministry. This missing element was supplied in the pregnant form of 'That it may please thee to send forth labourers into thy harvest.' This suffrage had in fact been found in Luther's Litany of 1529,[27] and in Marshall's Primer of 1535.[28]

The last American Revision of 1928 simplified the initial Invocations of the Holy Trinity into closer correspondence with the Latin originals, and divided them between Minister and People, instead of having the congregation repeat the entire 'O God the Father of heaven, have mercy upon us miserable sinners,' etc. 'From earthquake, fire, and flood' was added to the Deprecation beginning 'From lightning and tempest,' no doubt inspired by the addition of 'fire and flood' in the Canadian Book of 1922. A new suffrage for the President of the United States was derived from one of the petitions for the King omitted in 1789, but conformed to the phrasing of the Prayer for the President in Evening Prayer. 'Or by air' was added to the suffrage for 'all who travel by land or by water.' And the provisions for shortening the Litany by omitting the Supplication In Time of War were improved by making the break come after the Lord's Prayer — leaving the Litany complete in itself under all circumstances. The matter of duplicating the Lord's Prayer was taken care of by a rubric in Morning Prayer providing for the omission of the Lord's Prayer from that service when the Litany is to follow.

The English revision proposed in 1928 directs that the Litany shall end with the *Kyries* when the Holy Communion is to follow: otherwise, the Lord's Prayer must be said. Then the remainder of the present Litany is printed under the subtitle, 'A Supplication.' Rubrics indicate that this 'Supplication' may be appended to the Litany; or if not, 'one may use one or more of the Occasional Prayers and Thanksgivings, ending with the Prayer of Saint Chrysostom and The Grace.' The Supplication 'may also be used separately on the Rogation Days, at penitential seasons, and in times of trouble.'

The directions of the Scottish Prayer Book of 1929 are much the same, except that the prayer 'We humbly beseech thee, O Father,' which is the proper

---

27. P. Drews, *Beiträge zu Luthers liturgischen Reformen* (Tubingen, 1910), 28.
28. Wv. E. Burton, *Three Primers of Henry VIII* (Oxford: Univ. Press, 1834), 127.

terminal Collect of the Supplication, is removed from it and printed in the Litany; and the rubric adds that the Supplication may be used at any other service.

Both the English and the Scottish books give some consideration to further shortenings of the Litany. The English rubric is: 'The Minister may, at his discretion, say such of the Suffrages as he thinks convenient, provided that some are drawn from each section, and that all are concluded by "Son of God: we beseech thee to hear us, &c."' This is a rather loose rubric. Apparently the term 'Suffrages' is intended to comprise the Deprecations and Obsecrations of the Litany, as well as the Intercessions which have hitherto been specifically designated by this word.

The present Scottish Prayer Book evidently considered these provisions too lax, and perhaps too much of a demand upon the supposed discretion of the Minister, for it prints out a 'Shorter Litany I,' which is the full normal Litany, abbreviated only by the omission of two Deprecations, eight Suffrages, and (as the English rubric implies) the invocations of Christ as the Son of God and the Lamb of God. Also, 'Saint Chrysostom' is made an alternative to the terminal Collect.

The Scottish Book also sets forth a 'Shorter Litany II' which is an adaptation of the Litany at the beginning of the Byzantine Liturgy. It consists of nothing but Intercessions, with the unvarying respond, 'Lord, have mercy.'

8. The Use of the Litany

There has been a marked reduction in the use of the English Litany in recent times. To a considerable extent, this has been due to reaction from an extended period when a wooden interpretation of rubrics brought this service into a constant, conceivably an excessive, employment in the regular worship of the Church. The history of this development is informative. In the medieval Latin rituals of the Church of England before the Reformation, there were two uses of the Litany: as an introduction to the Mass, and really an integral part of it; and as a separate office of devotion.

In its liturgical connection, it was a direct inheritance of the 'Gelasian' Litany. In the Vigil services of Easter and Whitsunday, and upon the Rogation Days, the Litany was actually tied in to the liturgy, since its terminal *Kyries* were solemnly sung by cantors in ninefold form, to be at once the conclusion of the Litany and the exordium of the Mass, leading up (after an interpolated *Gloria* of later origin) to its original goal of the Collect of the Day. The same things were once true of the Litany at Ordinations; though the rearrangements which were made in order to interpolate the conferring of all the Orders, minor and major, into successive stages of the Ember Mass, caused the Litany to be displaced with relation to the text of the Mass, and its integrating connection broken.

As a separate service, the Litany was used in solemn procession on days appointed for special supplications for rain or fair weather, and in time of war, famine, pestilence, or any other public necessity. And it was also employed as an extra office, to be said in choir after Nones on Wednesdays and Fridays in Lent, in the Sarum Breviary.

Cranmer's Litany of 1544 was such a war-time intercession, appointed for use on Wednesdays and Fridays, after the Lenten pattern. But in 1547 Cranmer, displeased at the people's vying for places in the procession, ordered the English Litany to be sung by the clergy and choir kneeling in the midst of the church before High Mass on Sundays. No doubt he got this idea from the use of the Bidding Prayer in cathedral churches as part of the Procession before High Mass — just as in turn this place for the Bidding Prayer was a reminiscence of a 'Gelasian' Litany before the service; — though in parish churches this feature occurred in its most ancient location between the Sermon and the Offertory.

But in his First Prayer Book in 1549, Cranmer made markedly different provisions:

> Vpon wednesdaies & frydaies, the Englishe Letanie shalbe saied or song in all places . . . . And though be there be none to communicate with the Prieste, yet these daies (after the Letany ended) the Priest shall put vpon him a plaine Albe or surplesse, with a cope, and saie all thinges at the Altare (appoynted to bee sayde at the celebracion of the lordes supper) vntill after the offertory,

This was the only direction for the use of the Litany in this Prayer Book. And the service was printed after the Communion, as if by way of afterthought, and for employment only with the 'Ante-Communion.' Just what did Cranmer have in mind?

Wednesdays and Fridays were the ancient Fast Days, which were observed in every week in the time of Tertullian at the beginning of the third century, and which are mentioned even in the *Didaché*. But ever since, there has been a continuous tendency to lighten the once heavy obligations of fasting, abstinence, and devotion: and Wednesdays, even in Lent, have now disappeared from the picture, except in the four Ember Weeks of the year. Their use as Litany Days in the Church of England is the last reminiscence of their former significant place in the devotional pattern of the week. Cranmer in fact restored them to every week with his Litany of 1544, from the Sarum employment of them in Lent only; abolished them in 1547; and reinstated them in 1549. Why?

The explanation is that Cranmer recognized one fact about the use of the Litany in conjunction with the Eucharistic Liturgy of which all subsequent revisers of the Prayer Book have seemed to be entirely unaware. This is that the Litany is an absolute duplication of the whole cycle of thought and expression of that completely equivalent form of the Great Intercession found in the Prayer for the Whole State of Christ's Church.

This is a factor which did not need to be taken into consideration as long as the Mass was in Latin. There, the Intercessions were recited inaudibly in their place in the 'Silent Canon,' while the choir was singing the *Sanctus*. Therefore a Processional Litany could be sung, or even a Bidding Prayer in the vernacular recited, in connection with High Mass, without reiterating anything heard by the congregation. That was still true in 1547, when Cranmer ordered the singing of the Litany before the Sunday Mass.

But the situation was entirely altered when both the Litany and the Intercession were said aloud in English. Cranmer revoked the direction for a prefatory Litany, and provided instead an elaborate system of whole Psalms for Introits. But he revived the use of Wednesdays and Fridays as Litany Days, and gave more substance to the service by adding the first portion of the Liturgy through the Offertory. It is presumable that Cranmer knew that this use of a part of the Liturgy without a Consecration was an early custom of the Church of Alexandria upon Wednesdays and Fridays, from the well-known mention in the church historian Socrates;[29] and indeed such a use continued throughout the Middle Ages under exceptional circumstances when no celebration was possible.[30] But it must be noted that in the First Prayer Book the order for the Ante-Communion stopped short of the Prayer for the Church, which was still part of the Canon. It is more than coincidence that Cranmer cancelled the use of the Litany with the Liturgy as a whole, where it would duplicate the Intercession, and restored it with the Ante-Communion, where it would not.

This conclusion becomes inevitable when we note that in the Second Prayer Book of 1552, which transferred the Intercession to become the last constituent of the Ante-Communion, he not only dropped all directions for the use of the Litany with that service, but he eliminated all provisions for the use of the Ante-Communion upon the traditional Litany Days.

In the Second Prayer Book, the Litany was printed in a more congruous place, after Morning and Evening Prayer, under the rubric: 'Here foloweth the Letanye, to be vsed vpon Sundayes, Wednesdayes, and Fridayes, and at other times, when it shal be commaunded by the Ordenarye.' The mention of Sundays is a reminiscence of the Injunctions of 1547, and represents the only possible loophole in an otherwise foolproof program of excluding the duplication of Litany and Prayer for the Church. This would happen if the Litany were conjoined with either Communion or Ante-Communion. Cranmer may not have supplied that rubric. If he did, he may have reasonably, if fallaciously, hoped that his successors would recognize and profit by the principles which he had built into the services.

This rubric of 1552 stood in the Prayer Books in both England and America until their revisions of 1928; and, partly because of its indefiniteness, it gave rise to some considerable distortions of Cranmer's intentions.

---

29. *Hist. Eccles.* V. xxii.

30. W. E. Scudamore, *Notitia Eucharistica* (London: Rivingtons, 1876) 815 ff.

It seems that at first, the original interpretation of this rubric was in accord with the customs in force before the Reformation. Morning Prayer was said in the first hour of daylight, normally between six and seven o'clock. Then, about midmorning, the Litany was used in its traditional function of prefacing the celebration of the Holy Communion.

But in 1571, the Puritan Grindal, at that time Archbishop of York, issued an Injunction ordering Morning Prayer, the Litany, and the Holy Communion or Ante-Communion to be said together, without any intermission between them. Later, as Archbishop of Canterbury, he enforced this order upon the whole Church.

This action linked up the Litany with Morning Prayer, with which it had never previously been considered to have any liturgical connection; an understanding confirmed in the Prayer Book of 1662, when Cosin inserted in the rubric 'to be sung or said *after Morning Prayer.*'

This 'accumulated' combination of the three services became the standard Morning Service of the Church, imposed by a universal custom more difficult to breach than any rubric.

In the nineteenth century, the clergy who instituted an early service alone, or who presumed to say Morning Prayer without its wonted adjuncts of Litany and Ante-Communion, were assailed as lawbreakers. The literal-minded refused to be persuaded that the rubrical expression 'To be used' might mean 'available for use,' and did not necessarily assert 'must always be used.' Tardy relief came in a new General Rubric 'Concerning the Service of the Church' in the American Prayer Book of 1892, incorporating a pronouncement proposed at the Convention of 1877:

> The Order for Morning Prayer, the Litany, and the Order for the Administration of the Lord's Supper or Holy Communion, are distinct Services, and may be used either separately or together; Provided, that no one of these Services be habitually disused.

But however desirable such a stipulation might be, in the nature of things it was not enforcible. The General Rubric went on to try to give more scope for the use of the Litany by indicating that it might be substituted for the prayer after the Third Collect of either Morning or Evening Prayer. But the moment they were free to choose, it became apparent that most clergy prefer the briefer and more flexible provisions of the Prayers of Intercession in the Daily Offices to the fixed solemnities of the Litany. Little use of this combination of services is made at any time of the year outside of Lent, and only sparsely then.

Hence the American revision of 1928 was only realistic in dropping from this General Rubric any mention of the stipulation that the Litany must not 'be habitually disused,' and in contenting itself with classifying the Litany along with Morning and Evening Prayer and the Communion as 'the regular Services appointed for Public Worship in this Church.' And the rubric before the Litany now reads: 'To be used after the third Collect of Morning or Evening Prayer; or before the Holy Communion; or separately.'

The English draft of 1928 has similar flexibility, in substituting for the 'To be used' rubric the statement that it 'may be sung or said after Morning Prayer upon Sundays, Wednesdays, and Fridays, and also upon any day at the discretion of the Minister. It shall be used on the Rogation Days, and at other times when it shall be commanded by the Ordinary.' The Scottish Book of 1929 incorporates these same provisions, but adds that 'it shall be said at least on one Sunday in the month, and on Ash Wednesday and Good Friday.'

All this has been a rather remarkable reversal in the place of the Litany in the public worship of the Church. For nearly three centuries and a half, it was considered to be a required element in every principal service. Now, it has been relegated to a marginal and optional position. Our present American Prayer Book does not demand its employment upon any occasion, except at Ordinations; and even then, the Great Litany has been almost entirely supplanted by a new alternative, the briefer and more specialized Litany for Ordinations. In many parishes, it has vanished from the principal services; and in some, it is not heard from one year's end to the other. It is a *terra incognita* to the majority of the present generation of Seminarians. We have seen that the Scottish Prayer Book has taken alarm at such a situation, and tried to take some steps to avert the extinction of the Litany entirely.

Manifestly, the pendulum has swung too far. Reaction against the impositions of grim old Grindal should not drive us to a neglect of a service which all commentators have always agreed is to be ranked in the same exalted class as the *Te Deum*, as the most perfect and most affecting form of words which the spirit of devotion has ever devised. The impressive and expressive powers of the Litany have never been exceeded. No other form of intercessory prayer is to be compared with it: the sequence of supplications at Morning Prayer, the Prayer for the Church in the Communion, worn to triteness by much handling and many paraphrasings in the course of the ages, the rhetorical periods of the Bidding Prayer — none of these can approach the incisiveness and the vivid appeal of the Litany, which has come down to us enriched and enhanced, but blunted of none of its poignancy, from the ardent devotions of the Primitive Church.

The Litany was quite strictly a 'popular' service in its origin — deliberately composed in the first place to give wings to the 'earnest common prayers' of the people. And 'popular' it still is, whenever the people are given opportunity to participate in it. The decline in its use is chiefly the fault of the clergy — not indeed because they are slack, but rather because they are overzealous, filling up a Sunday morning with a very tight schedule of a multiplication of other services until one more thing cannot be fitted into the plan; or because they are oversolicitous about the staying powers of a modern congregation. Anyone who has seen a congregation emerge fresh as daisies from the solemnities of an Ordination of a Priest lasting nearly two hours, perfectly content with a long rite composed of many constituents, which does and says things of importance at every point, will realize that no congregation is going be intimidated by a service which has been lengthened by ten minutes by the inclusion of a Litany.

So the Roman Church since the sixteenth century has seen the evolution of four more official Litanies, those of St. Mary, St. Joseph, the Holy Name, and the Sacred Heart; besides an innumerable swarm of such forms employed in private devotion.

Current Protestantism likewise has quite abandoned the scornful attitude toward the Litany held by the Puritans at the time of the Restoration. Then they objected to all forms of 'repetitions and responsals,' holding that the 'Minister' was 'appointed for the people in all Public Services appertaining to God: and the Holy Scriptures . . . intimating the people's part in public prayer to be only with silence and reverence to attend thereto, and to declare their consent in the close, by saying *Amen*.'[31] Now, with the way perfectly prepared by a universal use of 'Responsive Readings,' all denominations have taken eagerly to the Litany form, and invented numerous variants of their own. The Presbyterian *Book of Common Worship* of 1946 contains no less than five Litanies. It is really rather extraordinary that at the very time when we have been showing ourselves neglectful of this element of our liturgical heritage, our former critics have been rediscovering its value and power. It seems just possible that we may not be quite so 'up-to-date' as we should like to think; still more possible that the very latest fashion in opinion or custom may not necessarily present a new pinnacle of human wisdom.

Proposed Text

1. Title

It is no longer satisfactory to speak of The Litany, as it was when the Prayer Book contained only one composition in that form. Our revision of 1928 brought into the picture two more Litanies, those for the Dying, and for Ordinations. We are now proposing to include two more Litanies — the Litany for the Church, from the 1949 *Book of Offices*, and a Litany of Saint Chrysostom, which is an adaptation of the Byzantine Litany as found in the Scottish Prayer Book of 1929. We recommend that we follow the solution which the Greek Church has found for a parallel problem. They distinguish their most comprehensive Litany of General Intercession from the numerous other adaptations of this form in the Liturgy by calling it 'The Great Litany.' This seems an adequate designation for the historic

---

31. W. E. Scudamore, *Notitia Eucharistica* (London: Rivingtons, 1876) 815 ff.

Western Litany which we have inherited which always has been, and doubtless always will be, the principal use of this method of General Supplication in the Church.

2. Initial Rubric

No revolutionary change in the current customs as to the use of the Litany can be hoped for from any modification of the directive rubric at the head of the service. We have thought it quite worth while to review the history of the use of the Litany, to emphasize its value, and to deprecate the decline in its employment in the devotions of the Church; but it is the lesson of liturgical history that the most that rubrics can do is to interpret living customs — they cannot create them. Therefore no important changes are advocated in the present perfectly lucid provisions. It would seem sufficient to add only some minor clarifications and suggestions.

For instance, there does not seem any point in trying to revive the ordering of the use of the Litany on Wednesdays and Fridays throughout the year. Even the Sarum Rite used those Litany Days only in Lent. Cranmer doubtless knew that he was restoring a feature of the Primitive Church when he ordered this observance in every week. But while it was perfectly practicable to secure the addition of the Litany to a scheme of Morning and Evening Prayer performed publicly and daily in the parish churches, it is not possible to enforce it in present-day America, where the Daily Offices are said in so few places.

We have to recognize that the Litany is a votive addition to the regular pattern of services: either an extra office, or a substitute for another form of General Intercession in one of the regular services. The only occasions on which it can really be said to be indispensable are the Rogation Days, and at Ordinations: and for the latter, another version has effectively supplanted the Great Litany. There are, however, other seasons to which the Litany is particularly appropriate. Though it is not in itself primarily a Penitential Office, its primitive heart-searching earnestness makes it especially harmonious with the penitential season of Lent, and with the solemn grandeur of the preparation season of Advent. Accordingly, these are suggested in the rubric.

At the same time, it is one of the glories of the Litany that it attains to great heights, as well as penetrating to great depths, of feeling. In these respects, it parallels the *Gloria in Excelsis* and in many ways is just as suitable to festal use. This is especially brought out when the Litany is sung in procession.

Much of the somber coloring of the rendition of the Litany, much of the idea that it is primarily a penitential exercise, has flowed from Cranmer's impatient action in 1547, in abolishing its processional use, and ordering it to be said kneeling. But processional Litanies have been revived during the last century, and used with great effect. Therefore these suggestions also have been incorporated into the rubric.

Although we have noted that it was a historical mistake to tie the Litany to Morning Prayer, and a greater breach of tradition to use it with Evening Prayer, there seems no reason to try to keep them apart now. The only cause for deprecating their conjunction by Archbishop Grindal was that it overloaded the required Sunday service. Upon occasion, and in particular in Lent, it may be very useful to substitute the most solemn form of General Intercession in the Litany for the concluding prayers of the Offices.

Liturgical purists have always opposed the use of the Litany as or with the evening service, maintaining that its proper function was to lead up to the Eucharist. That was true in the days before Gregory the Great, when the Litany was an integral part of the Mass. But in England, it was true only in the years 1547 to 1549, for anything that any authoritative regulations had to say about it. In both of his Prayer Books, Cranmer took pains to avoid directing the combination of the Litany with the Holy Communion, or even with the first part of it, if this would bring two forms of the General Intercession into the same service. The Second Prayer Book did indeed open Sundays to the use of the Litany. But the custom of saying the Litany immediately before the Communion, which seems to have originated unthinkingly, and to have been hardened into an immutable decree by Grindal's Injunctions, held its sway in defiance of the basic principles Cranmer thought he had established for the proper employment of the General Intercession. The liturgiologists never seem to have recognized this, and urged as the chief justification for the use of the Litany its conjunction with the Eucharistic Liturgy which had given it birth. But the users of the services could not help feeling the repetition of this important constituent; and their largely unconscious resentment for that reason has a great deal to do with the present reaction which has seen the Litany so generally disused now. All this furnishes a very infirm basis for a doctrinaire eschewing of the Litany as an evening service.

As a matter of fact, one of the most useful, and therefore probably most frequent, employments of the Litany is at an afternoon or evening service on a Lenten weekday, when it is not possible to have the assistance of a choir. The Litany ranks itself along with the Holy Communion as a service which loses nothing of its quality as a satisfactory congregational ritual when it is deprived of the adornment of music. Though the clergy of course are thoroughly habituated to saying the Daily Offices without music, the people regard them as very flat. But the Litany retains its vitality under all circumstances.

It remains true that the noblest and most effective use of the Litany is as an introduction to the Eucharist. It is essential that we should take account of that matter of the doubling of the Great Intercession which Cranmer recognized perfectly, but which no subsequent reviser has faced. This cannot be done by any alteration of the rubrics of the Litany. But our Committee on the Eucharistic Liturgy is proposing measures in the rubrics of that service which should be sufficient. They provide that a Litany may be substituted, if desired, for the Prayer for the Church; or, if a Litany has already been said, then this Prayer may be reduced to the dimensions and function of an Offertory Collect by employing its first and last sentences only. Some such arrangements seem to be the only way to open the door to a wider use of the Litany in connection with the Eucharist, which is certainly so desirable, but which is so little practicable now. It may be noted that in recent times one combination of services has sprung up and come into fairly wide use, which has considerable significance. Though it is not directly suggested by our rubrics, many clergy have taken to varying the routine of the Sunday services by substituting the Litany and Ante-Communion for Morning Prayer upon occasion. This is especially true in the Southern States, and the occasion is commonly the Fifth Sunday of the month. This move seems to be entirely spontaneous, and not from archeological reasons at all, though its effect is precisely to reconstitute the service which Cranmer prescribed for Wednesdays and Fridays in the First Prayer Book. In the American Prayer Book, as in 1549, the Ante-Communion comes to an end before the Prayer for the Church. This leaves the Ante-Communion, even if combined with Morning Prayer, as a service without any General Intercession; which is one reason why it is so little used. The Litany supplies that lack. And it shows that the clergy are conscious of that principle of the undesirability of duplicating the Great Intercession in the same service, which Cranmer realized, and his successors ignored, since though they tend to avoid the use of the Litany with the Holy Communion, they have reached out to make this employment of it with the Ante-Communion: a combination to which that objection does not apply. Its users find it a well-balanced and satisfactory service.

3. Arrangement

The chief defect of the Litany — perhaps its only appreciable flaw — and the principal source of dimly felt dissatisfactions with its use, is a certain lack of organizing plan in the order of the intercessory Suffrages. There is quite a little repetition of very similar devotional ideas, which keep recurring without any particular reason for their arrangement. This gives an effect of eddying around in circles, instead of a stream flowing directly to its destined goal. In spite of the vivid brilliancy of the Litany's expressions, and the free fluency of its phrases, the form seems to drag.

Most of the offending clauses upon examination turn out to be those which Cranmer derived from Luther's Litany. That is nothing against them: we must realize that we owe much of the most deeply moving and spiritually inspiring elements in this service to constituents which are *evangelical* in the highest and truest sense, which Cranmer drew from his German sources. But they do badly stand in need of rearrangement, to fit them in to the clear traditional plan of the primitive Litany form, so that there will be a consistent forward development of thought throughout, and so that at every point there will be a sense of *progress*.

This primitive plan is quite simple: I. For the Universal Church, with its Rulers, its Clergy, and its Laity; II. For all those in any Affliction or Necessity; III. For the whole World; and IV. For the Faithful Departed.

The last-named is an addition to the Litany, to conform its content with that of the Prayer for the Church. It is also a return to the most ancient form of the Litany and the General Intercession; and furnishes a most logical conclusion and *terminus ad quem* for the thought of such a general supplication.

The addition of this fourth section relieves the present 18th Suffrage from the duty of fulfillment a terminal function, and enables us to transfer it to a place after the sixth (present eighth), where it will be in logical progressive sequence. Then the ninth Suffrage may well be omitted, since 'to hear meekly thy word, . . . and to bring forth the fruits of the Spirit' is too obviously a doublet of 'to endue us with the grace of thy Holy Spirit to amend our lives according to thy holy Word.'

The seventh Suffrage, for the peace of the world, may profitably be put in the 4th place, in the intercessions for All Mankind; and the 10th, for the Erring, after the 15th (present 16th), for our Enemies.

These relatively simple rearrangements would give us four suffrages for the Church and the Clergy; four for the Laity, introduced by 'to bless and keep all thy people'; three for Those in Necessity; six for the World in general, beginning 'to have mercy upon all men'; and two for the Faithful Departed and the Saints. It is hoped that they will clarify the structure of thought, and lend purposiveness and movement to the office.

4. Alterations

A few expressions have been altered, either to give a more Christian meaning to certain Old Testament phrases, or to make the sense clearer. So far as possible, this has been done without disturbing the familiar rhythm.

In the penitential Introduction 'Remember not,' the expression 'neither take thou vengeance of our sins' — a somewhat exacerbated translation of Tobit 3:3 — has been altered to 'neither reward us according to our sins,' taken from the Sarum versicle (Ps. 103:10) after the Lord's Prayer on p. 58. 'Be not angry with us for ever' is another resounding phrase from the Apocrypha, from 2 Esdras 8:45. No doubt our present age does not think enough of the reality of God's wrath against sin. The fact remains that to most people such an expression would imply only his hatred of sinners — which is not true at all. Since this phrase provokes only incomprehension and revulsion, it may be well to substitute some intimation of God's saving care, such as 'by Thy mercy preserve us for ever.'

The first Deprecation, 'From all evil and mischief,' contains similar difficulties. The word 'mischief' was intended in its classical sense of 'harm.' Unfortunately, its modern connotation is trivial, that of 'vexatious annoyance.' The 'crafts and assaults of the devil' is too close to the following deceits of 'the world, the flesh, and the devil.' 'Thy wrath' is misleading, as we have said. And 'everlasting damnation' voices a medieval idea which to few people nowadays has any semantic reality at all. We recommend that after 'From all evil; from sin': the first Deprecation should go on to include the third, 'from all inordinate and sinful affections; and from all the deceits of the world, the flesh, and the devil.'

The order of the Deprecations would be more logical if this combination of the first and third were succeeded by the second, 'From all blindness of heart,' the fifth, 'From all sedition,' and the fourth, 'From lightning and tempest.' In the last Deprecation, the expression 'sudden death,' bracketed as it is with 'battle and murder,' has given rise to an idea that a *speedy* death is to be deplored: which is in no wise the case. The Latin original was a 'subitanea *et improvisa* morte.' Unfortunately, that does not translate well into English: 'unprepared *for*' is an impossible qualification of the word 'death.' There is in fact no satisfactory substitute for the present phrase, which has made itself a part of the English language: and we have been constrained to leave it as it is.

The second intercessory Suffrage, for Rulers, belongs exactly where it is, as part of the primeval supplication for the Peace of the Church. However, the present paraphrase of the corresponding passage in the General Intercession of the Liturgy has lost all sense of this meaning. It is a little difficult to recover it in phrases which will be distinctive, and which will not duplicate existing expressions to this effect in other prayers. We propose that 'thy Church, being hurt by no persecutions, may serve Thee in security and peace': taking the salient note from the Litany-Collect, 'O God, merciful Father,' which we propose to omit from the Litany.

In our third (present fourth) Suffrage, it might be as well to substitute the word 'enlighten' for 'illuminate,' because the latter is sometimes disconcertingly misread as 'eliminate'! In the 16th Suffrage, the word 'kindly' is intended to convey the archaic sense of 'after their kind.' The impression actually conveyed by the word to modern ears is pleasing, but fallacious. Since in all the old Intercessions this is intrinsically a prayer for Plenty of the Fruits of the Earth, perhaps we can somewhat enrich instead of apparently impoverishing the graciousness of the phrase, by substituting the word 'bountiful.'

On the other hand, we do not propose any change in the expression 'and finally to beat down Satan under our feet' in our eighth (present 11th) Suffrage. The question has been raised as to whether the word 'finally' means 'conclusively,' or 'eventually.' It might be nice to think it is the former; but the best that the original in Rom. 16:20 can offer us is 'shortly.' We have to face the fact that the perfecting of our human nature is an arduous and gradual process. It is a salvation painfully wrought *in* us, rather than one instantaneously accomplished *for* us. The present phrase is true to the facts, and accurate in either sense in which it may be understood.

The word 'comfort' is repeated in our present 11th and 12th Suffrages. In the first of these, it bears the sense in which it is exclusively understood in modern times, 'to comfort and help the weak-hearted,' and therefore may be left unchanged. But in the second, 'to succour, help, and comfort all who are in danger, necessity, and tribulation,' it calls for the more vigorous, but now wholly archaic, meaning of 'strengthen.' Moreover, the word 'succour' has fallen out of spoken English, and public speakers have learned to avoid it on account of its unfortunate coincidence with a slang word. We propose instead 'to help, support, and strengthen,' a phrase with identical rhythm.

5. Additions

The English and Scottish versions of the Litany have now adopted our present fifth Suffrage, 'to send forth labourers into thy harvest,' which appeared in our Prayer Book of 1892, and have added to it petitions for missionaries, and for the extension of the Church. We in turn have followed their lead as to these additions, but have not copied their language.

We propose a new Suffrage, the first after the petition for 'all men,' for the various vocations of human life.

The present seventh Suffrage, 'to give to all nations unity, peace, and concord,' which we propose to transfer to this section of Intercessions for the World in general, may profitably be expanded by supplications 'to make wars to cease in all the world,' and 'to bestow upon all peoples the liberty to serve thee without fear.' It would appear that the great 'Fourth Freedom' of the Atlantic Charter may be a long time in being realized upon earth:[32] and this seems a suitable contribution for our times to offer to the General Supplication of the Litany. The concluding Suffrages for the Faithful Departed and the Communion of the Saints have been put in simple and unexceptionable language: 'to grant to all the faithful departed eternal life and peace,' and 'to grant that with all thy Saints we may attain to thy heavenly kingdom.'

The *Agnus Dei* in the Litany has been restored to the familiar threefold form in which it is traditionally used in the Liturgy. There does not seem to be any sufficient reason to require the congregation to be alert to transpose the responses in the reverse order from that to which they are most accustomed, as is the case at present.

The fine but little used Collect, 'Almighty God, who hast promised to hear the petitions of those who ask in thy Son's Name,' from p. 50 of the Prayer Book, has been substituted for the prayer 'O God, merciful Father,' on p. 58, which is

---

32. Ed. Note: This is a reference to President Franklin D. Roosevelt's 1941 State of the Union address. Speaking against American isolationism, he discussed the four universal freedoms that all people should enjoy. The fourth, mentioned here, is "freedom from fear." The actual Atlantic Charter, a document signed by Churchill and Roosevelt regard the post-war world, contained eight common principles of which worldwide peace is the eighth, not the fourth.

structurally the proper Litany-Collect of our present arrangement[33] — although the final Collect 'We humbly beseech thee, O Father,'[34] which concludes the Supplication In Time of War, is now directed when the Litany is shortened. The new Collect is really a more adequate summation of the Litany as a General Supplication than either of the present Collects, which have done much to overstress the quality of the Litany as a penitential exercise.

6. Conjunction with the Liturgy

When Morning Prayer is to be followed by the Litany, the rubrics direct that the Lord's Prayer shall be omitted from Morning Prayer, and said in the Litany. This requires no rubric in the Litany.

But when the Litany is said before the Liturgy, then, as Dr. Frere pointed out,[35] the proper point of junction of the two services is the *Kyries*, which in Roman use are solemnly sung in a dual function, as we have noted.[36] A rubric after 'Son of God, we beseech thee to hear us,' intimates that at that point one may proceed at once to the *Kyries* of the Liturgy: avoiding duplicating the *Agnus Dei*, *Kyries* and Lord's Prayer in the combined service. A correlative rubric in the Liturgy will provide for omitting everything in that service before the *Kyries*.

7. The Supplication

The most useful change which can be made in the use of the Litany, the one which best brings its overlong extent into manageable compass, which best integrates its progress toward a purposed goal, and which thus furnishes the most cogent inducement for its more frequent use, is to be found in the proper treatment of

---

33. Ed. Note: The first-mentioned prayer on p. 50 is "ALMIGHTY God, who hast promised to hear the petitions of those who ask in thy Son's Name; We beseech thee mercifully to incline thine ears to us who have now made our prayers and supplications unto thee; and grant that those things which we have faithfully asked according to thy will, may effectually be obtained, to the relief of our necessaity, and to the setting forth of thy glory; through Jesus Christ our Lord. *Amen.*"

The second is: "O GOD, merciful Father, who despisest not the sighing of a contrite heart, nor the desire of such as are sorrowful; Mercifully assist our prayers which we make before thee in all our troubles and adversities, whensoever they oppress us; and graciously hear us, that those evils which the craft and subtilty of the devil or man worketh against us, may, by thy good providence, be brought to nought; that we thy servants, being hurt by no persecutions, may evermore give thanks unto thee in thy holy Church; through Jesus Christ our Lord. *Amen.*"

34. Ed. Note: "WE humbly beseech thee, O Father, mercifully to look upon our infirmities; and, for the glory of thy Name, turn from us all those evils that we most justly have deserved; and grant, that in all our troubles we may put our whole trust and confidence in thy mercy, and evermore serve thee in holiness and pureness of living, to thy honour and glory; through our only Mediator and Advocate, Jesus Christ our Lord. Amen."

35. *Some Principles of Liturgical Reform* (London: Murray, 1911), 156 ff.

36. P. 14 above.

the Supplication In Time of War which Cranmer added to his inherited material in 1544, and which has continued to lengthen and weight down the Litany form ever since, even at times when its original justification has been completely lacking.

We have seen that the American Prayer Books since the beginning have found means to leave it out. Similar steps were taken in the English and Scottish revisions of 1928-9. But in none of these have the revisers understood the structure of the forms upon which they were attempting surgery, and in none of them are the results satisfactory.[37]

The Litany proper extends through the prayer 'O God, merciful Father,' on p. 58, which is its terminal Collect. The Supplication begins with the Antiphon, 'O Lord, arise, help us,' and continues through its own terminal Collect, 'We humbly beseech thee, O Father,' on p. 59. The American and Scottish books treat this Collect of the Supplication as the Litany-Collect. No doubt this is a matter of taste and judgment: but in any case we propose to substitute another Collect as the terminus of the Litany. But both English and Scottish forms begin the Supplication as a separate office with the versicle and Collect after the Lord's Prayer, which organically are part of the Litany itself. This badly obscures the lucid structure of the Supplication, as Dr. Frere describes it:

> It consists properly of an opening Antiphon ('O Lord, arise,') and processional Psalm (reduced to a single verse, 'O God, we have heard') together with the *Gloria Patri* in the primitive shape which is elsewhere retained in the introits, these followed by a set of choir versicles, a priest's versicle, and the Collect of the occasion. This form is eminently suitable for its purpose; and in fact it was much used as an intercession during the Boer War.[38]

Dr. Frere recommended that this 'group of prayers intended for use in time of war and national anxiety,' which is 'unsuitable for perpetual use, . . . should be removed bodily from the Litany, restored to its proper form, and set in the collection of Intercessions.' This recommendation was adopted in general at the last English and Scottish revisions: but they did not 'restore it to its proper form.' We trust that our proposal does so.

---

37. Ed. Note: This point appears to follow the same complaint as Percy Dearmer's in his 1919 work *The Art of Public Worship*: "The one fact, that in all our revisions no attempt has been made so to print the Communion Service or the Litany as to show the dramatic culminations of its divisions, may serve as sufficient illustration of our lack of liturgical instinct in the past." (Dearmer, *The Art of Public Worship* (Oxford: Mowbray, 1919), 24).

38. *Some Principles of Liturgical Reform*, p. 169

The Supplication is of great value in such 'times of war and national anxiety' as overshadow the world at present.[39] It is perhaps too brief to be usable as a separate office. It can be added to the Litany, as of old; or used after the Third Collect of the services of Morning or Evening Prayer; or inserted before the Sermon at the Liturgy. These uses are therefore suggested by its rubric.

'The Litany of Saint Chrysostom'

We have noted that the Scottish 'Shorter Litany II' has a kind of adaptation of the Byzantine Liturgical Litany. Its style and arrangement are Eastern, but it is rather freely supplemented by congruous supplications: it might be called a sort of 'St. Chrysostom up to date.'

We on the other hand have had the idea of reconstructing the full original form of the Byzantine Litany-Intercessions. We have observed that in the time of Justin Martyr the General Intercession occurred after the Sermon and before the Offertory: and in the fourth-century text of the parent Liturgy of Antioch as recorded in the *Apostolic Constitutions* we find the Great Litany in exactly that place. Also, that in the early fifth century, when forms of the Litany first appeared in the West, this was apparently still true in the Liturgy of Constantinople, from which these forms were derived, since the structural framework is that of the present Litany after the Gospel, though the content of the supplications covers that of the Great Litany as well. It seems to have been since that time that the Litany has been duplicated at the Offertory, and at the beginning of the service: and the latter of these, the so-called Enarxis Litany, has absorbed the majority of the heads of intercession, and thus become the 'Great Litany' of that rite. To recover the full text of the Byzantine Litany as it stood about the year 400, one must collate the three present variants.

Evidence for this is found in the Litanies in the Stowe Missal, the Fulda Codex, and the Ambrosian Missal. When we find one or the other of the Byzantine variants supported by these, and also attested by the parent form in the *Apostolic Constitutions*, we may be fairly sure that it was present in the original form at Constantinople. The Western texts in fact furnish direct evidence for the state of the Byzantine Litany at the start of the fifth century, though no Greek texts have come down to us from that period.

We have therefore added to the basic text of the Great Litany at the Enarxis of the Byzantine service the following expressions:

From the Byzantine Litany after the Gospel:

> With all our heart and with all our mind, let us pray to the Lord, saying,
> Lord, have mercy. (Stowe, Fulda, Milan.)

---

39. Ed. Note: It is unclear when this passage was written. The earlier reference to Roosevelt's 1941 State of the Union address in conjuction with this comment raises the question whether this material address the post-war setting when it was published or war-time work.

For all who bring forth fruit and do good works of mercy (AC, Stowe, Fulda, Milan: though 'of mercy' is not in the Byzantine).

From the Byzantine Litany at the Offertory:

For things good and profitable to our souls and bodies (AC, 'St. James').
That the end of our lives may be Christian, without suffering and without reproach (AC, Stowe, Fulda).

From the parent rite of Antioch:

and the loving-kindness of God (James).
and all those in authority (AC, Stowe, Fulda).
for the aged and infirm (AC, James).
for widows and orphans (AC, Stowe, Fulda, Milan).

The two phrases derived from the original Antiochene sources, and not supported by the Western versions, cannot, of course, be certified as ever having been in the Byzantine text, though we deem their inclusion in our form to be desirable. Otherwise, we consider we are on firm ground in our undertaking to restore the content of the original Great Litany of Constantinople.

As to our proposed title for this form, of course it is true that this is a 'Litany of St. Chrysostom' only in the same sense that the Collect at the end of Morning Prayer is a 'Prayer of St. Chrysostom.' Both belong to the common framework of the Byzantine Liturgy, into which the Anaphoras of St. Basil and St. Chrysostom are inserted on different occasions. But the latter is much the dominant form, used on all but a few occasions of the year. To speak of the 'Liturgy of St. Chrysostom' when referring to the major rite of the Eastern Orthodox Churches is much more convenient than to say 'Byzantine' or 'Constantinopolitan,' and as natural as to say 'Sarum' instead of 'pre-Reformation English.'

Furthermore, there is a strong possibility that the Great Litany of Constantinople was actually composed by the author of the Anaphora of St. Chrysostom. Compared with the parent forms of Antioch, in the *Apostolic Constitutions* or even in 'St. James,' this Litany has an extraordinary condensation. All the 'result-clauses' are left out, and the text reduced to the minimal heads of intercession, This is all entirely in the spirit of the Anaphora of St. Chrysostom, which reduced the long Thanksgiving for the Redemption to — John 3: 16!

There is nothing in the very voluminous liturgical quotations of St. John Chrysostom to indicate that he ever used any liturgy at Constantinople except the parent rite of Antioch, in the ample form in which it is presented in the *Apostolic Constitutions*. He is the last man in the world to have composed the drastically abbreviated Anaphora which now goes by his name. Nevertheless, it may have been made in his time, and with his sanction: with the result that we have the name of the *imprimatur*, not the author. And there seems to be every reason to think that it was the same author who condensed the Byzantine litany-forms to their essentials.

Since therefore we have a Liturgy, and a Prayer, 'commonly called' after St. Chrysostom, it would seem entirely in order to use the same identification for the Litany. It would be a more convenient — to say nothing of being a more attractive designation than the Scottish 'Shorter Litany II.'

We believe it will be a real enrichment to the Prayer Book to have this ancient form, which is at once so comprehensive, and so brief, trenchant, and vivid in its language. Upon occasion, it would furnish a useful alternative to the General Intercession in the Liturgy — a substitution which a rubric in that service proposes expressly to permit.

BAYARD H. JONES
MORTON C. STONE
for the Commission

The Revised Version

The Great Litany

¶ To be said or sung, kneeling, standing, or in procession; after the Third Collect of Morning or Evening Prayer; or before the Liturgy; or separately; especially in Advent, Lent, and upon the Rogation Days.

The Invocations

O God the Father, Creator of heaven and earth,
Have mercy upon us.

O God the Son, Redeemer of the world,
Have mercy upon us.

O God the Holy Ghost, Sanctifier of the faithful,
Have mercy upon us.

O holy, blessed, and glorious Trinity, one God,
Have mercy upon us.

REMEMBER not, Lord, our offences, nor the offences of our forefathers; neither reward us according to our sins: Spare us, good Lord, spare thy people, whom thou hast redeemed with thy most precious blood, and by thy mercy preserve us forever,
Spare us, good Lord.

The Deprecations

FROM all evil; from sin; from inordinate and sinful affections; and from all the deceits of the world, the flesh, and the devil,
Good Lord, deliver us.
From all blindness of heart; from pride, vainglory, and hypocrisy; from envy, hatred, and malice, and all uncharitableness,
Good Lord, deliver us.
From all sedition, privy conspiracy, and rebellion; from all false doctrine, heresy, and schism; from hardness of heart, and contempt of thy Word and Commandment,
Good Lord, deliver us.
From lightning and tempest; from earthquake, fire, and flood; from plague, pestilence, and famine; from battle and murder, and from sudden death,
Good Lord, deliver us.

The Obsecrations

BY the mystery of thy holy Incarnation; by thy Baptism, Fasting, and Temptation,
Good Lord, deliver us.
By thine Agony and Bloody Sweat; by thy Cross and Passion; by thy precious Death and Burial; by thy glorious Resurrection and Ascension; and by the Coming of the Holy Ghost,
Good Lord, deliver us.
In all time of our tribulation; in all time of our prosperity; in the hour of death, and in the day of judgment, Good Lord, deliver us.

The Intercessions

WE sinners do beseech thee to hear us, O Lord God, and that it may please thee to rule and govern thy holy Church Universal in the right way,
We beseech thee to hear us, good Lord.
That it may please thee so to rule the hearts of thy servants, The President of the United States, and all others in authority, that thy Church, being hurt by no persecutions, may serve thee in security and peace,
We beseech thee to hear us, good Lord.
That it may please thee to enlighten all Bishops, Priests, and Deacons, with true knowledge and understanding of thy Word, and that both by their preaching and living they may set it forth, and show it accordingly,
We beseech thee to hear us, good Lord.

That it may please thee to send forth labourers into thy harvest; and to extend thy Church over all the earth,

We beseech thee to hear us, good Lord.

That it may please thee to bless and keep all thy people,

We beseech thee to hear us, good Lord.

That it may please thee to give us an heart to love and fear thee, and diligently to live after thy commandments,

We beseech thee to hear us, good Lord.

That it may please thee to give us true repentance; to forgive us all our sins, negligences, and ignorances; and to endue us with the grace of thy Holy Spirit to amend our lives according to thy holy Word,

We beseech thee to hear us, good Lord.

That it may please thee to strengthen such as do stand; and to comfort and help the weak-hearted; and to raise up those who fall; and finally to beat down Satan under our feet,

We beseech thee to hear us, good Lord.

That it may please thee to help, support, and strengthen all who are in danger, need, and tribulation,

We beseech thee to hear us, good Lord.

That it may please thee to preserve all who travel by land, by water, or by air, all women in child-birth, all sick persons and young children; and to show thy pity upon all prisoners and captives,

We beseech thee to hear us, good Lord.

That it may please thee to defend and provide for the fatherless children, and widows, and all who are desolate and oppressed,

We beseech thee to hear us, good Lord.

That it may please thee to have mercy upon all men,

We beseech thee to hear us, good Lord.

That it may please thee to bless all who serve in medicine or the law, all who minister in commerce, industry, or agriculture; and to guide with thy wisdom all who seek thy truth in art, science, or education,

We beseech thee to hear us, good Lord.

That it may please thee to make wars to cease in all the world; to give to all nations unity, peace, and concord; and to bestow upon all peoples the liberty to serve thee without fear,

We beseech thee to hear us, good Lord.

That it may please thee to forgive our enemies, persecutors, and slanderers, and to turn their hearts,

We beseech thee to hear us, good Lord.

That it may please thee to bring into the way of truth all such as have erred, and are deceived,
We beseech thee to hear us, good Lord.
That it may please thee to give and preserve to our use the bountiful fruits of the earth, so that in due time we may enjoy them,
We beseech thee to hear us, good Lord.
That it may please thee to grant to all the faithful departed eternal life and peace,
We beseech thee to hear us, good Lord.
That it may please thee to grant that with all thy Saints we may attain to thy heavenly kingdom,
We beseech thee to hear us, good Lord.

SON of God, we beseech thee to hear us.
Son of God, we beseech thee to hear us.

¶ *When the Liturgy followeth immediately the Litany may end here, and the Liturgy may begin with the Kyrie eleison.*

Agnus Dei

LAMB of God, who takest away the sins of the world,
Have mercy upon us.
O Lamb of God, who takest away the sins of the world,
Have mercy upon us.
O Lamb of God, who takest away the sins of the world,
Grant us thy peace.

Kyrie eleison

¶ *Minister and People*

Lord, have mercy upon us.
Christ, have mercy upon us.
Lord, have mercy upon us.

Lord's Prayer

OUR Father, who art in heaven, Hallowed be thy Name. Thy kingdom come. Thy will be done, On earth as it is in heaven. Give us this day our daily bread. And forgive us our trespasses, As we forgive those who trespass against us. And lead us not into temptation, But deliver us from evil. Amen.

O Lord, let thy mercy be showed upon us,
As we do put our trust in thee.
The Lord be with you,
And with thy spirit.
Let us pray.

The Collect

ALMIGHTY God, who hast promised to hear the petitions of those who ask in thy Son's Name; We beseech thee to incline thine ear to us who have now made our supplications unto thee; and grant that those things which we have asked faithfully according to thy will, may be obtained effectually, to the relief of our necessity, and to the setting forth of thy glory; through Jesus Christ our Lord, to whom, with thee and the Holy Ghost, be all honour and glory, world without end. *Amen.*

† † †

The Supplication

¶ For use after the Great Litany; or after the Third Collect of Morning or Evening Prayer; or before the Sermon at the Liturgy, especially on penitential days and in times of war or national anxiety.

Antiphon. O Lord, arise, help us; * *and deliver us for thy Name's sake.*

Psalm 44:I. *Deus auribus.*

O GOD, we have heard with our ears, and our fathers have declared unto us,
The noble works that thou didst in their days, and in the old time before them.
Glory be to the Father, and to the Son, and to the Holy Ghost,
As it was in the beginning, is now, and ever shall be, world without end. Amen.
Antiphon. O Lord, arise, help us; * *and deliver us for thy Name's sake.*

FROM our enemies defend us, O Christ.
Graciously look upon our afflictions.
With pity behold the sorrows of our hearts.
Mercifully forgive the sins of thy people.

Favourably with mercy hear our prayers.
O Son of David, have mercy upon us.
Both now and ever vouchsafe to hear us, O Christ.
Graciously hear us, O Lord Christ.
The Lord be with you,
And with this spirit.
Let us pray.

The Collect

WE humbly beseech thee, O Father, mercifully to look upon our infirmities; and, for the glory of thy Name, turn from us all those evils that we most justly have deserved; and grant, that in all our troubles we may put our whole trust and confidence in thy mercy, and evermore serve thee in holiness and pureness of living, to thy honour and glory; through our only Mediator and Advocate, Jesus Christ our Lord. *Amen.*

The Litany of Saint Chrysostom

¶ For use in place of the Great Litany; or in place of the Prayer for the Church in the Liturgy; or separately.

With all our heart and with all our mind, let us pray to the Lord, saying:
    Lord, have mercy.

FOR the peace from above, for the loving-kindness of God, and for the salvation of our souls, let us pray to the Lord,
Lord, have mercy.
For the peace of the whole world, and for the welfare and unity of the holy Church of God, let us pray to the Lord,
Lord, have mercy.
For the President of the United States, and for all those in authority, let us pray to the Lord,
Lord, have mercy.
For our Bishop, and for all the clergy and people, let us pray to the Lord,
Lord, have mercy.
For this place, and for all the faithful who dwell here, let us pray to the Lord,
Lord, have mercy.
For all who bring forth fruit, and do good works of mercy, let us pray to the Lord,

Lord, have mercy.

For deliverance from all tribulation, hostility, danger, and privation, let us pray to the Lord,

Lord, have mercy.

For those who travel by land, by water, or by air, and for all prisoners and captives, let us pray to the Lord,

Lord, have mercy.

For the aged and infirm, for widows and orphans, and for all the sick and suffering, let us pray to the Lord,

Lord, have mercy.

For seasonable weather, and for an abundance of the fruits of the earth, let us pray to the Lord,

Lord, have mercy.

For all things good and profitable to our souls and bodies, let us pray to the Lord,

Lord, have mercy.

That the end of our lives may be Christian, without suffering and without reproach, let us pray to the Lord,

Lord, have mercy.

In the Communion of Saints, let us commend ourselves, and one another, and all our life, to Christ our God.

O THOU who hast given us grace at this time with one accord to make our common supplications unto thee; and dost promise that when two or three are agreed together in thy Name thou wilt grant their requests; Fulfil now, O Lord, the desires and petitions of thy servants, as may be most expedient for them; granting us in this world knowledge of thy truth, and in the world to come life everlasting; through thy mercy, O Christ, to whom with the Father and the Holy Ghost be all honour and glory, world without end. *Amen.*

PRAYER BOOK STUDIES VI: MORNING AND EVENING PRAYER

The Standing Liturgical Commission
of the Protestant Episcopal Church in the
United States of America

1957

PREFACE

The last revision of our Prayer Book was brought to a rather abrupt conclusion in 1928. Consideration of it had preoccupied the time of General Convention ever since 1913. Everyone was weary of the long and ponderous legislative process, and desired to make the new Prayer Book available as soon as possible for the use of the Church.

But the work of revision, which sometimes has seemed difficult to start, in this case proved hard to stop. The years of debate had aroused widespread interest in the whole subject: and the mind of the Church was more receptive of suggestions for revision when the work was brought to an end than when it began. Moreover, the revision was actually closed to new action in 1925, in order that it might receive final adoption in 1928: so that it was not possible to give due consideration to a number of very desirable features in the English and Scottish revisions, which appeared simultaneously with our own. It was further realized that there were some rough edges in what had been done, as well as an unsatisfied demand for still further alterations.

The problem of defects in detail was met by continuing the Revision Commission, and giving it rather large 'editorial' powers (subject only to review by General Convention) to correct obvious errors in the text as adopted, in the publication of the new Prayer Book. Then, to deal with the constructive proposals for other changes which continued to be brought up in every General Convention, the Revision Commission was reconstituted as a Standing Liturgical Commission. To this body all matters concerning the Prayer Book were to be referred, for preservation in permanent files, and for continuing consideration, until such time as the accumulated matter was sufficient in amount and importance to justify proposing another Revision.

The number of such referrals by General Convention, of Memorials from Dioceses, and of suggestions made directly to the Commission from all regions and schools and parties in the Church, has now reached such a total that it is evident that there is a widespread and insistent demand for a general revision of the Prayer Book.

The Standing Liturgical Commission is not, however, proposing any immediate revision. On the contrary, we believe that there ought to be a period of study and discussion, to acquaint the Church at large with the principles and issues involved, in order that the eventual action may be taken intelligently, and if possible without consuming so much of the time of our supreme legislative synod.

Accordingly, the General Convention of 1949 signaled the Fourth Centennial Year of the First Book of Common Prayer in English by authorizing the Liturgical Commission to publish its findings, in the form of a series of *Prayer Book Studies*.

It must be emphasized that the liturgical forms presented in these *Studies* are not — and under our Constitution, cannot be — sanctioned for public use. They are submitted for free discussion. The Commission will be grateful for copies or articles, resolutions, and direct comment, for its consideration, that the mind of the Church may be fully known to the body charged with reporting it.

In this undertaking, we have endeavored to be objective and impartial. It is not possible to avoid every matter which may be thought by some to be controversial. Ideas which seem to be constructively valuable will be brought to the attention of the Church, without too much regard as to whether they may ultimately be judged to be expedient. We cannot undertake to eliminate every proposal to which anyone might conceivably object: to do so would be to admit that any constructive progress is impossible. What we can do is to be alert not to alter the present *balance* of expressed or implied doctrine of the Church. We can seek to counterbalance every proposal which might seem to favor some one party of opinion by some other change in the opposite direction. The goal we have constantly had in mind — however imperfectly we may have succeeded in attaining it — is the shaping of a future Prayer Book which *every* party might embrace with the well-founded conviction that therein its own position had been strengthened, its witness enhanced, and its devotions enriched.

The objective we have pursued is the same as that expressed by the Commission for the Revision of 1892: "*Resolved*, That this Committee, in all its suggestions and acts, be guided by those principles of liturgical construction and ritual use which have guided the compilation and amendments of the Book of Common Prayer, and have made it what it is."

THE STANDING LITURGICAL COMMISSION:

GOODRICH R. FENNER, *Chairman*
ARTHUR C. LICHTENBERGER
BAYARD H. JONES, *Vice Chairman*
JOHN W. SUTER, *Custodian*
MASSEY H. SHEPHERD, JR.
CHARLES W. F. SMITH
FRANCIS B. SAYRE, JR.
BERTRAM L. SMITH
SPENCER ERVIN, *Secretary*
JOHN ASHTON

The Commission desires to express its gratitude to the Reverend Paul Hartzell for much preliminary work in connection with the Study on the Daily Offices; and to two former members of the Commission, the Reverend Morton C. Stone and the Reverend Walter Williams, for drafting materials in the earlier stages of work on the Penitential Office. The sub-committee on the Daily Offices has been headed by Dr. Shepherd; that on the Penitential Office, by Bishop Lichtenberger.

History of Revision

The genius of our Common Prayer is in no instance more clearly exemplified than in the Daily Offices of Morning and Evening Prayer. Out of the elaborate, complicated Canonical Hours of the medieval Breviary the sixteenth century Reformers produced a pattern of daily, praise and prayer that was loyal to tradition, solidly Scriptural in content, simple and convenient in execution, balanced and artful in design. The older Latin Offices had been a primary duty of the clergy, the monks and the friars, upon whom their recitation was imposed by canonical law. But the Reformers intended their simpler, vernacular forms to be a means of corporate worship and of edification in the knowledge of God's Word for all the laity no less than for the clergy. In this purpose their labors have borne abundant fruit. To no other part of the Prayer Book have the lay people shown greater attachment and responsiveness.

The arrangement of the Offices in the 1549 Prayer Book has remained basic through all subsequent revisions. The Lord's Prayer and opening versicles introduce the appointed psalmody. Then follow the two lessons, first from the Old Testament, then from the New, with each lesson followed by a responsive canticle. The Apostles' Creed, a set of suffrages, and three Collects, the first one of the Day, bring them to a close. To this pattern each successive revision since 1549 has made some addition or modification, but never has any alteration of the essential structure of the Offices been proposed.

The 1552 Book gave us the penitential introduction, and the 1661 revision appended the intercessions for the State and the Clergy and People, the Prayer of St. Chrysostom and the Grace.

Our first American Book of 1789 made a number of changes and additions. Several new opening Sentences were included, and the Absolution from the Holy Communion was provided as an alternative. The conclusion of the *Venite* was altered by substituting verses 9 and 13 of Psalm 96 for the last four verses of Psalm 95. The *Gloria in excelsis* was permitted as an alternative to the Gloria Patri. According to Bishop White it was thought that its addition "would add to the beauty of the service."[1] A long-standing Puritan prejudice against the use of the Gospel canticles caused the lamentable excision of the Gospel canticles, except for the first four verses of the Benedictus in Morning Prayer. To make up for this loss new psalm-canticles were introduced as alternatives in Evening Prayer. A curious innovation was the provision of the Nicene Creed as an alternative to the Apostles' Creed. This was done, no doubt, with a view to satisfying the objections of the English bishops to the omission of the Nicene Creed altogether from the Proposed Prayer Book of 1786. At Morning Prayer the versicles before the

---

1. The *Gloria in excelsis* was removed from Morning Prayer in the 1928 Book, but not from Evening Prayer. It has never been very much used in the Daily Offices.

Collects were reduced from six pairs to two. Finally, the Prayer for All Conditions of Men and the General Thanksgiving were moved from the occasional Prayers and Thanksgivings to a place within the Offices proper.

In their review of the liturgy in 1789 our founding fathers adopted a new guiding principle which was to be extended and developed in later revisions: namely, the avoidance of unnecessary duplications. At that time, the ordinary Sunday morning service consisted of Morning Prayer, Litany and Ante-Communion, with the full Holy Communion rite celebrated, in most parishes, about four times a year. In order to remove the repetitions of material, which such a combination of offices entailed, the revisers omitted the Lord's Prayer in its second occurrence in the Offices, immediately after the Creed, and allowed its omission also at the beginning of the Communion.

Likewise the Collect for the Day was omitted from Morning Prayer "when the Communion Service is read." After the Prayer for the President a new rubric was inserted: "The following Prayers are to be omitted here, when the Litany is read."[2] One should note also that the Ante-Communion was concluded with the Gospel, not with the Prayer for the Church, as in the English Book; for this provision may explain in part why the Nicene Creed was placed in Morning Prayer as an alternative to the Apostles' Creed. If a creed had once been said in Morning Prayer, it seemed unnecessary to say the same creed or another one in Ante-Communion. At the same time the English bishops could be reassured that the Nicene Creed would not be altogether neglected.

Over a hundred years elapsed before the next revision of the American Prayer Book was completed. In the meantime the Memorialist Movement had made a telling impression upon the mind of the Church, with its insistence upon a more flexible use of the Church's liturgical offices. The rapid growth of our parishes and the more varied make-up of their congregations demanded an increase in parish schedules for worship, not only on Sundays but also on weekdays. With this new need came a correspondent demand for more freedom in adapting the length of the Prayer Book rites to suit varying occasions and different types of worshippers. The Catholic revival of the mid-nineteenth century awakened in many a greater appreciation for some of the liturgical treasures of the past that had been lost in successive revisions of the Prayer Book; and this circumstance, combined with the controversies over "ritualism," pointed up the need not only for flexibility but for enrichment.

The 1892 Prayer Book made great advances in these new directions. For the first time substantial provisions were made for shortening the Offices. The

---

2. The rubric was placed after the Prayer for the President instead of the third Collect because of George Washington's desire to hear this prayer read, inasmuch as he was seldom able to attend Evening Prayer. It will be recalled that the Litany did not include a specific petition for the President until the 1928 revision.

penitential introduction of the Offices could be omitted at Morning Prayer on any day when the Holy Communion was to follow immediately, and at Evening Prayer it could be omitted on any weekday. A brief bidding to the General Confession was allowed as a substitute for the long Exhortation at any time in Evening Prayer, and on a weekday at Morning Prayer. The prayers after the Prayer for the President were to be optional, not only when the Litany was read, but whenever the Holy Communion followed Morning Prayer. At the evening office the minister was allowed to end the service after the third Collect with any prayer or prayers from the Book that he might deem fitting.

Notable enrichments were also made in the 1892 Book. The Gospel canticles were restored, although the full *Benedictus* was not required to be used in entirety except when sung during the season of Advent. The opening Sentences were much revised, with many new passages proper to the seasonal themes of the Christian Year added. An anthem after the third Collect at Evening Prayer was allowed, as in the English Book, but this provision was not made for Morning Prayer.

Our last revision of 1913-28 continued along the lines laid down in the 1892 Book. The opening Sentences were again reworked to afford greater seasonal variety. The penitential introduction could now be omitted at any time except at Morning Prayer on days of fasting and abstinence. Seasonal antiphons were provided for use with the *Venite*; and the canticle *Benedictus es*, proposed for the 1892 revision, was adopted for Morning Prayer. In place of the alternative Absolution from Holy Communion, allowed at Evening Prayer, a new Absolution, taken from the ancient Office of Compline, was substituted. The most notable concession to flexibility, however, was the option granted of omitting all of Morning Prayer after the first lesson and canticle whenever the Holy Communion immediately followed, as also the permission to omit one lesson and canticle any time the minister so desired in Evening Prayer. This new provision was the first trespass upon the original, basic structure of the Office and one of its essential elements; namely the lectionary.

Such in brief is the record of our present inheritance. Without doubt, future revisions of the Prayer Book will witness new modifications of addition or subtraction. The Liturgical Commission has already received many suggestions for improvements in detail. In some cases these suggestions have been so unanimously in accord as to imply that the Church as a whole is ready to proceed with the desired changes. On other points, however, there is sharp disagreement. The Commission has tried to assess the respective arguments for or against this or that alteration as impartially as possible in the light of the larger perspectives of historical tradition, liturgical fitness, and practical value. We turn therefore to a consideration of the proposals made to us, first the more general problems and principles, and secondly the more detailed points.

Proposed Revisions

There have been many voices raised against any further extension of the principle of flexibility and the provision of alternative forms, and in favor of a more strict uniformity of observance of the Offices with the elimination of some of the alternate forms now provided. It is believed that overmuch variability is confusing to the laity and makes it difficult for them to follow the service in their Prayer Books, when many pages of alternative forms have to be skipped in order to keep up with the officiant. Certainly some of the less used variations can be eliminated, such as the Nicene Creed and (in Evening Prayer) the *Gloria in excelsis*, inasmuch as both of these already have their established place in the Eucharistic liturgy. There is also general agreement that the Lord's Prayer should be removed from its early position after the Absolution so that it always occurs in the same place, *i.e.,* at the point of climax in the Office, after the Creed and before the prayers. Another point at which variability seems unwise is the use of the canticle *Benedictus* in its shortened form of four verses. Such a mutilation of a Gospel canticle is unjustifiable, not only from the standpoint of liturgical tradition, but also from the vantage point of the inherent value of the text of the canticle itself.

There are weighty considerations, however, against the imposing of restrictions upon the flexibilities of use which recent revisions have given us. The experience of using the Offices with so many different types of congregation with varying needs of time and occasion has proved their larger effectiveness when they can be adapted in length and content. The Offices are not occasional ones, infrequently used. Their basic structure is well known to the laity who use them regularly. Confusion arising from constant employment of alternatives can be exaggerated. Those who read the Offices regularly, as they were intended to be used, are the ones who appreciate most the variations now available. They should not be penalized by the tedium of rigid uniformity in order to satisfy the difficulties of casual and uninstructed worshippers. There are points at which further possibilities of variation may very well be tried. Many requests have been made, for example, for greater freedom in the choice of canticles. These will be discussed in due course. The Commission does wish to go on record, however, in opposing any rubrical provision for shortening the Offices beyond what is now allowed, lest there be real sacrifice of basic material such as the Psalter and the lessons of Scripture.

Of a quite different character have been the proposals made to the Commission for such a reconstruction of the Offices as to make them more serviceable for general occasions of worship of a catechetical or missionary character. Specifically this would involve the permission to substitute metrical hymns for the Psalms and canticles, and greater freedom given to the officiant to select lessons of his choice so as to give a central topicaltheme to the entire service. It is argued, not without some reason, that many congregations exhibit little enthusiasm for chanting, and that the vicarious rendition of much of the Office by trained choirs robs the people of active participation which is rightfully theirs in any true liturgical act. Furthermore it is contended that the majority of the laity shares in the Office once a week at most, and not daily, and that therefore a service built around one dominant theme is more meaningful to them than one containing varied strands of teaching derived from continuous course readings.

Somewhat akin to this proposal is the suggestion made from time to time that we need two different types of non-sacramental, general services of worship in the Prayer Book: one similar to our present Daily Offices, another of a more general character with maximum freedom allowed the minister in choosing psalms and hymns, lessons and prayers. In line with this view is the criticism frequently made that Morning and Evening Prayer are too exactly similar in outline and content. Two offices constructed in different ways would be of value. Inasmuch as no adequate substitute has been advanced to take the place of either Morning or Evening Prayer, the Commission does not consider itself responsible for the construction of such a new office. We would in turn call attention to a provision already existing in the Prayer Book under the general rubric "Concerning the Service of the Church," where such services of a general character are permitted in lieu of Morning or Evening Prayer when authorized by the Ordinary.

The Commission is not unsympathetic to the very real pastoral and practical problems which these more radical proposals present. The hearty participation of our congregations in the liturgical offices should be for all of us a primary desideratum. But hymn-singing in many of our congregations is often as much of a problem as lack of zeal in chanting. The lectionary passed by General Convention in 1943 provides related psalms and lessons for Sundays and special occasions. Clergy who take the trouble to study these schedules will discover many topical themes, giving unity of thought to the entire service without sacrifice of the broader doctrinal framework which the fixed portions of the Office give them. It should also be pointed out that inasmuch as so many of the laity do not participate publicly in both the Offices so much as weekly, much less daily, there is little evidence that they find the two Offices tiresome by reason of their close similarity of structure.

A constant occasion of criticism of our Prayer Book rites is the archaisms of its language. The ideal of our liturgy is always that it be "understanded of the people." Every revision of our liturgy has attempted to fulfill this purpose by alterations or retranslations of words and phrases which have ceased to convey their proper meanings. The clergy are sometimes not fully aware of the extent of semantic difficulties which the laity have with some of our inherited terminology in the liturgy. Yet it is always a delicate problem to reword traditional forms without loss of dignity of expression and rhythm of style, not to speak of the more indefinable emotional overtones which familiar and long-used phrases carry with them. In this matter, questions of taste are no less important than considerations of reason. The Commission has tried to steer a middle course amongst the various suggestions presented to us for alterations of text in the Daily Office. We should not be afraid to make changes in the direction of a more modern English, provided the new expressions are forceful and clear. At the same time we do not reject older ways of expression merely because they are old or somewhat different from modern idiom. We must remember that each generation has contributed something of its style and vocabulary to our corporate prayer. Our own distraught times can also make an offering to the continuing, living voice of aspiration and petition.

We must ever bear in mind the primary ends for which the Daily Offices exist and the purposes they are meant to serve. They are not mere devotional adjuncts to the preaching and teaching ministries of the Church. They have a rationale of their own, independent in their own right, as complete acts of meditation and worship. They are the Church's day-by-day offerings of praise and supplication to God for His wondrous and manifold acts of love, mercy, and judgment towards all His creatures. Their proper impact upon our lives is cumulative in effect. For this reason the elements in them that are particular and immediate in reference are subsumed within the larger framework of what is universal in our faith and continuous in our experience. Their abiding value unto edification lies in such a well-knit balance.

Outline and Arrangement

Every well-constructed liturgical office has an inherent design whereby its several parts are arranged in logical sequence and rhythmic movement. Our Daily Offices are noteworthy examples of this liturgical art, yet curiously their structural pattern is not readily grasped by many who participate in them. The long Exhortation appointed before the General Confession gives their outline. But this Exhortation is frequently not read; and when it is used, it suggests a greater preponderance given to the penitential elements in the Offices than is actually the case. Another source of confusion is the fact that some of the most important elements in the Offices require much less printed space than others of a minor significance. For example, the optional antiphons to the *Venite*, though printed in smaller type, take up half a page, whereas the lessons are referred to in two brief rubrics.

Our congregations would profit by the insertion of captions in capital letters that mark off the chief divisions of the Offices, in addition to the titles now appearing in italics for the several canticles and prayers. These larger subheads are comparable to those the Commission has already proposed in its Study of Baptism and Confirmation and the Holy Communion. Steps in this direction, so far as the Offices are concerned, were made in the English Proposed Book of 1928, the Scottish Book of 1929, and the South African Book of 1944. The captions are uniform for both Morning and Evening Prayer: The Introduction, The Psalter, The Word of God, The Apostles' Creed and The Prayers.

In addition, the long Exhortation has been revised in part to make these divisions more clear:

- to make humble confession of our sins;
- to set forth his most worthy praise;
- to hear his most holy Word;
- to declare our faith in him;
- to ask. . . those things which are necessary; to offer to him the service of our lives; and to receive his blessing.

Of course, these divisions overlap. A psalm may make confession of our sins or declare our faith; the reading of the Scriptures is a means of setting forth God's most worthy praise. In the main, however, these divisions correspond to the major portions of the Offices in their most distinctive elements.

Another question of arrangement involves the advisability of printing twice, *i.e.,* in both Morning and Evening Prayer, those parts which both Offices have in common: the introduction and the prayers after the Third Collect. The English Proposed Book and the Scottish 1929 Book have suggested the plan of a single printing of the introduction; and the English Proposed Book and the South African Book have omitted the intercessions after the Third Collect and removed them to the occasional Prayers and Thanksgivings. The plan which we propose is somewhat different, being suggested by the actual uses now generally prevailing in our parishes.

Our Sunday congregations for Morning and Evening Prayer are seldom composed of the same group of worshippers. Hence it would seem advisable to repeat the printing of the introduction as a preface to Evening Prayer, inasmuch as all the people join in the General Confession. It would be inconvenient, if not confusing, for the evening congregation to begin its worship with forms printed at the beginning of Morning Prayer, and then turn some fourteen or fifteen pages in order to resume the service. Most of the Opening Sentences, however, we propose to print once, in Morning Prayer, leaving only the few that are especially appropriate to evening worship to be retained in the preface to Evening Prayer. A rubric makes clear that the Minister may use any of the Sentences in Morning Prayer at the evening service also if he so desires.

The intercessions now printed at the end of Evening Prayer are omitted. They are provided in full in Morning Prayer, as this Office is commonly used by many congregations as their principal service of worship on Sunday morning. The Minister is therefore more likely to use them at Morning Prayer, in their entirety. It may be that a second printing of the General Thanksgiving at Evening Prayer would be desirable, since it has become customary to recite this form by all the people joining with the Minister. The advisability of retaining the Prayer for the President which now occurs in Evening Prayer will be discussed later.

Recommended Changes

The Introduction

The introductory section of the Offices has been the subject of the largest number of proposals for change and revision. This has been due in large measure to widespread dissatisfaction with much of its phraseology. In many parishes the reading of the long Exhortation has virtually fallen out of use. Yet the alternative short bidding, when used in its place, has seemed overly abrupt. It gives the congregation scarce time for any recollection before making confession of their sins together. There have been many requests for at least some period of silence preceding this solemn act of penitent approach before the presence of God.

Various suggestions have also been offered with respect to the rubrical directions for the use of the introduction. Some would have it required on Sundays of Lent no less than on days of fasting and abstinence, in order to assure its reading at least sometime to a Sunday morning congregation. (In the English Proposed Book the long Exhortation was so required on the first Sunday of Advent and the first Sunday of Lent.) Others have suggested a "once a month" requirement. Experience has shown, however, that such rubrical directions are consistently ignored by many of the clergy — not so much from captious individualism on their part, as from a sense of the artificiality of such regulations. The various propers of the Lenten season contain much penitential material. There is no necessity to underscore this aspect of our common prayer in Lent by a set of forms which must be repeated for six successive Sundays. Such rubrics also have the unhappy effect of suggesting to some clergy that the full penitential introduction is *only* suitable in Lent, or on the first Sunday of the month.

The Commission does not recommend, therefore, that any change be made in the present rubrical directions for beginning the Offices. Instead we plead for a serious consideration of the review of its content, as here proposed, in the hope that the alterations offered for study will commend themselves as more effective with present-day congregations, than what is now provided in the Prayer Book. Thus many of the clergy will be less tempted to take the maximum liberty allowed by the rubrics for omitting the penitential introduction altogether.

The Opening Sentences

We have noted that each successive revision of the Prayer Book in America has revised and enriched the appointed selections of opening Sentences. There is room for further improvements. Most of the present Sentences certainly should be retained. But a few of them can well be replaced by better selections, either because they are incomplete sentences (such as Eph. i.7) or because their seasonal symbolism is no longer readily apparent to the laity (as Isa. lii.1, Psalm cxviii.24). A new section is proposed under the caption "Saints' Days," and the Thanksgiving Day theme is subsumed under a larger title, "National Days." For the most part three Sentences have been provided for each season, except Lent, which has five. This exception is made because the Lenten sentences are always very apt for use on any occasion when the General Confession and Absolution are to follow.

By combining into one group the Sentences now separated and divided between Morning and Evening Prayer, with rubrical permission to use any of the Sentences at either service, the Minister is given a much richer body of material to draw upon than is allowed at present. Four Sentences, however, have been reserved for exclusive use at Evening Prayer — three of them already long familiar in association with this Office. The fourth (Psalm xcii.1, 2) is also familiar as the opening verses of the present evening canticle *Bonum est confiteri*. Inasmuch as we shall propose the excision of this canticle, we suggest that these verses may very well be retained for use at this place because of their suitability as an invitatory call to evening worship.

The Exhortations

Our present long Exhortation is a statement of consummate dignity and has a further merit in that it affords a succinct summary of the structure and contents of the Office. Yet more and more its repeated use falls into disfavor. In part this is due to the fact that a short alternative is always preferred by some officiants to a long one. But there are more weighty reasons. When the Exhortation was composed by Cranmer it was designed to follow opening Sentences that were invariably penitential in content. Hence the Exhortation itself stresses the penitential approach to the worship of God. Now that we employ more frequently the Sentences of a seasonal note, the Exhortation does not seem to fit so logically in the sequence of thought. For there is little point in saying that the Scripture moveth us, in sundry places, to confess our sins, unless such passages have actually been read as a reminder.

There is, however, a deeper difficulty in the use of the Exhortation by reason of the unconvincing *a fortiori* clause which it contains; namely, that we ought chiefly to acknowledge our sins when we assemble and meet together to render thanks, etc. As the late Dr. Brightman remarked, "it is not in fact intelligible to any one why he should confess his sins *to God, most chiefly* when *the Church* 'assembles and meets together.'"[3] This curious phraseology is the result of one of those conflations of sources to which Cranmer was addicted ever so often. (We shall have occasion to note another one in discussing the Prayer of St. Chrysostom.) From Hermann of Cologne, Cranmer took the perfectly acceptable idea that

---

3. F. E. Brightman, *The English Rite* (Rivingtons, 1951), I, clix.

"it is in accordance with true piety, that so often as we appear before God in his Church, we should first of all acknowledge and confess our sins and pray for remission." From the ninth century liturgist, Florus of Lyons, he took another equally justifiable statement: "although we ought, at all times, to acknowledge from our hearts that we are sinners, yet ought we most chiefly so to do the more attentively and perform the same, when in that holy Mystery [i.e., the Eucharist] is celebrated the grace of remission and forgiveness of sins." It will at once be noted that Cranmer has confused the two principles by making it appear that an act of penitence is the chief response of piety at any assemblage of the Church for worship, whether to receive the Eucharistic grace of forgiveness or not. What he apparently meant to say was that confession of sin is the first thing the Church ought to do before it proceeds to render thanks and praise and hear God's holy Word. Yet even this is open to question. It may well be that praise may at many times be a more fitting beginning of our worship than penitence.

The form which the Commission proposes as a substitute for the long Exhortation is designed to preserve the values of the older bidding while avoiding the pitfall of attempting to evaluate the respective merits of penitence as over against other elements of corporate worship. This form has been suggested by the one in the English Proposed Book of 1928, but it is by no means identical with it. It preserves much more of the language of the old Exhortation, than did the English substitute. We believe that it is an improvement on our present form in the following respects:

1. it states more objectively the divine presence in worship, and less subjectively man's attitudes in response to that presence;
2. it underscores the larger communion of saints in associating our common prayer with the whole company of heaven;
3. it gives a more complete outline of the several parts of the Office than does the present form; and
4. it provides for a period of silent recollection in the presence of God.

This last point has been made in response to numerous requests that a place be found in our Offices for the effective use of silence. The need for silence has especially been noted when the short bidding has been so frequently used before the General Confession. We therefore propose that a moment of silent waiting upon God always precede the act of confession, first that we may be fully aware of the momentous and awesome fact of God's presence in our midst and of our own unworthiness to stand in that presence without sincere penitence and contrition.

The Confession and Absolution

The General Confession in the Daily Offices has the strength of Biblical language, and, for common liturgical use, the advantage of objectivity of statement. It declares in forthright language both the fact of human sin, whether of commission or omission, and the assured promise of God to forgive sin for Christ's sake. The Confession does not betray the penitents into expressions of subjective emotions which they may not feel at the moment, and thereby arouse in them unnecessary anxieties of unreality. The worshipper may feel as deeply as he wishes, without embarrassment among his fellows. The confession objectifies this in a concrete statement that demands the rational assent of the will. Thus it is true to the proper genius of corporate, liturgical worship.

Two changes in the form, however, are herewith proposed. One is the dropping of the phrase: "And there is no health in us." The words are based upon passages in the Psalms. According to some authorities, it derives from Psalm xxxviii.3; others refer it to Psalm cxlvi.2, in which older versions of the Psalters read "health" for "help." Whatever the source, the word in this context means "saving health," the same as in the Prayer for All Conditions of Men. This archaic connotation of "health" is largely missed by modern congregations, and many worshippers are puzzled by it because the word speaks to them of physical, rather than of spiritual health. Another common misunderstanding is to take the phrase as a reference to the doctrine of man's total depravity — a doctrine never taught in our Communion. If the phrase is to be retained at all, it should be corrected to: "And there is no saving health in us," *i.e.*, there is no capacity in man to restore himself into God's graces. Our forgiveness is a free gift of God, and not contingent upon any ability of man to make amends for his sin in his own nature. The phrase "saving health" is itself archaic and demands careful explanation. It does not add anything to what has been said in the prayer. The Commission believes that the Confession would be more effective, if it were omitted altogether.

The other change recommended in the General Confession has to do with the re-arrangement of the final clauses, for greater clarity and smoothness of rhythm. It also shortens the prayer slightly.

In the 1928 revision, the Sarum Absolution was introduced as an alternative to the longer Declaration that came into the Prayer Book in 1552. It has proved popular, not merely because of its brevity, but because it is direct and to the point. The older form is argumentative, for Cranmer in writing it had in mind the extremists who would deny to the priesthood the right to pronounce absolution. More than that, the force of the longer Declaration is weakened by the exhortation contained in the second paragraph. We have just confessed our sins, and been declared forgiven. But the Declaration goes on to bid us to pray once more for "true repentance." The shorter Sarum form contains all the essential elements of the longer Declaration. The Commission believes that its use in Morning Prayer, in addition to Evening Prayer, would be advantageous. The oblation clause "through Jesus Christ our Lord" is added, in both Offices, for obvious reasons. At the same time, the rubric continues to permit the priest to substitute the form of Absolution in Holy Communion, if he so desires.

The omission of the Lord's Prayer after the Declaration has long been needed. The Lord's Prayer in all other offices of the Prayer Book comes at a climactic position, and generally introduces the prayers and intercessions of these offices. Its position in the preparatory part of the Daily Offices is a relic of the time when it was said privately, as a personal devotion, before the Office began. There is also an advantage in having the Lord's Prayer always come at the same place in the service, whether the penitential preparation has been said or not. Both the Scottish and the South African Prayer Books have removed the Lord's Prayer from the preparatory section, to give it its full climax after the Creed.

Psalms and Canticles

The versicles after the Absolution provide a neat transition to the next section of the Offices: the Psalms. The *Gloria Patri* of these versicles is a "common" antiphon to the whole body of psalms read or sung, and with the *Gloria* after the psalms gives a Christian doxological frame enclosing the whole psalmody. In the medieval Offices, the versicle was enriched by the singing of Alleluia immediately after the *Gloria* in festal seasons. Cranmer preserved this custom in the First Prayer Book; but in the Book of 1552 he omitted the Alleluia, presumably because he felt that "Praise ye the Lord," a literal translation of Alleluia, would be sufficient for any season of the Christian Year. This bidding led directly into the *Venite*. The 1662 revisers, however, seemed to have thought that a response was necessary to "Praise ye the Lord," and consequently they added the inane and tautological "The Lord's Name be praised." The Commission believes that a return to Cranmer's arrangement is desirable, so that the *Venite* itself become once again the congregational response to "Praise ye the Lord."

A more radical proposal with respect to Prayer Book tradition is the removal of the *Jubilate* from its place after the Second Lesson to a position alternative to the *Venite*. At first sight, this proposal may seem altogether too radical and unprecedented. The *Venite* has for centuries — long before the Reformation — served as the invitatory psalm of the Daily Offices. And it is pre-eminently suitable to this use. The problem here is not with the *Venite*, but with the *Jubilate* in its present position in the Prayer Book Offices. The *Jubilate* is an invitatory psalm, a summons to enter God's courts with praise. In the Jewish temple worship it was probably used to accompany processions before the sacrifices. Cranmer introduced it in the Second Prayer Book as an alternative to the *Benedictus*, doubtless with the aim of mollifying those more "Puritan" circles that objected — for reasons that seem to us most irrational — to the use of the Gospel canticles. But the 1662 Book went so far as to modify Cranmer's arrangement by inserting an express rubrical direction that the *Jubilate* was to supplant the *Benedictus* only on such occasions when the text of the *Benedictus* was included in the Second Lesson.

The lesson from the New Testament surely calls for a response of praise that is Christian in reference. This the *Jubilate* does not supply, and its obvious invitatory character makes it anti-climactic and incongruous in the position it now enjoys. At the same time, the *Jubilate* (Old Hundredth) is one of the finest and most beloved psalms. Congregations would not wish to give it up, except for the few occasions when it is appointed among the psalms for the day. We believe that its use, when desired, as an invitatory psalm, would satisfy both the desire of the laity for a more frequent use of the psalm and the greater appropriateness of its use near the beginning of the service. There is, of course, no inherent liturgical reason why both the *Venite* and the *Jubilate* might not be used together.

The removal of the *Jubilate* from its place after the Second Lesson led the Commission to a re-examination of the whole arrangement of canticles at Morning Prayer. It is known that Cranmer placed them in the order in which they appeared in the older Offices of the medieval Church: first those from Matins, and secondly those from Lauds. The result of this, however, was just the opposite in its rationale to that inherent in the order of the canticles at Evening Prayer. At Evening Prayer, the pre-Incarnation psalm *Magnificat* serves as a link between the Old and the New Testament, and the post-Incarnation psalm *Nunc Dimittis* supplies a responsory to the New Testament. The *Magnificat* summarizes the hope of the people of the Old Covenant as they looked forward to the manifestation of the Messiah-Redeemer. It thus leads logically into the New Testament lesson. The *Nunc Dimittis* looks back upon the birth of our Lord and celebrates its implications for all men. Now the same logical sequence can be obtained in Morning Prayer if the *Benedictus*, which like the *Magnificat* is a pre-Incarnation psalm, is placed after the First Lesson, and the *Te Deum*, a post-Incarnation hymn, follows and is responsory to the Second Lesson. And there is an additional advantage in this new arrangement, in that the *Te Deum* enjoys a more climactic place. The Commission, therefore, strongly recommends that favorable attention be given to this proposal.

By exchanging the positions of *Benedictus* and *Te Deum*, we found that further study of the morning canticles was demanded. The question in our minds was this: what would be suitable substitutes for these two canticles in the places where we have put them? (We assumed, of course, that at least one alternative to each of these canticles was desirable.) The *Benedictus es*, introduced in the 1928 revision, has proved very popular, though largely because it is a short canticle allowed to replace one or the other of two long ones. It does not have the richness of content of other canticles in the Prayer Book, and its language, or much of it, is not very plain to the average worshipper. There has been a strong demand from many quarters for something better. The Commission is agreed that there are better texts, and for this reason is ready to see the *Benedictus es* dropped from the Prayer Book. In its place, we propose a canticle drawn from Isaiah lx. This psalm is of Messianic character, like the *Benedictus*, and an excellent summary of the

Old Testament faith in God's promises of redemption. We have taken the text, with slight changes, from the Canadian Prayer Book, where it is set in a Special Service for Missions. Experiments have shown that this new canticle, *Surge Illuminator*, is easily pointed for chanting, and lends itself admirably to settings either of plainsong or of Anglican chants.

We were not so successful in finding a good alternative to the *Te Deum*. That would be almost comparable to finding a good substitute for the Creed! We have therefore left the *Benedicite*, its traditional alternative in the Prayer Book; and allowed the *Benedictus* to be used here, if it has not been used after the First Lesson. The Commission, however, would welcome suggestions of a good Christian canticle that serves as responsory to the New Testament lesson. In printing the *Benedicite* we recommend a shorter form — without prejudice to those who would wish to sing it in its present long version, with refrains after each verse. The version we propose is that found in Fr. Ray F. Brown's, *The Oxford American Psalter* (New York: Oxford University Press, 1949), number 25. This version has been used experimentally in several of our theological seminaries. Its sixteen verses make it suitable to either single or double Anglican chants.

It will be observed that we have utilized only the first two sections of the *Te Deum* as a canticle, and reserved the third section for use as versicles and responses after the Creed and before the prayers. This corresponds to the actual history of the *Te Deum* and its inherent structure. The third section was a later addition to it, a kind of appendage in the form of versicles and responses, drawn from the Scriptures and woven about a petition: "Vouchsafe, O Lord, to keep us this day without sin." The true ending and climax of the *Te Deum* was the responsory or petition that concluded the second part. We believe that the new arrangement of *Te Deum* sections is sound liturgically, and that the shortening of the hymn as a canticle will do much to restore it to frequent use in our congregations. For the *Benedictus es* has, alas, almost driven it out of the worship of many parishes, — a poor substitute indeed for the greatest hymn of the Church!

A very constant request that has come in to the Commission has been a proposal to allow the canticles of Morning and Evening Prayer to be alternative one to the other. This arises from the fact that in so many places there is either no regular service of Evening Prayer, or there is a different congregation at Evening Prayer from that at Morning Prayer. Quite a few of our congregations are now almost ignorant of Evening Prayer as a corporate office of worship, or else it is so infrequently observed (usually during Lent, if at all), that the people are not so familiar with the evening canticles as they should be. We have accordingly introduced a rubrical provision that in places where only one of the two Daily Offices is said, the canticles of Morning Prayer may be used in the evening office, or *vice versa*. The purpose of this rubric is purely practical, in view of present circumstances. We do not believe it to be ideal, of course, for the ideal situation is that both Offices be a regular part of the normative experience of each and every parish and mission.

This Study is not designed to deal with lectionary problems. Suffice it to say that the rubrics concerning the lessons have been revised so as to give a better form for introducing the lections. The logical order is that the reader announce first the book, then the chapter, then the verse — just the reverse of the present rubrical direction. There are still many people who like to follow the lessons in their Bibles. The present rubrics are the poorest devices for helping them find the places readily. One looks for a passage first of all by the title of the book, certainly not by the number of a verse.

The Creed and Prayers

No change is proposed in the Creed, but the Commission believes that the time has come to drop the cumbrous rubric concerning the "Descent into Hell" clause. Whatever purpose this theological explanation may have served in generations past, the clause is no longer a live issue in the Church. It would be interesting to know if any parish ever takes advantage of the substitute clause. The difficulty is that it is impractical to do so. One does not stop in the middle of reciting the Creed, recollect that a clause is not to be said, and then hunt the fine print of the rubric to find out what is a permissible substitute.

The *Kyrie* has been introduced before the Lord's Prayer, as in the other Anglican Prayer Books. The omission of the doxology from the Lord's Prayer is not a matter upon which the Commission has strong feelings. We have omitted it here merely to make the form of the Lord's Prayer correspond to other places in the Prayer Book where it is preceded by the *Kyrie*, instead of by a solemn bidding.[4] There may be some advantage in reserving the fuller form with doxology for those great sacramental occasions, when the Lord's Prayer has a peculiar emphasis of praise no less than of petition. The use of the versicles from the third section of the *Te Deum* has already been commented upon in the previous section of this Study.

A slight alteration has been made in the Third Collect — the Collect for Grace. The final clauses have been restored to a wording more nearly akin to their original and the version of the other Prayer Books. It places the verb in the active, rather than in the passive voice, and gives a greater vigor to the rhythm. We suspect that it will also have a subtle effect upon the worshipper in suggesting to his mind and will the need of positive Christian action in his life.

The first Prayer for the President, in the present Prayer Book, has been omitted. It is an adaptation of the old prayer for the King, and implies a life-long ruler who is temporal head of the Church. The alternative form, introduced in 1928, is more generally favored in current use in any case, for it speaks more relevantly to the American scene. It is known that the older prayer was marked for omission in the last revision of 1928. But an odd circumstance of history led to its retention.

---

4. See the discussion of this in E. L. Parsons and B. H. Jones, *The American Prayer Book* (New York: Scribners, 1937), pp. 140-41.

The Convention was discussing the prayer for the President at its meeting in 1919, soon after President Wilson's collapse of health. Many felt at that time that the old prayer, with its more personal references, was desirable; and so it was retained.[5]

A number of alterations have been made in the Prayer of St. Chrysostom. It has long been known that Cranmer mismanaged the translation of this prayer, which he derived from the Greek Liturgy of St. Chrysostom. Bishop Dowden in a careful essay on the subject showed that he was misled by a Latin version of the prayer that induced him to translate the verb *convenire* as "gather together" rather than "agree."[6] Much worse than a mistranslation, however, was his conflation of two sayings of our Lord in St. Matthew xviii. 19-20. The result was not only unfortunate; it was definitely wrong in its teaching about prayer. Our Lord said that when two or three were gathered together in His name, He would be in the midst of them; but only if two or three agreed in His name would their requests be granted. There is a difference. Another problem with the English version of this prayer has been the confusion as to whether it was addressed to the Father or to the Son. Our present form makes it clear that it is addressed to the Father. We have also proposed the word "befitting" as a substitute for "expedient." The latter word has lost in current English usage its old sense of profitableness and has become associated with very dubious policies. We feel certain that here is a case where the retention of archaic language is not only misleading, but possibly even harmful to modern worshippers.

Evening Prayer

The changes proposed in Evening Prayer are not so extensive as those outlined in Morning Prayer. We have commented above on the position and number of the Opening Sentences. We propose to retain only those appropriate to an evening office at this place, but to allow the officiant to use any of the Sentences printed before Morning Prayer if he so desires. The Exhortation, General Confession and Absolution are the same as in Morning Prayer. One may note also that the rubric allows, as at Morning Prayer, the use of the Absolution in Holy Communion as an alternative.

The versicles of transition into the psalmody are different. We suggest here the restoration of a set of versicles, still used in the other Anglican Prayer Books, drawn from Psalm lxx.i. In the morning office the psalmody always begins with an invitatory of praise, hence the suitability of the versicle and response asking God to open our lips in praise. In the evening office, the psalm appointed may not always be a hymn of praise. The new versicles avoid, therefore, an inappropriate introduction on such occasions.

---

5. E. L. Parsons and B. H. Jones, *The American Prayer Book* (New York: Scribners, 1937), p. 116.

6. John Dowden, *The Workmanship of the Prayer Book* (2d ed.; London: Methuen, 1904), pp. 227-29.

The second set of alternative psalm-canticles has been omitted. Neither of them, *Bonum est confiteri* and *Benedic, anima mea*, is a good substitute for the Gospel canticles, since they do not deal with the same themes. Moreover these two canticles are only pieces of psalms, fragments that omit many of the finer verses of the psalms from which they are drawn. The great popularity of the Gospel canticles (restored since 1892) has almost driven them out of use. The other two psalm-canticles, *Cantate Domino* and *Deus misereatur*, are also seldom used. But it is perhaps best to leave them in the Office, for those congregations which desire some variety in their daily use of Evening Prayer. These canticles also in their content are more closely akin to the themes of the Gospel canticles especially the *Deus misereatur*, which celebrates, as does the *Nunc Dimittis*, the universality of God's redemptive purpose, for Gentile no less than for Jew.

An alteration is proposed in the response of the last pair of versicles in the Office, before the Collects. In place of, "And take not thy Holy Spirit from us," we suggest the substitution of the original parallel of the versicle, "And renew a right spirit within us." Many people are confused by the present ending of these versicles, and rightly so, for they are used entirely out of their original and proper context. A reference to the relevant verses in Psalm 51 will make this obvious:

Make me a clean heart, O God,
and renew a right spirit within me.

Cast me not away from thy presence,
and take not thy holy Spirit from me.

The psalmist prays, out of the deep penitence for his sin, for renewal and forgiveness, rather than for condemnation and rejection. His prayer is intensely personal. But these words have another meaning entirely when put into the plural, as in our Office. God does not take His Holy Spirit away from His Church, when it is at prayer. His Spirit is rather all the more present to "renew" the hearts of His people.

The prayers after the Third Collect have been omitted. The officiant, if he desires, may take them from Morning Prayer. The only loss here is the Prayer for the President, peculiar to Evening Prayer in our present Prayer Book. Some may feel keenly the loss, though we suspect that many American churchmen have little taste for its implication of passive obedience. Like the older prayer for civil rulers at Morning Prayer, this intercession belongs to a different kind of temporal order and Church-State relation from that obtaining in our own land today. The twentieth century prayers for the State and its institutions, that entered our Prayer Book in the last revision, are far superior to the older forms coming down from Tudor England. We should welcome them as a fruitful contribution of our own age to the ever ongoing heritage and tradition of common prayer that is our special blessing in the Anglican Communion.

The Order for Daily Morning Prayer

The Introduction

¶ The Minister shall begin Morning Prayer by reading one or more of the following Sentences of Scripture.

GRACE be unto you, and peace, from God our Father, and from the Lord Jesus Christ, *Phil. i.*2.

The Lord is in his holy temple: let all the earth keep silence before him. *Hab. ii.*20.

I was glad when they said unto me, We will go into the house of the Lord. *Psalm cxxii.*1.

Let the words of my mouth, and the meditation of my heart, be alway acceptable in thy sight. O Lord, my strength and my redeemer. *Psalm xix.*14.

O send out thy light and thy truth, that they may lead me, and bring me unto thy holy hill, and to thy dwelling. *Psalm xliii.*3.

The hour cometh, and now is, when the true worshippers shall worship the Father in spirit and in truth: for the Father seeketh such to worship him. *St John iv.* 23.

Advent

Repent ye; for the Kingdom of heaven is at hand. *St. Matt. iii.*2.

The night is far spent, the day is at hand: let us therefore cast off the works of darkness, and let us put on the armour of light. *Rom. xiii.*12.

Watch ye, for ye know not when the master of the house cometh, at even, or at midnight, or at the cock-crowing, or in the morning: lest coming suddenly he find you sleeping. *St. Mark xiii.* 35, 36.

Christmas

Behold, I bring you good tidings of great joy, which shall be to all the people. For unto you is born this day in the city of David a Saviour, which is Christ the Lord. *St. Luke ii.*10,11.

In this was manifested the love of God toward us, because that God sent his only begotten Son into the world, that we might live through him. *1 St. John iv.*9.

Behold, the tabernacle of God is with men, and he will dwell with them, and they shall be his people, and God himself shall he with them, and be their God. *Rev. xxi.*3.

Epiphany

From the rising of the sun even unto the going down of the same my Name shall be great among the Gentiles; and in every place incense shall be offered unto my Name, and a pure offering; for my Name shall be great among the heathen, saith the Lord of hosts. *Mal. i.*11.

Thus saith God the Lord, I the Lord have called thee in righteousness, and will hold thine hand, and will keep thee, and give thee for a covenant of the people, for a light of the Gentiles. *Isa. xlii.*5,6.

Sing unto the Lord, and praise his Name; be telling of his salvation from day to day. Declare his honour unto the heathen, and his wonders unto all peoples. *Psalm xcvi.*2,3.

Lent

Thus saith the high and lofty One that inhabiteth eternity, whose name is Holy; I dwell in the high and holy place, with him also that is of a contrite and humble spirit, to revive the spirit of the humble, and to revive the heart of the contrite ones. *Isa. lvii.*15.

The sacrifices of God are a broken spirit: a broken and a contrite heart, O God, thou wilt not despise. *Psalm li.*17.

To the Lord our God belong mercies and forgivenesses, though we have rebelled against him; neither have we obeyed the voice of the Lord our God, to walk in his laws which he set before us. *Dan. ix.*9,10.

If we say that we have no sin, we deceive ourselves, and the truth is not in us; but if we confess our sins, God is faithful and just to forgive us our sins, and to cleanse us from all unrighteousness. *1 St. John i.*8,9.

I will arise and go to my father, and will say unto him, Father, I have sinned against heaven, and before thee, and am no more worthy to be called thy son. *St. Luke xv.* 18,19.

Holy Week

Is it nothing to you, all ye that pass by? behold, and see if there be any sorrow like unto my sorrow which is done unto me, wherewith the Lord hath afflicted me. *Lam. i.*12.

All we like sheep have gone astray; we have turned every one to his own way; and the Lord hath laid on him the iniquity of us all. *Isaiah liii.*6.

God commendeth his love toward us, in that, while we were yet sinners, Christ died for us. *Rom. v.* 8.

Easter

He is risen. The Lord is risen indeed. *St. Mark xvi.*6; *St. Luke xxiv.*34.

Thanks be to God, which giveth us the victory through our Lord Jesus Christ. *1 Cor. xv.*57.

If ye then be risen with Christ, seek those things which are above, where Christ sitteth on the right hand of God. *Col. iii.*1.

Ascension

Christ is not entered into the holy places made with hands, which are the figures of the true; but into heaven itself, now to appear in the presence of God for us. *Heb. ix.* 24.

Seeing that we have a great High Priest, that is passed into the heavens, Jesus the Son of God, let us come boldly unto the throne of grace, that we may obtain mercy, and find grace to help in time of need. *Heb. iv.*14,16.

Blessing, and honour, and glory, and power, be unto him that sitteth upon the throne, and unto the Lamb for ever and ever. *Rev. v.* 13.

Whitsunday

Ye shall receive power, after that the Holy Ghost is come upon you: and ye shall be witnesses unto me both in Jerusalem, and in all Judaea, and in Samaria, and unto the uttermost part of the earth. *Acts i.* 8.

As many as are led by the Spirit of God, they are the sons of God. For ye have not received the spirit of bondage again to fear; but ye have received the Spirit of adoption, whereby we cry, Abba, Father. *Rom. viii.*14,15.

Jesus said, If ye love me, keep my commandments, and I will pray the Father, and he shall give you another Comforter, that he may abide with you for ever; even the Spirit of truth. *St. John xiv.*15,16,17.

Trinity Sunday

Holy, holy, holy, is the Lord of hosts: the whole earth is full of his glory. *Isaiah vi.*3.

Blessed be the Name of the Lord from this time forth for evermore. *Psalm cxiii.*2.

Saints' Days

The souls of the righteous are in the hand of God; for God proved them, and found them worthy for himself. *Wisd. iii.*1,5.

Therefore are they before the throne of God, and serve him day and night in his temple: and he that sitteth on the throne shall dwell among them. *Rev. vii.*15.

Now therefore ye are no more strangers and foreigners, but fellow citizens with the saints, and the household of God. *Eph. ii.*19.

National Days

O let the nations rejoice and be glad; for thou shalt judge the folk righteously, and govern the nations upon earth. *Psalm lxvii*.4.

The earth is the Lord's, and all that therein is; the compass of the world, and they that dwell therein. *Psalm xxiv*.I.

If ye walk in my statutes, and keep my commandments, and do them: then will I give you rain in due season, and the land shall yield her increase, and the trees of the field shall yield their fruit. *Lev. xxvi*. 3,4.

¶ *Then the Minister shall say this Exhortation:*

¶ *And* NOTE, *Upon any day except a Day of Fasting or Abstinence, or upon any day when the Litany or Holy Communion is immediately to follow, the Minister may, at his discretion, pass at once from the Sentences to the Versicles, O Lord, open thou our lips, etc.*

DEARLY beloved, we are come together in the presence of Almighty God, and of the whole company of heaven, to make humble confession of our sins unto him; to set forth his most worthy praise; to hear his most holy Word; to declare our faith in him; to ask, for ourselves and all men, those things which are necessary for the body and the soul; to offer unto him the service of our lives; and to receive his blessing.

Wherefore, let us kneel in silence before God our heavenly Father, and remember his presence with us now; and let us with humble and obedient hearts make confession of our sins before him, that we may obtain forgiveness of the same, by his infinite goodness and mercy.

¶ *And* NOTE, *The Minister may, at his discretion, begin the Exhortation with the words, Let us kneel in silence, etc.*

A General Confession

¶ *After silence has been kept for a space, the whole Congregation shall say, after the Minister, all kneeling,*

ALMIGHTY and most merciful Father, we have erred, and strayed from thy ways like lost sheep. We have followed too much the devices and desires of our own hearts. We have offended against thy holy laws. We have left undone those things which we ought to have done; And we have done those things which we ought not to have done. But thou, O Lord, have mercy upon us; Spare thou those who confess their faults; Restore thou those who are penitent; According to thy promises declared unto mankind in Christ Jesus our Lord; And grant that hereafter, we may live a godly, righteous and sober life, for his sake, to the glory of thy holy Name. Amen.

The Absolution

¶ To be made by the Priest alone, the People still kneeling.

¶ And NOTE, *That the Priest may use, at his discretion, instead of what follows, the Absolution from the Holy Communion.*

THE Almighty and merciful Lord grant you Absolution and Remission of all your sins, true repentance, amendment of life, and the grace and consolation of his Holy Spirit; through Jesus Christ our Lord. Amen.

¶ Then likewise he shall say,
O Lord, open thou our lips.
Answer. And our mouth shall show forth thy praise.

The Psalter

¶ Here, all standing up, the Minister shall say,

Glory be to the Father, and to the Son, and to the Holy Ghost.
Answer. As it was in the beginning, is now, and ever shall be, world without end. Amen.
Minister. Praise ye the Lord.

¶ Then shall be said the Invitatory Psalm following, except on Easter Day and seven days after, and on Thanksgiving Day, for which other Anthems are appointed.

¶ And NOTE, *That Psalm 95 may be used instead of the* Venite *on Days of Fasting or Abstinence, or when Psalm 96 is to follow; and that on Ash Wednesday and Good Friday the* Venite *may be omitted.*

¶ Immediately before and after the Venite, *the following Antiphons may be said.*

Advent. Our King and Saviour draweth nigh; * O come, let us adore him.
Christmastide. Alleluia. Unto us a child is born; * O come, let us adore him. Alleluia.
Epiphanytide, and on the Feast of the Transfiguration. Alleluia. The Lord hath manifested forth his glory; * O come, let us adore him, Alleluia.
The Purification, and the Annunciation. The Word was made flesh, and dwelt among us; * O come, let us adore him.

Holy Week. Christ our Saviour hath redeemed us by his Cross; * O come, let us adore him.

Eastertide. Alleluia. The Lord is risen indeed; * O come, let us adore him. Alleluia.

Ascentiontide. Alleluia. Christ the Lord ascendeth into heaven; * O come, let us adore him. Alleluia.

Whitsuntide. Alleluia. The Spirit of the Lord filleth the whole world; * O come, let us adore him. Alleluia.

Trinity Sunday. Father, Son, and Holy Ghost, one God; * O come, let us adore him.

Saints' Days. The Lord is glorious in his saints; * O come, let us adore him.

Venite, exultemus Domino

O COME, let us sing unto the Lord; * let us heartily rejoice in the strength of our salvation.

Let us come before his presence with thanksgiving; * and show ourselves glad in him with psalms.

For the Lord is a great God; * and a great King above all gods.

In his hand are all the corners of the earth; * and the strength of the hills is his also.

The sea is his, and he made it; * and his hands prepared the dry land.

O come, let us worship and fall down; * and kneel before the Lord our Maker.

For he is the Lord our God; * and we are the people of his pasture, and the sheep of his hand.

O worship the Lord in the beauty of holiness; * let the whole earth stand in awe of him.

For he cometh, for he cometh to judge the earth; * and with righteousness to judge the world, and the peoples with his truth.

Glory be to the Father, and to the Son; * and to the Holy Ghost.

As it was in the beginning, is now, and ever shall be; world without end. Amen.

¶ *In place of the* Venite, *the following Psalm may be used,*

Jubilate Deo. Psalm c

O BE joyful in the Lord, all ye lands; * serve the Lord with gladness, and come before his presence with a song.

Be ye sure that the Lord he is God; it is he that hath made us, and we are his; * we are his people, and the sheep of his pasture.

O go your way into his gates with thanksgiving, and into his courts with praise; * be thankful unto him and speak good of his Name.

For the Lord is gracious, his mercy is everlasting; * and his truth endureth from generation to generation.

Glory be to the Father, and to the Son; * and to the Holy Ghost.

As it was in the beginning, is now, and ever shall be; * world without end. Amen.

> ¶ *Then shall follow a Portion of the Psalms, according to the Use of this Church. At the end of every Psalm, or at the end of the whole Portion from the Psalter, shall be said the* Gloria Patri.

The Word of God

> ¶ *Then shall be read the First Lesson, from the Old Testament, as it is appointed in the Table of Lessons. And NOTE, That before every Lesson, the Minister appointed to read it shall say,* The Lesson from the Book of --------, in the ---- Chapter, at the ------ Verse; *and after the Lesson,* Here endeth the First (or, Second) Lesson

> ¶ *Here shall be said or sung the following Hymn, called the* Benedictus. *And NOTE, That in place of the* Benedictus, *the Hymn called* Magnificat, *appointed at Evening Prayer, may be said or sung, if there be no evening service on that day.*

Benedictus. St. Luke i.68

BLESSED be the Lord God of Israel; * for he hath visited and redeemed his people.

And hath raised up a mighty salvation for us; * in the house of his servant David;

As he spake by the mouth of his holy Prophets, * which have been since the world began;

That we should be saved from our enemies, * and from the hand of all that hate us.

To perform the mercy promised to our forefathers, * and to remember his holy covenant;

To perform the oath which he sware to our forefather Abraham, * that he would give us;

That we being delivered out of the hand of our enemies * might serve him without fear;

In holiness and righteousness before him, * all the days of our life.

And thou, child, shalt be called the prophet of the Highest: * for thou shalt go before the face of the Lord to prepare his ways;

To give knowledge of salvation unto his people * for the remission of their sins,

Through the tender mercy of our God; * whereby the day-spring from on high hath visited us;

To give light to them that sit in darkness, and in the shadow of death, * and to guide our feet into the way of peace.

Glory be to the Father, and to the Son, * and to the Holy Ghost.

As it was in the beginning, is now, and ever shall be, * world without end. Amen.

¶ Or this Canticle.

Surge illuminator. Isaiah lx

ARISE, shine, for thy light is come, * and the glory of the Lord is risen upon thee.

For, behold, the darkness shall cover the earth, * and gross darkness the people;

But the Lord shall arise upon thee, * and his glory shall be seen upon thee.

And the Gentiles shall come to thy light, * and kings to the brightness of thy rising.

Thy gates shall be open continually; * they shall not be shut day nor night.

They shall call thee, The city of the Lord, * the Zion of the Holy One of Israel.

Violence shall no more be heard in thy land, * wasting nor destruction within thy borders;

But thou shalt call thy walls Salvation, * and thy gates Praise.

The sun shall be no more thy light by day; * neither for brightness shall the moon give light unto thee:

But the Lord shall be unto thee an everlasting light, * and thy God thy glory.

Glory be to the Father, and to the Son, * and to the Holy Ghost.

As it was in the beginning, is now, and ever shall be, * world without end. Amen.

¶ On any day when the Holy Communion is immediately to follow, the Minister at his discretion, after any one of the Canticles of Morning Prayer has been said or sung, may pass at once to the Communion Service.

¶ Then shall be read, in like manner, the Second Lesson, taken out of the New Testament, according to the Table of Lessons.

¶ And after that shall be said or sung the Hymn, Te Deum. *And* NOTE, *That the* Te Deum *shall not be used in the seasons of Advent or Lent; and* NOTE *also, That if the Hymn* Benedictus *has not been said after the First Lesson it may be used in this place; or else the Hymn* Nunc Dimittis *appointed in Evening Prayer, if there be no evening service on that day.*

Te Deum Laudamus

WE praise thee, O God; we acknowledge thee to be the Lord. All the earth doth worship thee, the Father everlasting.
    To thee all angels cry aloud; the Heavens, and all the Powers therein;
    To thee Cherubim and Seraphim continually do cry, Holy, Holy, Holy, Lord God of Sabaoth;
    Heaven and earth are full of the Majesty of thy glory.

The glorious company of the Apostles praise thee.
The goodly fellowship of the Prophets praise thee.
The noble army of Martyrs praise thee.
The holy Church throughout all the world doth acknowledge thee,
The Father, of an infinite Majesty;
Thine adorable, true, and only Son;
Also the Holy Ghost the Comforter.

THOU art the King of Glory, O Christ.
    Thou art the everlasting Son of the Father.
    When thou tookest upon thee to deliver man,
Thou didst humble thyself to be born of a Virgin.
When thou hadst overcome the sharpness of death,
Thou didst open the Kingdom of Heaven to all believers.
Thou sittest at the right hand of God, in the glory of the Father.
We believe that thou shalt come to be our Judge.
We therefore pray thee, help thy servants, whom thou hast redeemed with thy precious blood.
    Make them to be numbered with thy Saints, in glory everlasting.

¶ *Or this Canticle.*

Benedicite, omnia opera Domini

O ALL ye works of the Lord, bless ye the Lord: * praise him and magnify him for ever.
    O ye Angels of the Lord, bless ye the Lord:* praise him and magnify him for ever.

O YE Heavens, bless ye the Lord: * O ye Waters that be above the firmament, bless ye the Lord.
    O all ye Powers of the Lord, O ye Sun and Moon: * O ye Stars of heaven, bless ye the Lord.
    O ye Showers and Dew, O ye Winds of God: * O ye Fire and Heat, bless ye the Lord.

O ye Winter and Summer, O ye Frost and Cold: * O ye Ice and Snow, bless ye the Lord.

O ye Nights and Days, bless ye the Lord: * O ye Light and Darkness, bless ye the Lord.

O ye Lightnings and Clouds, bless ye the Lord: * praise him and magnify him for ever.

O LET the Earth bless the Lord: * yea, let it praise him and magnify him for ever.

O ye Mountains and Hills, O all ye Green Things upon the earth: * O ye Wells, O ye Seas and Floods, bless ye the Lord.

O ye Whales, and all that move in the waters, bless ye the Lord: * O ye Fowls of the air, O all ye Beasts and Cattle, bless ye the Lord.

O ye Children of Men, bless ye the Lord: * praise him and magnify him for ever.

O LET Israel bless the Lord: * praise him and magnify him for ever.

O ye Priests of the Lord, O ye Servants of the Lord: * O ye Spirits and Souls of the Righteous, bless ye the Lord.

O ye holy and humble Men of heart, bless ye the Lord: * praise him and magnify him for ever.

LET us bless the Father, and the Son, and the Holy Ghost: * praise him and magnify him for ever.

The Apostles' Creed

¶ *Then shall be said the Apostles' Creed by the Minister and the People, all standing.*

I BELIEVE in God the Father Almighty, Maker of heaven and earth:

And in Jesus Christ his only Son our Lord: Who was conceived by the Holy Ghost, Born of the Virgin Mary: Suffered under Pontius Pilate, Was crucified, dead, and buried: He descended into hell; The third day he rose again from the dead: He ascended into heaven, And sitteth on the right hand of God the Father Almighty: From thence he shall come to judge the quick and the dead.

I believe in the Holy Ghost: The Holy Catholic Church; The Communion of saints: The Forgiveness of Sins: The Resurrection of the body: And the Life everlasting. Amen.

The Prayers

¶ Then shall be said these Prayers following, the People devoutly kneeling; the Minister first pronouncing,

The Lord be with you.
Answer. And with thy spirit.
Minister. Let us pray.

¶ Minister and People.

Lord, have mercy.
Christ, have mercy.
Lord, have mercy.

OUR Father, who art in heaven, Hallowed be thy Name. Thy kingdom come. Thy will be done, On earth as it is in heaven. Give us this day our daily bread. And forgive us our trespasses, As we forgive those who trespass against us. And lead us not into temptation, But deliver us from evil. Amen.

Minister. O Lord, save thy people, and bless thine heritage.
People. Govern them, and lift them up for ever.
Minister. Day by day we magnify thee;
People. And we worship thy Name ever, world without end.
Minister. Vouchsafe, O Lord, to keep us this day without sin.
People. O Lord, have mercy upon us, have mercy upon us.
Minister. O Lord, let thy mercy be upon us, as our trust is in thee.
People. O Lord, in thee have we trusted; let us never be confounded.
Minister. Let us pray

¶ Then shall follow the Collect for the Day, and the two following Collects. And NOTE, *The Collect for the Day shall be omitted when the Holy Communion is immediately to follow this Service.*

A Collect for Peace

O GOD, who art the author of peace and lover of concord, in knowledge of whom standeth our eternal life, whose service is perfect freedom; Defend us thy humble servants in all assaults of our enemies; that we, surely trusting in thy defence, may not fear the power of any adversaries, through the might of Jesus Christ our Lord. *Amen.*

A Collect for Grace

O LORD, our heavenly Father, Almighty and everlasting God, who hast safely brought us to the beginning of this day; Defend us in the same with thy mighty power; and grant that this day we fall into no sin, neither any kind of danger; but that we, being ordered by thy governance, may do always what is righteous in thy sight; through Jesus Christ our Lord. *Amen.*

¶ *Here may be sung a Hymn or an Anthem.*

¶ *The Minister may here end the Morning Prayer with Prayers and Thanksgivings taken out of this Book, or authorized by the Ordinary; or with the Grace.*

A Prayer for the United States and the President, and for All in Authority

O LORD, our Governor, whose glory is in all the world; We commend this nation to thy merciful care, that being guided by thy Providence, we may dwell secure in thy peace. Grant to THE PRESIDENT OF THE UNITED STATES, *The Governor of this State*, and all in authority, wisdom and strength to know and to do thy will. Fill them with the love of truth and righteousness; and make them ever mindful of their calling to serve this people in thy fear; through Jesus Christ our Lord, who liveth and reigneth with thee and the Holy Ghost, one God, world without end. *Amen.*

A Prayer for the Clergy and People

ALMIGHTY and everlasting God, from whom cometh every good and perfect gift; Send down upon our Bishops, and other Clergy, and upon the Congregations committed to their charge, the healthful spirit of thy grace; and, that they may truly please thee, pour upon them the continual dew of thy blessing. Grant this, O Lord, for the honour of our Advocate and Mediator, Jesus Christ. *Amen.*

A Prayer for all Conditions of Men

O GOD, the Creator and Preserver of all mankind, we humbly beseech thee for all sorts and conditions of men; that thou wouldest be pleased to make thy ways known unto them, thy saving health unto all nations. More especially we pray for thy holy Church universal; that it may be so guided and governed by thy good Spirit, that all who profess and call themselves Christians may be led into the way of truth, and hold the faith in unity of spirit, in the bond of peace, and in righteousness of life. Finally, we commend to thy fatherly goodness all those who are any ways afflicted, or distressed, in mind, body, or estate;

(* *especially those for whom our prayers are desired;*)   [* *This may be said when any desire the prayers of the Congregation.*]   that it may please thee to comfort and relieve them, according to their several necessities; giving them patience under their sufferings, and a happy issue out of all their afflictions. And this we beg for Jesus Christ's sake. *Amen.*

A General Thanksgiving

¶ *The General Thanksgiving may be said by the Congregation with the Minister.*

ALMIGHTY God, Father of all mercies, we thine unworthy servants, do give thee most humble and hearty thanks for all thy goodness and loving-kindness to us, and to all men. We bless thee for our creation, preservation, and all the blessings of this life; but above all for thine inestimable love in the redemption of the world by our Lord Jesus Christ; for the means of grace, and for the hope of glory. And, we beseech thee, give us that due sense of all thy mercies, that our hearts may be unfeignedly thankful; and that we show forth thy praise, not only with our lips, but in our lives, by giving up ourselves to thy service, and by walking before thee in holiness and righteousness all our days; through Jesus Christ our Lord, to whom, with thee and the Holy Ghost, be all honour and glory, world without end. *Amen.*

A Prayer of St. Chrysostom

ALMIGHTY God, who hast given us grace at this time with one accord to make our common supplications unto thee; and dost promise, through thy well-beloved Son, that when two or three shall agree in his Name thou wilt grant their requests; Fulfil now, O Lord, the desires and petitions of thy servants, as may be most befitting for them; granting us in this world knowledge of thy truth, and in the world to come life everlasting; through the same thy Son, Jesus Christ our Lord. *Amen.*

The Grace. 2 Cor. xiii. 14

THE grace of our Lord Jesus Christ, and the love of God, and the fellowship of the Holy Ghost, be with us all evermore. *Amen.*

Here endeth the Order of Morning Prayer.

The Order for Daily Evening Prayer

The Introduction

¶ The Minister shall begin Evening Prayer by reading one or more of the following Sentences of Scripture; or, at his discretion, any of the Sentences appointed at Morning Prayer.

LORD, I have loved the habitation of thy house, and the place where thine honour dwelleth. *Psalm xxvi.8.*

Let my prayer be set forth in thy sight as the incense; and let the lifting up of my hands be an evening sacrifice. *Psalm cxli.2.*

O worship the Lord in the beauty of holiness; let the whole earth stand in awe of him. *Psalm xcvi.9.*

It is a good thing to give thanks unto the Lord, and to sing praises unto thy Name, O Most Highest; to tell of thy loving-kindness early in the morning, and of thy truth in the night season. *Psalm xcii.1,2.*

¶ Then shall the Minister say this Exhortation; and NOTE, *That the Minister may, at his discretion, omit all that follows after the Sentences, and pass at once to the Versicles,* O God, make speed to save us, *etc.*

DEARLY beloved, we are come together in the presence of Almighty God, and of the whole company of heaven, to make humble confession of our sins; to set forth his most worthy praise; to hear his most holy Word; to declare our faith in him; to ask, for ourselves and all men, those things which are necessary for the body and the soul; to offer unto him the service of our lives; and to receive his blessing.

Wherefore, let us kneel in silence before God our heavenly Father, and remember his presence with us now; and let us with humble and obedient hearts make confession of our sins before him, that we may obtain forgiveness of the same, by his infinite goodness and mercy.

¶ And NOTE, *The Minister may, at his discretion, begin the Exhortation with the words,* Let us kneel in silence, *etc.*

A General Confession

¶ After silence has been kept for a brief space, the whole Congregation shall say, after the Minister, all kneeling.

ALMIGHTY and most merciful Father, we have erred and strayed from thy ways like lost sheep. We have followed too much the devices and desires of our own hearts. We have offended against thy holy laws. We have left undone those things which we ought to have done; And we have done those things which we ought not to have done. But thou, O Lord, have mercy upon us; Spare thou those who confess their faults; Restore thou those who are penitent; According to thy promises declared unto mankind in Christ Jesus our Lord; And grant that hereafter, we may live a godly, righteous and sober life, for his sake, to the glory of thy holy Name. Amen.

The Absolution

¶ To be made by the Priest alone, the People still kneeling.

¶ And NOTE, *That the Priest may use, at his discretion, instead of what follows, the Absolution from the Holy Communion.*

THE Almighty and merciful Lord grant you Absolution and Remission of all your sins, true repentance, amendment of life, and the grace and consolation of his Holy Spirit; through Jesus Christ our Lord. *Amen.*

¶ Then likewise he shall say,

O God, make speed to save us.
Answer. O Lord, make haste to help us.

The Psalter

¶ Here, all standing up, the Minister shall say,

Glory be to the Father, and to the Son, and to the Holy Ghost.

Answer. As it was in the beginning, is now, and ever shall be, world without end. Amen.
Minister. Praise ye the Lord.

¶ Then shall follow a Portion of the Psalms, according to the Use of this Church. And at the end of every Psalm, or at the end of the whole Portion of Psalms for the day, shall be said the Gloria Patri:

Glory be to the Father, and to the Son, * and to the Holy Ghost.
 As it was in the beginning, is now, and ever shall be, * world without end. Amen.

The Word of God

¶ Then shall be read the First Lesson, from the Old Testament, as it is appointed in the Table of Lessons. And NOTE, *That before every Lesson, the Minister appointed to read it shall say,* The Lesson from the Book of -------, in the ---- Chapter, at the ----- verse; *and after the Lesson,* Here endeth the First (or, Second) Lesson.

¶ But NOTE, *That the Minister, at his discretion, may omit one of the two Lessons in Evening Prayer, the Lesson read being followed by one of the Canticles.*

¶ After the First Lesson shall be sung or said the following Hymn called Magnificat. *And* NOTE, *That if Morning Prayer hath not been said, the Minister may, at his discretion, appoint in place of the* Magnificat *one of the Canticles appointed after the First Lesson at Morning Prayer.*

Magnificat. St. Luke i.46

MY soul doth magnify the Lord, * and my spirit hath rejoiced in God my Saviour.

For he hath regarded * the lowliness of his handmaiden.

For behold, from henceforth * all generations shall call me blessed. For he that is mighty hath magnified me; * and holy is his Name.

And his mercy is on them that fear him * throughout all generations.

He hath showed strength with his arm; * he hath scattered the proud in the imagination of their hearts.

He hath put down the mighty from their seat, * and hath exalted the humble and meek.

He hath filled the hungry with good things; * and the rich he hath sent empty away.

He remembering his mercy hath holpen his servant Israel; * as he promised to our forefathers, Abraham and his seed, for ever.

Glory be to the Father, and to the Son, * and to the Holy Ghost.

As it was in the beginning, is now, and ever shall be, * world without end. Amen.

¶ Or this Psalm.

Cantate Domino. Psalm xcviii

O SING unto the Lord a new song; * for he hath done marvellous things.

With his own right hand, and with his holy arm, * hath he gotten himself the victory.

The Lord declared his salvation; * his righteousness hath he openly showed in the sight of the heathen.

He hath remembered his mercy and truth toward the house of Israel; * and all the ends of the world have seen the salvation of our God.

Show yourselves joyful unto the Lord, all ye lands; * sing, rejoice, and give thanks.

Praise the Lord upon the harp; * sing to the harp with a psalm of thanksgiving.

With trumpets also and shawms, * O show yourselves joyful before the Lord, the King.

Let the sea make a noise, and all that therein is; * the round world, and they that dwell therein.

Let the floods clap their hands, * and let the hills be joyful together before the Lord;

For he cometh to judge the earth; * with righteousness shall he judge the world, and the peoples with equity.

Glory be to the Father, and to the Son, * and to the Holy Ghost.

As it was in the beginning, is now, and ever shall be, * world without end. Amen.

¶ Then shall be read a Lesson of the New Testament, as it is appointed.

¶ And after that shall be sung or said the Hymn called Nunc Dimittis. And NOTE, *That if Morning Prayer hath not been said, the Minister may, at his discretion, appoint in place of the Nunc Dimittis, the Te Deum.*

Nunc Dimittis. St. Luke ii. 29

LORD, now lettest thou thy servant depart in peace, according to thy word.
For mine eyes have seen thy salvation, * which thou hast prepared before the face of all people:

To be a light to lighten the Gentiles, * and to be the glory of thy people Israel.

Glory be to the Father, and to the Son, * and to the Holy Ghost.

As it was in the beginning, is now, and ever shall be, * world without end. Amen.

¶ Or this Psalm.

Deus misereatur. Psalm lxvii

GOD be merciful unto us, and bless us, * and show us the light of his countenance, and be merciful unto us;

That thy way may be known upon earth, * thy saving health among all nations.

Let the peoples praise thee, O God; * yea, let all the peoples praise thee.

O let the nations rejoice and be glad; * for thou shalt judge the folk righteously, and govern the nations upon earth.

Let the peoples praise thee, O God; * yea, let all the peoples praise thee.

Then shall the earth bring forth her increase; * and God, even our own God, shall give us his blessing.

God shall bless us; * and all the ends of the world shall fear him.

Glory be to the Father, and to the Son, * and to the Holy Ghost.

As it was in the beginning, is now, and ever shall be, * world without end. Amen.

The Apostles' Creed

¶ *Then shall be said the Apostles' Creed by the Minister and the People, all standing.*

I BELIEVE in God the Father Almighty, Maker of heaven and earth:
And in Jesus Christ his only Son our Lord: who was conceived by the Holy Ghost, Born of the Virgin Mary: Suffered under Pontius Pilate, Was crucified, dead, and buried: He descended into hell; The third day he rose again from the dead: He ascended into heaven, And sitteth on the right hand of God the Father Almighty: From thence he shall come to judge the quick and the dead.

I believe in the Holy Ghost: The holy Catholic Church: The Communion of Saints: The Forgiveness of sins: The Resurrection of the body: And the Life everlasting. Amen.

The Prayers

¶ *Then shall be said these prayers following, the People devoutly kneeling; the Minister first pronouncing,*

The Lord be with you.

Answer. And with thy spirit.

Minister. Let us pray.

¶ *Minister and People.*

Lord, have mercy.
Christ, have mercy.
Lord, have mercy.

OUR Father, who art in heaven, Hallowed be thy Name. Thy kingdom come. Thy will be done, On earth as it is in heaven. Give us this day our daily bread. And forgive us our trespasses, As we forgive those who trespass against us. And lead us not into temptation, but deliver us from evil. Amen.

Minister. O Lord, show thy mercy upon us.
People. And grant us thy salvation.
Minister. O Lord, save the State.
People. And mercifully hear us when we call upon thee.
Minister. Endue thy Ministers with righteousness.
People. And make thy chosen people joyful.
Minister. O Lord, save thy people.
People. And bless thine inheritance.
Minister. Give peace in our time, O Lord.
People. For it is thou, Lord, only, that makest us dwell in safety.
Minister. O God, make clean our hearts,
People. And renew a right spirit within us.

¶ Then shall be said the Collect for the Day, and after that the Collects following.

A Collect for Peace

O GOD, from whom all holy desires, all good counsels, and all just works do proceed; Give unto thy servants that peace which the world cannot give; that our hearts may be set to obey thy commandments, and also that by thee, we, being defended from the fear of our enemies, may pass our time in rest and quietness; through the merits of Jesus Christ our Saviour. *Amen.*

A Collect for Aid Against Perils

LIGHTEN our darkness, we beseech thee, O Lord; and by thy great mercy defend us from all perils and dangers of this night; for the love of thy only Son, our Saviour, Jesus Christ. *Amen.*

¶ Here may be sung a Hymn or an Anthem.

¶ The Minister may here end Evening Prayer with such Prayers and Thanksgivings taken out of this Book, or authorized by the Ordinary, as he shall think fit; or with the Grace.

THE grace of our Lord Jesus Christ, and the love of God, and the fellowship of the Holy Ghost, be with us all evermore. Amen.

Here endeth the Order of Evening Prayer.

PRAYER BOOK STUDIES VII: THE PENITENTIAL OFFICE

The Standing Liturgical Commission
of the Protestant Episcopal Church in the
United States of America

1957

PREFACE

The last revision of our Prayer Book was brought to a rather abrupt conclusion in 1928. Consideration of it had preoccupied the time of General Convention ever since 1913. Everyone was weary of the long and ponderous legislative process, and desired to make the new Prayer Book available as soon as possible for the use of the Church.

But the work of revision, which sometimes has seemed difficult to start, in this case proved hard to stop. The years of debate had aroused widespread interest in the whole subject: and the mind of the Church was more receptive of suggestions for revision when the work was brought to an end than when it began. Moreover, the revision was actually closed to new action in 1925, in order that it might receive final adoption in 1928: so that it was not possible to give due consideration to a number of very desirable features in the English and Scottish revisions, which appeared simultaneously with our own. It was further realized that there were some rough edges in what had been done, as well as an unsatisfied demand for still further alterations.

The problem of defects in detail was met by continuing the Revision Commission, and giving it rather large 'editorial' powers (subject only to review by General Convention) to correct obvious errors in the text as adopted, in the publication of the new Prayer Book. Then, to deal with the constructive proposals for other changes which continued to be brought up in every General Convention, the Revision Commission was reconstituted as a Standing Liturgical Commission. To this body all matters concerning the Prayer Book were to be referred, for preservation in permanent files, and for continuing consideration, until such time as the accumulated matter was sufficient in amount and importance to justify proposing another Revision.

The number of such referrals by General Convention, of Memorials from Dioceses, and of suggestions made directly to the Commission from all regions and schools and parties in the Church, has now reached such a total that it is evident that there is a widespread and insistent demand for a general revision of the Prayer Book.

The Standing Liturgical Commission is not, however, proposing any immediate revision. On the contrary, we believe that there ought to be a period of study and discussion, to acquaint the Church at large with the principles and issues involved, in order that the eventual action may be taken intelligently, and if possible without consuming so much of the time of our supreme legislative synod.

Accordingly, the General Convention of 1949 signalized the Fourth Centennial Year of the First Book of Common Prayer in English by authorizing the Liturgical Commission to publish its findings, in the form of a series of *Prayer Book Studies*.

It must be emphasized that the liturgical forms presented in these *Studies* are not — and under our Constitution, cannot be — sanctioned for public use. They are submitted for free discussion. The Commission will be grateful for copies or articles, resolutions, and direct comment, for its consideration, that the mind of the Church may be fully known to the body charged with reporting it.

In this undertaking, we have endeavored to be objective and impartial. It is not possible to avoid every matter which may be thought by some to be controversial. Ideas which seem to be constructively valuable will be brought to the attention of the Church, without too much regard as to whether they may ultimately be judged to be expedient. We cannot undertake to eliminate every proposal to which anyone might conceivably object: to do so would be to admit that any constructive progress is impossible. What we can do is to be alert not to alter the present *balance* of expressed or implied doctrine of the Church. We can seek to counterbalance every proposal which might seem to favor some one party of opinion by some other change in the opposite direction. The goal we have constantly had in mind — however imperfectly we may have succeeded in attaining it — is the shaping of a future Prayer Book which *every* party might embrace with the well-founded conviction that therein its own position had been strengthened, its witness enhanced, and its devotions enriched.

The objective we have pursued is the same as that expressed by the Commission for the Revision of 1892: "*Resolved*, That this Committee, in all its suggestions and acts, be guided by those principles of liturgical construction and ritual use which have guided the compilation and amendments of the Book of Common Prayer, and have made it what it is."

THE STANDING LITURGICAL COMMISSION:

GOODRICH R. FENNER, *Chairman*
ARTHUR C. LICHTENBERGER
BAYARD H. JONES, *Vice Chairman*
JOHN W. SUTER, *Custodian*
MASSEY H. SHEPHERD, JR.
CHARLES W. F. SMITH
FRANCIS B. SAYRE, JR.
BERTRAM L. SMITH
SPENCER ERVIN, *Secretary*
JOHN ASHTON

The Commission desires to express its gratitude to the Reverend Paul Hartzell for much preliminary work in connection with the Study on the Daily Offices; and to two former members of the Commission, the Reverend Morton C. Stone and the Reverend Walter Williams, for drafting materials in the earlier stages of work on the Penitential Office. The sub-committee on the Daily Offices has been headed by Dr. Shepherd; that on the Penitential Office, by Bishop Lichtenberger.

Introduction

The American Penitential Office is derived from, and is a great improvement on, the Commination service of the English Prayer Book. In the opening exhortation of that service, we read that "it is thought good, that at this time should be read the general sentences of God's cursing against impenitent sinners." There follows a series of curses to which the people reply Amen, after which another long and gloomy exhortation is read, which begins, "Now seeing that all they are accursed who do err and go astray from the commandments"; and continuing in this vein, there comes at long last the idea that if we repent, "Christ will deliver us from the curse of the law." Then follow the familiar Psalm and Prayers, which we have in the American Office.

Cranmer derived the Commination from the much more appealing service in the Sarum Missal for the Blessing and Distribution of Ashes on Ash Wednesday. The exhortations are his substitute for the sermon or homily which often preceded the ceremony. However, Cranmer was obviously influenced by the exaggerated value placed upon the Old Testament by the Continental Reformers. While we may not think lightly of sin or of the just judgment of God, we ought rather to emphasize His love and mercy for penitent sinners.

Though the American Penitential Office uses only that part of the Commination which comes from the Sarum Missal rejecting the cursings — there is still much to be desired in making it a constructive service of penitence. The Liturgical Commission has received more criticisms of this service than of almost any other in the Prayer Book, the consensus being that it is really not penitential at all, but rather a morbid dwelling on our sinfulness. While we have eliminated the attempt to frighten people into repentance by invoking the wrath of God, still nothing is said about what our sins are, or how we may be rid of them and be restored to holiness of life. Altogether it is a most discouraging office.

The proposed service is, therefore, a quite radical revision of our present office. The attempt is made to compose a really penitential service, based upon the parts of repentance: namely, Contrition, Self-examination, Confession, Absolution, and Amendment, for both public and private use.

The clergy talk a good deal about the necessity for careful self-examination and confession in preparation for Holy Communion, but there is no official form in the Prayer Book to give point to their remarks. Then, too, there are an increasing number of people who avail themselves of the invitation in the Exhortation after the Communion office to make their confession before a priest. While many of the clergy do not emphasize this voluntary act of discipline, they are often placed in a position where it is necessary to hear a confession, and sometimes they do not know what to do. An official form in the Prayer Book would solve this difficulty. In the section "Confession and Absolution" such a form is provided, and the rest of the service may be used by the penitent in preparation and thanksgiving. Subjects involved in the relation of the priest and the penitent in private confession are not properly matters which can be handled in a form primarily designed for public use, and must be left to the discretion of the priest in dealing with the individual.

Proposed New Office

The first rubric suggests that this office may be used appropriately, not only on Ash Wednesday, but also at other times. A second rubric gives guidance for the use of the form in private confession.

The service begins, after an opening Collect from the present Office, with an act of contrition, for which the traditional *Miserere* is most fitting. The controversial verses of the Psalm have been omitted, and it is arranged for responsive recitation according to the natural parallelism of thought in the verses.

The self-examination, as such, is new both to the Office and to the Prayer Book. But all of it is derived from Prayer Book material, mostly from the Offices of Instruction. This self-examination is positive, dealing with the ideal of our duty, rather than with the negative thought of the sins which we might commit. The examinations found in books of private devotion, based on the Ten Commandments or the Seven Deadly Sins, are often completely negative, and give long lists of sins, which sometimes have the quite unintended effect of suggesting to the penitent sins that he never thought of before. Both theologically and psychologically this method of examination is unsound. In examining oneself by a particular, but always incomplete, list of sins, one may be quite self-satisfied, if those particular sins have not been committed. But in comparing oneself with the ideal of our duties, it is easy to see how we have "missed the mark" of "the high calling of God in Christ Jesus"; and one's energy can be directed towards practicing the virtues, rather than towards the mere avoiding of sins.

Certainly, some such positive summary of our duty is needed. Many people have only a vague idea as to what the Church teaches, and what its requirements are. Here is the standard of the Prayer Book, which shows the goal towards which we should strive. Most of the statements are taken directly from the "duties" in the Offices of Instruction, with some slight expansions from other parts of the same Offices, and other parts of the Prayer Book. Positive statements are substituted for negative ones wherever they occur.

The section entitled "Confession and Absolution" is intended not only for use in the public recitation of the Office, but, as indicated by a rubric at the beginning of the service, for private confession as well. The first bidding is a form in common use. The Confession is the familiar one from the Holy Communion, but in the revised form proposed for the Liturgy (*Prayer Book Studies*, IV, vol. 1, page 363). At a public service, a pause may be made after the words, "Against thy Divine Majesty," for the recollection of particular sins. In a private confession the penitent will confess his sins at this point. The Absolution is the Sarum form familiar in Evening Prayer, but with the addition of an oblation clause.

The service concludes with the Lord's Prayer, a selection of versicles from Psalm 103, and a blessing.

The Penitential Office

¶ *For use on Ash Wednesday, and at other times, at the discretion of the Minister.*

¶ *And* NOTE, *The Confession and Absolution, and the Blessing, may be used at private confession before a Priest, the rest of the Office being used by the Penitent in preparation and thanksgiving.*

Contrition

Minister. The Lord be with you.
Answer. And with thy spirit.
Minister. Let us pray.

¶ *Then, all kneeling, the Minister shall say,*

O LORD, we beseech thee, mercifully hear our prayers, and spare all those who confess their sins unto thee; that they, whose consciences by sin are accused, by thy merciful pardon may be absolved; through Christ our Lord. *Amen.*

¶ *After which, still kneeling, the Minister and People shall say the following, responsively,*

From Psalm li. *Miserere mei, Deus.*

HAVE mercy upon me, O God, after thy great goodness;
According to the multitude of thy mercies do away mine offences.
Wash me throughly from my wickedness,
And cleanse me from my sin.
For I acknowledge my faults,
And my sin is ever before me.
Against thee only have I sinned,
And done this evil in thy sight.
But lo, thou requirest truth in the inward parts,
And shall make me to understand wisdom secretly.

Thou shalt purge me with hyssop, and I shall be clean;
Thou shalt wash me, and I shall be whiter than snow.
Turn thy face from my sins,
And put out all my misdeeds.
Make me a clean heart, O God,
And renew a right spirit within me.
Cast me not away from thy presence,
And take not thy Holy Spirit from me.
O give me the comfort of thy help again,
And stablish me with thy free Spirit.
Then shall I teach thy ways unto the wicked,
And sinners shall be converted unto thee.
Thou shalt open my lips, O Lord,
And my mouth shall show thy praise.
The sacrifice of God is a troubled spirit;
A broken and contrite heart, O God, shalt thou not despise.

Minister. Let us pray.

O GOD, whose nature and property is ever to have mercy and to forgive; Receive our humble petitions; and though we be tied and bound with the chain of our sins, yet let the pitifulness of thy great mercy loose us; for the honour of Jesus Christ, our Mediator and Advocate. *Amen.*

Self-Examination

BESEECHING the help of the Holy Spirit, let us examine ourselves as to our fulfillment of our Duties to God and to our Neighbour.
  Examine me, O Lord, and prove me; search out the thoughts of my heart.
My duty towards God is:
To believe in him;
To love him with all my heart, and with all my soul, and with all my mind;
To stand in awe of him;
To put my whole trust in him;
To call upon him in daily prayer;
To intercede for others;
To worship him every Sunday in his Church;
To receive the Holy Communion;
To work and pray and give for the increase of his kingdom;
And to serve him truly all the days of my life.

My Duty towards my Neighbour is:
To love him as myself, and to do unto all men as I would they should do unto me;
To be loving, helpful, and loyal to all my family;

To be a responsible citizen;
To learn and labour diligently;
To minister humbly to the needs of others, as unto Christ;
To be patient, kind, and forgiving;
To keep my body in temperance, soberness, and chastity;
To be true and just in all my dealings;
To work and pray for the good of all men everywhere;
And to seek that vocation through which I best can serve God and my fellow men.

¶ *If the Holy Communion is to follow immediately, the rest of this Office shall be omitted.*

Confession and Absolution

¶ *Then the Priest alone shall say, standing,*

THE LORD be in your heart and on your lips, that you may rightly and truly confess all your sins.

¶ *Then the Priest and People shall say together the Confession, all kneeling,*

ALMIGHTY GOD, Father of our Lord Jesus Christ, Maker of all things, Judge of all men; We acknowledge and confess our manifold sins, Which we have committed by thought, word, and deed, Against thy Divine Majesty. [*Here, in a private confession, the penitent shall confess his particular sins.*] We do earnestly repent, And are heartily sorry for these our misdoings. Have mercy upon us, most merciful Father; For thy Son our Lord Jesus Christ's sake, Forgive us all that is past; And grant that we may ever hereafter Serve and please thee in newness of life, To the honour and glory of thy Name; through the same Jesus Christ our Lord. Amen.

¶ *Then shall the Priest alone, standing and turning to the People, say,*

The Absolution

THE Almighty and merciful Lord grant you Absolution and Remission of all your sins, true repentance, amendment of life, and the grace and consolation of his Holy Spirit; through Jesus Christ our Lord. *Amen.*

¶ *Then shall the Priest and People say, all kneeling,*

OUR Father, who art in heaven, Hallowed be thy Name. Thy kingdom come. Thy will be done, On earth as it is in heaven. Give us this day our daily bread. And forgive us our trespasses, As we forgive those who trespass against us.

And lead us not into temptation, But deliver us from evil. For thine is the kingdom, and the power, and the glory, for ever and ever. Amen.

The Blessing

>   *Minister.* Praise the Lord, O my soul;
>   *Answer.* And forget not all his benefits.
>   *Minister.* Who forgiveth all thy sin,
>   *Answer.* And healeth all thine infirmities.
>   *Minister.* He hath not dealt with us after our sins;
>   *Answer.* Nor rewarded us according to our wickedness.
>   *Minister.* Look how wide the east is from the west;
>   *Answer.* So far hath he set our sins from us.

> ¶ *Then shall the Priest stand and say,*

GO in peace, for the Lord hath put away thy sin; And the blessing of God Almighty, the Father, the Son, and the Holy Ghost, be with you, and remain with you always. *Amen.*

PRAYER BOOK STUDIES VIII: THE ORDINAL

The Standing Liturgical Commission
of the Protestant Episcopal Church in the
United States of America

1957

PREFACE

The last revision of our Prayer Book was brought to a rather abrupt conclusion in 1928. Consideration of it had preoccupied the time of General Convention ever since 1913. Everyone was weary of the long and ponderous legislative process, and desired to make the new Prayer Book available as soon as possible for the use of the Church.

But the work of revision, which sometimes has seemed difficult to start, in this case proved hard to stop. The years of debate had aroused widespread interest in the whole subject: and the mind of the Church was more receptive of suggestions for revision when the work was brought to an end than when it began. Moreover, the revision was actually closed to new action in 1925, in order that it might receive final adoption in 1928: so that it was not possible to give due consideration to a number of very desirable features in the English and Scottish revisions, which appeared simultaneously with our own. It was further realized that there were some rough edges in what had been done, as well as an unsatisfied demand for still further alterations.

The problem of defects in detail was met by continuing the Revision Commission, and giving it rather large 'editorial' powers (subject only to review by General Convention) to correct obvious errors in the text as adopted, in the publication of the new Prayer Book. Then, to deal with the constructive proposals for other changes which continued to be brought up in every General Convention, the Revision Commission was reconstituted as a Standing Liturgical Commission. To this body all matters concerning the Prayer Book were to be referred, for preservation in permanent files, and for continuing consideration, until such time as the accumulated matter was sufficient in amount and importance to justify proposing another Revision.

The number of such referrals by General Convention, of Memorials from Dioceses, and of suggestions made directly to the Commission from all regions and schools and parties in the Church, has now reached such a total that it is evident that there is a widespread and insistent demand for a general revision of the Prayer Book.

The Standing Liturgical Commission is not, however, proposing any immediate revision. On the contrary, we believe that there ought to be a period of study and discussion, to acquaint the Church at large with the principles and issues involved, in order that the eventual action may be taken intelligently, and if possible without consuming so much of the time of our supreme legislative synod.

Accordingly, the General Convention of 1949 signaled the Fourth Centennial Year of the First Book of Common Prayer in English by authorizing the Liturgical Commission to publish its findings, in the form of a series of *Prayer Book Studies*.

It must be emphasized that the liturgical forms presented in these *Studies* are not — and under our Constitution, cannot be — sanctioned for public use. They are submitted for free discussion. The Commission will be grateful for copies or articles, resolutions, and direct comment, for its consideration, that the mind of the Church may be fully known to the body charged with reporting it.

In this undertaking, we have endeavored to be objective and impartial. It is not possible to avoid every matter which may be thought by some to be controversial. Ideas which seem to be constructively valuable will be brought to the attention of the Church, without too much regard as to whether they may ultimately be judged to be expedient. We cannot undertake to eliminate every proposal to which anyone might conceivably object: to do so would be to admit that any constructive progress is impossible. What we can do is to be alert not to alter the present *balance* of expressed or implied doctrine of the Church. We can seek to counterbalance every proposal which might seem to favor some one party of opinion by some other change in the opposite direction. The goal we have constantly had in mind — however imperfectly we may have succeeded in attaining it — is the shaping of a future Prayer Book which *every* party might embrace with the well-founded conviction that therein its own position had been strengthened, its witness enhanced, and its devotions enriched.

The objective we have pursued is the same as that expressed by the Commission for the Revision of 1892: "*Resolved*, That this Committee, in all its suggestions and acts, be guided by those principles of liturgical construction and ritual use which have guided the compilation and amendments of the Book of Common Prayer, and have made it what it is."

THE STANDING LITURGICAL COMMISSION:

GOODRICH R. FENNER, *Chairman*
ARTHUR C. LICHTENBERGER
* BAYARD H. JONES, *Vice Chairman*
JOHN W. SUTER, *Custodian*
MASSEY H. SHEPHERD, JR.
CHARLES W. F. SMITH
FRANCIS B. SAYRE, JR.
BERTRAM L. SMITH
SPENCER ERVIN, *Secretary*
JOHN ASHTON
* Died, April 27, 1957

The Commission's sub-committee on the Ordinal has been in charge of Bishop Fenner. The fact that this study only concerns the three rites of ordination does not imply that the Commission does not recommend the inclusion of other rites in the Ordinal, such as are at present contained therein. But studies on these other rites will appear at a later time.

The Ordinal

This introduction to the proposed Ordinal sets forth in brief form the development of the Ordinal from the first intimations of ordinations given in the New Testament to the revision of the American Prayer Book in 1928. No attempt is made to give a detailed historical development or the theology of the Sacred Ministry. These would be beyond the scope or needs of these Studies. Our effort has been confined to showing the place Holy Order occupies in the long worshipping life of the Church and the changes in the Ordinal which we think will make for greater enrichment.

Nothing, of course, is suggested that would tend in the least to draw our Church away from the Ordinals of the Anglican Church generally, nor from those basic elements of the historic Ordinals that have been continuous in the life of the Church. The changes here proposed are wholly contained within the structure of the Ordinal as it has developed in the Western Church.

The Development of the Ordinal

Early Sacramentaries

What the Church means by Order is well described by St. Augustine when he states that order is "an arrangement of things like and unlike which assigns to each its place." (*De civ. Dei* xix. 13). Holy Order began very early to mean the assignment of each to his place. In the beginnings of the Church's life, assignment is referred to as "lot." In Acts 1:17, Judas is spoken of as having had his part and place in the Apostolic Ministry; and, to take the place from which he had fallen, the Apostles "gave forth their lots; and the lot fell upon Matthias; and he was numbered with the eleven Apostles" (Acts 1:26). By the time of Hippolytus, lot and assignment had developed into *leitourgeia* and meant "ministry" in a technical sense. Each Order has its own particular function in the corporate life of the Church. The clergy receive the Holy Spirit to empower them to perform those functions which belong to their Order in the Ministry.

According to a later strand of New Testament tradition the first ordination and commission were bestowed by Christ Himself in one of His Resurrection appearances. "He breathed on them, and saith unto them, Receive ye the Holy Ghost." (John 20:22.) This action in breathing on His Apostles was never repeated. The laying on of hands, however, had been a consistent gesture of our Lord. In healing, He laid His hands upon those who were diseased. In thanksgiving, He laid His hands and consecrated. At Bethany, He "lifted up His hands and blessed them." His commissioning and sending forth were uniformly stated in the declarative. Forthwith, in the New Testament, the only ceremony at Ordination was the laying on of hands with prayer.

By the laying on of hands with prayer, the ordinand received the endowment of the Holy Spirit for the twofold purpose of extending the gift of Christ to His Apostles down through the ages and of manifesting from within himself the abiding presence and power of his Lord in the Order to which he has been called and ordained. No minister in any Order can do anything apart from the operation of the Holy Spirit. It is through the minister that the Holy Spirit presents the things of Christ to the Church. The minister of the Church does everything through the power and presence of the Holy Spirit, for he is chosen and ordained by the one abiding Priest to be His living instrument in the world. He uses this ministry that He Himself may reach His children in baptism; bestow upon them the sevenfold gifts of His Holy Spirit in Confirmation; consecrate the elements in the Holy Communion for them; absolve and reconcile the penitent; ordain men to be His ministers; join a man and woman in holy wedlock; and strengthen the sick. "I am the vine, ye are the branches . . . without me, ye can do nothing."

The New Testament makes clear that it is the one Lord who by His spirit calls, endows and uses His ministers to carry on His redemptive mission in the world, and through those already so called and endowed, others are to be added that His ministry may be continued in each succeeding generation.

Outside the New Testament the first Christian writer to make record of this continuing ministry in the Church is Clement of Rome. In his epistle to the Corinthians, he tells in chapter 42 how the Apostles, having received a charge, went forth with full assurance of the Holy Ghost to preach the Gospel that the Kingdom of God was about to come. So proclaiming everywhere in the country-sides and cities, they appointed their first-fruits, after they had proved them by the Spirit, to be bishops and deacons unto them that should believe.

Our knowledge of the Ordinal is derived chiefly from Sacramentaries and Pontificals and by the nature of these documents they are scarce. A Sacramentary or Pontifical contained only those parts of the services that pertained to the office of the bishop. They were always regarded as the personal property of the bishop and on his death they were frequently withdrawn from the safekeeping of the cathedral and placed with his personal belongings. This made them liable to mutilation and loss.

The earliest text we have of the Ordinal appears in the *Apostolic Tradition* of Hippolytus of Rome, and dates from the beginning of the third century. The three Orders are taken for granted and they are set forth as the Ministry of the Church. The minister in each order was elected by the Church and ordained by a single prayer accompanied by the laying on of hands. In his directions, Hippolytus states that the bishop alone laid his hand upon the deacon. He was ordained to be the pastoral and liturgical assistant to the bishop. The presbyters joined the bishop in laying hands upon the presbyter. This gesture of the presbyters was not considered as ordaining, but as assenting to and welcoming the ordinand into their ranks. When a bishop was consecrated, the act of consecration was delegated to one bishop who imposed his hands and said the prayer of ordination.

The prayer for the ordering of deacons in the *Apostolic Tradition* has changed less in detail than in any of the other orders.

In the prayer for the consecration of a bishop, his functions are stated as feeding the flock, offering the holy gifts, absolving penitents, and making choice of clergy. To him is given the high priesthood of the Church and he is the minister of all Sacraments.

There is scant definition of the ministry of the presbyter in the Apostolic Tradition. He is to assist the bishop as a member of his advisory council, as Moses chose elders to assist him in ruling the chosen people. There is no indication of any sacerdotal function given to the presbyter. In his celebration of the Eucharist and in Baptism and Absolution, the bishop had the assistance of the deacons.

The next text, and the earliest Eastern one, is that of the Sacramentary of the Egyptian bishop, Serapion. It dates from the middle of the fourth century and is similar in all significant respects to the *Apostolic Tradition* of Hippolytus, with the exception of the greater recognition given to the duties of the presbyter. While he is still to serve in a subordinate capacity, he is now mentioned as one who is to be a minister of the Word and of reconciliation, and to be responsible for the administration of the parish — "To be a steward of thy people and an ambassador of thy divine oracles and to reconcile thy peoples to thee." It was a natural development that between the times of Hippolytus and Serapion the populous centers saw the considerable growth of parishes and that which the bishop did, in performing all sacramental functions for all the people of the city, had to be supplemented by the preaching, pastoral and administrative ministry of the presbyter.

In the last quarter of the eighth century in the Frankish kingdom, Charlemagne made an effort to bring unity to the great variety of liturgical usage that prevailed. Some churches were using the Gallican rite and some the Roman rite, and each with local adaptations. Charlemagne applied to Pope Hadrian I for an authentic copy of the Roman Sacramentary. Apparently, from lack of interest in Charlemagne's project, Hadrian sent something that was partial and inadequate. It did, however, contain the Ordinal. Although Hadrian's letter to Charlemagne described the work as "The Book of the Sacraments published by St. Gregory the Great," it is now known as the "Sacramentary of Hadrian."

This sacramentary did not meet the needs of the Frankish or any other Church, and to supply its deficiencies a supplement was added. This supplement is the work of Alcuin. It became known as the Gregorian Sacramentary, and to a considerable extent it is the source of the essential prayers in the later Missals and Pontificals.

Another document of importance in the development of the Ordinal is the sacramentary which came to be called the Gelasian. It has been attributed to Pope Gelasius I (492-496). It is a Roman book, but it is characterized by the deletion of most things that were merely of local Roman interest and by the addition of certain things that were Gallican.

The last of the more prominent medieval sacramentaries is known as the "Leonine." It was assumed by an earlier editor that it was the work of Pope Leo the Great (440-461). In strict definition it is not a sacramentary, but out of its haphazard arrangement of material a sacramentary might be assembled. A considerable amount of the Leonine material appears in later sacramentaries and service books, and through them a few prayers, verbatim or by paraphrase, came into the Book of Common Prayer. Among them is the final Collect in the Ordination of Deacons.

The Leonine and Gelasian rites conform in essential matters to the rites as set forth in the *Apostolic Tradition*, but there are some significant additions. A litany makes its first appearance in the Leonine rite, and in the Gelasian rite is recorded the first use of the "Instruments." The priest's and the bishop's hands are anointed and the open book of the Gospels is imposed upon the neck and head of the bishop.

The most important addition in the Gelasian rite, as it developed in the Gallican Church before Charlemagne, is that of sacerdotal character being given to the priest. It is a new and important departure. There are differing interpretations, due to conflicting readings, yet it does seem to point definitely to the fact that the presbyter had occupied a place as a minister of the Eucharist. In H. A. Wilson's edition of the Gelasian Sacramentary, the petition in the ordination of a priest states that he may "through the service of thy people transform the Body and Blood of Thy Son by a stainless benediction and by an inviolate charity into a perfect man, into the measure of the age of the fullness of Christ." It may be argued from this that if the Gelasian Sacramentary is really the work of Pope Gelasius I, the sacerdotal functions of the presbyter began at least as early as the fifth century.

English Ordinals

The development of rites in the Church of England had even more diversity than that of the Gallican Church. There were notably those of Salisbury, Hereford, Bangor, York and Lincoln. But this does not exhaust the list. In theory each church was supposed to follow the usage of the Metropolitan Church of its province, but in fact most of the larger and more ancient churches in each diocese had their own Use. They were not so much different rites, for in structure and text they were approximately the same, but there were differences in detail. All of them, however, expressed in bold outline a definite adherence to the Roman rite.

What is known as the Sarum Use contained an Ordinal set forth early in the thirteenth century by Richard le Poer, dean and later bishop of Salisbury. The Sarum Use began to be adopted quite readily, and it is apparent that by the middle of the fifteenth century the Ordinal known as the "New Use of Sarum" was in general use in the Churches in England, Wales and Ireland.

The English Prayer Book of 1549 did not contain an Ordinal. The Roman version of the Ordinal, as set forth in the "New Use of Sarum," was soon to be displaced. By an Act of Parliament on January 31st, 1550, the King was empowered to appoint a commission to prepare and publish a "Form and Manner of Making and Consecrating Archbishops, Bishops, Priests and Deacons, and Other Ministers of the Church." There are several items of evidence which show that an Ordinal had already been prepared. The commissioners were appointed three days after Parliamentary authorization and the book was actually published about two months later.

The permission to draw up rites of ordination 'for the Other Ministries of the Church' was ignored, for there was a determination not to continue Minor Orders. Persons in Minor Orders could claim immunity from criminal prosecution in the secular courts and could demand that they be turned over to the jurisdiction of their bishops. This abuse of privilege had grown to such an extent that there was considerable outcry against it.

The essential forms of ordination — the laying on of hands and prayer — had never been used for the Minor Orders. Theirs was a commissioning to perform certain duties rather than an ordination. Their commissioning was accomplished by prayer that they might rightly perform their duties and the presentation of a proper instrument to signify their office. The sub-deacon received an empty paten and chalice from the bishop, and from the archdeacon he received a cruet with water and a bowl and napkin. The acolyte received a candlestick with candle and an empty cruet. The exorcist received a booklet containing the exorcisms. The reader had delivered to him the Bible, and the doorkeeper received the keys to the church.

The Tradition of the Instruments, while beginning with the Minor Orders, was added to the ordinations of bishops, priests and deacons in the eleventh century. Generally, the instruments consisted of vesting the ordinand in the vestment proper for his order. The deacon received a book of the Gospels and was enjoined to read it to the people. The priest received the paten and chalice with hosts and wine in them, and was charged with the duty of offering the Holy Sacrifice. The bishop was given the ring and pastoral staff, and he was charged with maintaining discipline and sound faith. The anointing of the hands had added to it the anointing of the head, but this was not continued in later Pontificals except in the case of a bishop.

This first commission, charged with providing an Ordinal, placed first the essentials of ordination — prayer and the imposition of hands — but they were careful also to retain the Tradition of the Instruments. While the revisers undoubtedly did not concur with the scholastic theories of the time, that the Instruments were essential, nevertheless, they must have concluded that they did not obscure the essential elements of ordination.

The Sarum Pontifical in all essentials had an identity with the Roman Pontifical. The revisers of the 1550 Ordinal, under the guidance of Cranmer, took into consideration other local rites with which they were familiar. These had retained several ancient features that the Roman Use had beclouded. While there were differences in the language and ceremonies in the new English Ordinal, yet it had exactly the same end in view as the Roman Pontifical. There is not the slightest evidence that their intention was otherwise. They stated in the Preface to the Ordinal that "from the Apostles' time there have been these Orders of Ministers in Christ's Church, — Bishops, Priests and Deacons, — and therefore, to the intent that these Orders may be continued and reverently used and esteemed in this Church . . ."

The Roman objection to Anglican Orders contained in the Bull *Apostolicae Curae* of Pope Leo XIII states that the English Ordinal is defective in its form and intention; that it does not mention priesthood as the power of offering sacrifice and that there is no intention of continuing the historic orders of the ministry as they are understood in the universal Church. With respect to form, it should be clear that those oldest ordination prayers found in the *Apostolic Tradition* of Hippolytus and the Sacramentary of Serapion make no specific mention of the priest offering sacrifice. It is not until the appearance of the Gelasian Sacramentary, in the fifth century, that we find the priest given a sacerdotal function. The power to offer the sacrifice also was not originally a part of the Roman rite. Nowhere is the "intent" set forth so explicitly by any historic church as in the Preface to the English Ordinal. The form and intention, not only of priesthood but also of the other ministries, are made clearer and are more in accord with the practice of the universal and undivided Church than those of the present-day Roman Pontifical itself.

Roman critics further charged that the Anglican Church recognized deficiencies in its form when it changed the form in the Edwardian Ordinals of Ordination of Priests and Bishops from the simple scriptural passage, " Receive the Holy Ghost: whose sins . . . ," to the particularizing of the office in the 1662 Ordinal — " Receive the Holy Ghost for the Office and Work of a Priest. . ." " — of a Bishop." The specification of the order was not made in anticipation of any Roman objections, but rather that the Presbyterians and Puritans would be under no misapprehensions as to the teaching of the English Church. Ordination is to an Order and not to any single function of that Order, and it is not necessary to specify every function. In giving the power to minister the sacraments, there is given obviously the power to offer sacrifice.

The changes made in the Ordinal since 1550, with the exception of the designation of the Order in the formulae in 1662, have been few. None of them affected the structure of the services.

In the revision of 1552, the Tradition of the Instruments with respect to the chalice for the priest, and the pastoral staff with the imposition of the Gospels on the neck for the bishop were omitted. No mention was made of vestments. In the 1550 Ordinal albs were required for the priests and deacons and a tunicle for the deacon who read the Gospel. Copes had been designated as the proper vestment for bishops.

The rite of 1662 recast the first paragraph of the Preface to make it still more definite that the English Church recognizes only episcopal ordination — "admitted thereunto according to the Form hereafter following or hath had Episcopal Consecration or Ordination." The deacons and priests are to be decently habited and the bishop-elect is to wear first a rochet and before the consecration he is to "put on the rest of the Episcopal habit." Heretofore the deacon had been authorized "to Baptize" but this was changed to read "in the absence of the priest to baptize infants." In this same question, as also in the address to the bishop-elect, "congregation" was changed to "church." In the ordination of priests, the shorter translation of the *Veni Creator* was added and, instead of its being sung immediately after the Gospel, it was placed in the position it now occupies. There was added also the question to the bishop-elect —"Will you be faithful in Ordaining, sending, or laying hands upon others?"

American Ordinals

The General Convention which met in New York City in September, 1792, formally omitted the Oath of the King's Sovereignty as contained in the Ordinal of 1662 and added an alternative formula for the ordination of a priest. "Take thou authority to execute the Office of a Priest . . . ," was made an alternative to "Receive the Holy Ghost for the Office and Work of a Priest . . ." The English rite in the Consecration of Bishops contained the pledge to render "all due reverence and obedience to the Archbishop." This was changed to a promise of "conformity and obedience to the doctrine, discipline, and worship of the Protestant Episcopal Church in the United States of America." A further promise was made "diligently to exercise such discipline as by the authority of God's Word and by the order of this Church is committed to you." This was a substitute for the English promise to "correct and punish all such as are unquiet, disobedient and criminous within your diocese."

The Ordinal was subjected to very slight and inconsequential changes in the Book of 1892. The provision was added for saying the Nicene Creed in the Ordination of Priests and the Consecration of Bishops. The longer paraphrase of the *Veni, Creator Spiritus* was omitted. In the Order for the Administration of the Lord's Supper appended to the Ordinal, the word "bishop" was substituted for "priest."

A notable change in the Ordinal of the 1928 Book was the provision for "The Litany and Suffrages for Ordinations." This is alternative to the General Litany that had been used in the Ordinal since 1550 and, before that, in the Roman Pontifical. It is considerably shorter than the General Litany and makes more specific the prayers of the congregation for God's blessing upon His Church and its ministry, and in particular for the one who is about to be ordained. Another change, reflecting perhaps the newer attitude towards the Scripture, is contained in the question asked of the deacon. Instead of the older, "Do you unfeignedly believe all the Canonical Scriptures of the Old and New Testament?" it became, "Are you persuaded that the Holy Scriptures contain all Doctrine required as necessary for salvation through faith in Jesus Christ?"

Proposed Revision

The changes made in the following proposed revision of the Ordinal in no way affect the basic structure of the rites. The revisers of the Ordinal in 1550 were careful to retain all the essentials that had come down to them from the New Testament. The thread of these essentials was to be found in the several Sacramentaries and Pontificals and also in the "New Use of Sarum." This last had considerable use in England when, by an Act of Parliament in early 1550, the commission was appointed by the King to provide an Ordinal that would be the "one Use" for the ordination of all clergy in the Church. Even with the recognition in our own century of the *Apostolic Tradition* of Hippolytus as a primary source of Church Order, the work done by the commission in 1550 is fully supported as to the essentials in ordinations found in later sources that were unknown at that time.

It has often been said that the great bond of unity in the Anglican communion is the Book of Common Prayer. This can be repeated with special emphasis in respect to the Ordinal. The intention of all Anglican Churches in the ordination of their ministers must be identical, one with another, and must be set forth clearly in the forms they use. These proposals are made in strict conformity with this principle.

There are certain significant and meaningful ceremonies, however, that were a part of ordination services at one time or another in the Church, and there are others that are used in a number of our dioceses in the American Church without having any rubric either providing for them or prohibiting their use. Some of the more meritorious of these should be recognized either in the text or by permissive rubric.

It will be noted also that certain rearrangements, substitutions and deletions have been made. These we regard as making for better order in the services and being in line with modern liturgical scholarship.

The changes made in several words and the deletion of some redundant phrases in this text will be apparent and do not need explanation. It is well to remember that there has been practically no revision of the Ordinal of the American Book since our first Book in 1792, and in these 165 years the shades of meaning of many words have changed and some modes of expression then in use are now obsolete.

Changes Common to the Three Rites

The Title Page

Both the title page and the title for the Office of the Ordination of Deacons use the term "Making of Deacons." This was a change made in the Book of 1662. The first English Ordinal, and the Ordinal of 1552 used the "Ordering of Deacons." The older title, however, continued to head the succeeding pages in both the Book of 1662 and the first and subsequent American Books. The word "Making" does not add or explain anything that is not already implicit in "Ordering" or Ordaining. The diaconate is, of course, the first order in the threefold ministry and is quite separate and apart from the Minor Orders. The laying on of hands is an essential in the ordination of a deacon, whereas the presentation of the appropriate instrument was sufficient to set apart the Minor Orders. The diaconate, moreover, should not be referred to (as is done in our present commendatory prayer at the end of the service) as "this inferior Office" in contrast to "the higher Ministries in thy Church." The diaconate has an integrity of its own as a part of the sacred Ministry.

To the title page of our American Ordinal has been added two other services — " The Form of Consecration of a Church" and "An Office of Institution of Ministers." These bear no particular relationship to the Ordinal and as they would be provided for in the index, no useful purpose is served by their being included in the title page.

The Preface

The reading of the Preface to the Ordinal at ordination services, and more particularly its first paragraph, has come into wide use in the Church. It is customarily read immediately after the sermon and before the candidate is formally presented to the Bishop. The Preface makes no argument respecting the threefold Orders of Ministers in the historic Church; it simply states the fact "that from the Apostles' time there have been these Orders of Ministers in Christ's Church." It further declares that it is the intention of the Church that these Orders shall be continued and that what is done in this present ordination is within the context of what the Church has done since the Apostles' time. The public reading of the Preface has the value of recalling to the minds of the worshipping congregation that they are a part of that ongoing stream of the Church's life as represented in its continuing and unbroken line of the ministry.

The use of the first paragraph of the Preface is suggested, for it is that portion which is common to all Churches of the Anglican communion. The succeeding paragraphs vary with the applicable canonical and traditional emphases in each Church.

The Litany

The General or "great" Litany is so rarely used at ordinations and the Litany for Ordinations is so uniformly substituted for it that it seems well to recognize this situation by a rubric which specifies the Litany for Ordinations with the appropriate suffrage for each order.

A suggested change is offered with respect to the position of the Litany in the ordination of a deacon and priest. The present position in both these rites breaks the service into two parts. In the Consecration of a Bishop, the Litany is provided for immediately before the examination and the laying on of hands, and this seems to be the proper place. To bring uniformity in the use of the Litany, it is proposed that it shall be said following the Epistle in the ordination of a deacon and the Gospel in the ordination of a priest. This provision would also have the advantage of bringing the supplication of the Litany into closer relation with the solemn moment of ordination.

It is proposed further that the *Kyrie eleison* and the Lord's Prayer be omitted from the Litany for Ordinations, since both will be said at the celebration of the Holy Communion.

To make the Litany for Ordinations more accessible to the congregation than it is in its present location, it should be printed immediately after the Preface to the Ordinal.

Promise of Conformity

In ordinations to the diaconate and priesthood, the canonical Promise of Conformity is usually read and signed before the bishop and other clergy in a robing room prior to the services. In the Consecration of a Bishop, this Promise is read publicly by the bishop-elect as a part of the service. It follows immediately after the presentation of the candidate for the episcopal office. The congregation needs no less to hear this public declaration from the person to be ordained deacon and priest. To this end it is placed as a part of the presentation and follows the bishop's inquiry of the presenter that the person is "apt and meet" for the order to which he is being ordained.

The Alternative 'Veni, Creator Spiritus'

The American Church in its revision of the Ordinal provided for an alternative to Bishop John Cosin's translation of *Veni, Creator Spiritus*. This alternative version is peculiar to the American Church. This translation does not measure up to the beauty and succinctness of Cosin's. While the *Veni, Creator Spiritus* is the only metrical hymn in the Prayer Book, it has had centuries of use. It was in the Pontifical that Cranmer had before him and it also was a part of the priest's preparation for Mass in the Sarum Missal. Inasmuch as the alternative version is rarely used, it is proposed that it be dropped from ordination to the priesthood and the consecration of a bishop, and that the Cosin translation in use since 1662 be the only one supplied.

The Eucharistic Preface

The ordination prayer which immediately precedes the laying on of hands in each Order is introduced by the Salutation, the *Sursum Corda* and the Eucharistic Preface. This dialogue and the Preface are found in two of the oldest sources we have — Hippolytus (c. A. D. 200) and Cyprian (c. A. D. 252). The form here offered is an adaptation of 2 Corinthians 13:14, and was retained in the Book of 1549. It disappeared in the 1552 revision, but the *Sursum Corda* and the Eucharistic Preface have introduced the Prayer of Consecration since the first American Book. It has been in the Scottish Book since 1637. The Salutation, the *Sursum Corda* and the Eucharistic Preface are now to be found in our 1928 revision of Holy Baptism. The proposed English Book of 1928 and the Scottish Book of 1929 use the dialogue and the Preface in all three ordination prayers.

The function of the Salutation, the *Sursum Corda* and the Eucharistic Preface has been that of calling special attention to a new turn in the service and to prepare the worshippers in their hearts with thanksgiving for that which is to follow. Similar to Holy Baptism, it should be used to introduce the ordination prayer and thereby give emphasis to the principal reason for the people coming together.

Tradition of the Instruments

It has been so well established historically that prayer and the laying on of hands are the essentials of ordination, that the danger of confusion by the use of the Instruments, other than the New Testament and Bible, has ceased to be a real one. In the First Edwardian Ordinal, the chalice and paten with the Bible delivered to the presbyter, and the pastoral staff with the Bible to the bishop, were retained; but due to the strident controversial spirit of the times they disappeared from the Second Edwardian Ordinal. While they are ceremonial accessories, they are, at the same time, meaningful ones. The authority given the deacon is embraced in the delivery of the New Testament. For the priest, the Bible symbolizes his authority to preach the Word of God. There should be added the Instruments employed in the Holy Communion to symbolize the commission to minister the sacraments. In the Consecration of a Bishop, the Bible is delivered again, with the exhortation that he is to derive his doctrine and his work from it. But along with his vocation within the Gospel, it is stated that he is also to be to the flock of Christ a shepherd. The pastoral staff from ancient times has been a symbol of the bishop's work as the chief shepherd of the flock, and, together with the Bible, should be delivered to him as the second symbolical instrument of the episcopal office.

"The Bishop Sitting in his Chair"

In our present Book, the rubric in each Office recites "The Bishop sitting in his chair near to the Holy Table." There have been so many and various interpretations and usages as to where the bishop's chair is placed that it seems best to delete from the rubric any reference to its location.

"These Persons"

In the words of presentation of candidates for both the diaconate and priesthood the plural is used — "these persons present." This derives from the English usage of having the archdeacon or some one person appointed by the bishop to make the presentation of all the candidates. In most instances in American ordinations only a single candidate is ordained, and even if several are ordained at the same time they are normally presented singly by different priests. For these reasons it seems simpler to cast the presentation in the singular and have the presenting priest say, "Reverend Father in God, I present unto you this person present . . ."

Commendatory Prayers

In line with the proposed revision of the Eucharistic Liturgy (Prayer Book Study IV), commendatory prayers or post-communion collects are omitted. The reasons usually given for the use of a post-communion collect are that we have a precedent set for us in ordination rites. A true post-communion collect is a prayer for grace that is derived from the sacrament that has just been received. The post-communion collects in the ordination rites do not do this, and moreover they are needless duplications of what has already been said in the ordination itself. (See Prayer Book Study IV, Vol. 1, pp. 334-337.)

Changes in Each Rite

Other proposed changes are set forth in the ordination rites for each of the Orders. In many instances where verbal changes have been made, no special attention is called to them as they do not change the meanings, but rather make for clarity of expression.

Deacon

In the second rubric, "decently habited" is changed to "vested in surplice or alb." As at present, only the rite for the Consecration of a Bishop makes any specification as to vestments. It is considered that in any revision it would be well to recognize the vestments worn by the other Orders and not leave the matter to our indefinite description, "decently habited." This description in our Book came undoubtedly from the English Book of 1662. This, however, pointed directly to the "Ornaments Rubric" contained in the Act of Uniformity of 1559. The framers of the Ordinal of the American Book of 1792 may not have realized that "decently habited" had this specific reference in the English Book. In specifying "surplice or alb," we do not go back to vestments authorized by the Ornaments Rubric, but rather to those which have developed and become customary in our own Church.

The first Epistle (1 Timothy 3:8-13) is omitted in favor of the second (Acts 6:2-11). The Epistle from Acts has always been interpreted by the Church as a narrative of the institution of the diaconate. It also provides for the qualification of deacons as does the Timothy Epistle, but it is given as a summary of qualifications by saying that they shall be "men of honest report."

It is proposed that there shall be a prayer of invocation prior to the laying on of hands. Both the Ordering of Priests and the Consecration of Bishops have such a prayer. The prayer submitted here, preceded by the *Sursum Corda* and the Eucharistic Preface, is taken from the proposed English Book of 1928 and the Scottish Book of 1929. It is fuller than our present post-communion collect. It makes no reference to the Order being "inferior" or to the ordinand being "called unto the higher Ministries in thy Church."

A new rubric has been introduced immediately before the reading of the Gospel which provides for the placing of a stole over the deacon's left shoulder.

The last rubric has been omitted. It has no function in view of the fact that the matters mentioned in it are all taken care of in the Canons, and they are properly a matter of canonical rather than liturgical regulation.

Priest

The only changes in the rite for the Ordering of Priests that have not been commented on in the proposed changes that are common to all three services are as follows:

The first Gospel in our present Book (St. Matthew 9:36-38) should be omitted. It is too short and moreover the theme of pastoral care as exemplified by the Good Shepherd is more fully and better developed for the purposes at hand in the second Gospel (St. John 10: 1-16). The Exhortation of the Bishop to the ordinand, which immediately follows, is based also on the Johannine Gospel and is a superb commentary upon it.

The alternative formula accompanying laying on of hands, "Take thou authority. . . ." is omitted from this proposed revision. No other Anglican Ordinal has an alternative formula. They uniformly use, "Receive the Holy Ghost . . ." The alternative formula was placed in the American Ordinal in 1792. Bishop Seabury made strenuous objection to it:

> "But the sacerdotal implications of the older form were objectionable to many, despite the Scriptural language. . . . Bishop White saw no essential difference between the two formularies, and he remarked of the first one that it related 'according to the intention of the service, principally, under due regulation to the power of passing ecclesiastical censures, and of releasing from them, and partly to the declaring of the forgiveness of sins, repented of and forsaken, such forgiveness not to apply independently of the sincerity of the receiver.' From the strictly historical standpoint, the power of declaring Absolution was given by our Lord to His Apostles, from whom it was transmitted to the bishops, but the bishops have delegated this privilege of their priestly powers to the presbyterate from the earliest times." (Shepherd — *The Oxford American Prayer Book Commentary*, pp. 546-547.)

Bishop

The only further change in the rite of the Consecration of a Bishop that must have special notice is that of the exhortation that follows the laying on of hands and accompanies the delivery of the instruments.

The questions addressed to the bishop-elect, with necessary modifications, carry back to those asked of candidates for the diaconate and priesthood. The answers given are promises to follow, "first, a pattern of life; second, a life of belief; third, a life of ministering." (*Liturgy and Worship*, edited by W. K. Lowther Clarke, pp. 681.) This third promise, in our judgment, needs specific reference to the priestly character of the episcopate; of his high-priestly office of ordaining and sending. Cranmer, the author of the present text, had thought chiefly in terms of the Gospel, and he placed the emphasis in the episcopal office upon the bishop's guardianship of the Bible and the administration of discipline. The episcopate, however, is not merely dependent upon the New Testament, but is coterminous with it and the continuation of the ministry of this Church derives from the bishop's high-priestly authority and power to ordain. To this end, along with certain simplifications and directness of expression, this exhortation has added to it a recognition of the continuing and heightened priestly character of the bishop to "ordain and send forth men to preach the Gospel and to administer the Holy Sacraments."

[Editor's Note: In the published edition of *Prayer Book Studies* VII, the old rite and the proposed rite are printed in parallel, the old rite on the left page, the proposed rite on the right page. Following the pattern established in PBS I-VII, I will produce the proposed text below.]

The Ordinal

The Form and Manner of Making, Ordaining, and Consecrating Bishops, Priests, and Deacons according to the Order of the Protestant Episcopal Church in the United States of America, as established by the Bishops, the Clergy, and Laity of said Church, in General Convention

The Preface

It is evident unto all men, diligently reading Holy Scripture and ancient Authors, that from the Apostles' time there have been these Orders of Ministers in Christ's Church, — Bishops, Priests, and Deacons. Which Offices were evermore had in such reverend estimation, that no man might presume to execute any of them, except he were first called, tried, examined, and known to have such qualities as are requisite for the same; and also by public Prayer, with Imposition of Hands, were approved and admitted thereunto by lawful Authority. And therefore, to the intent that these Orders may be continued, and reverently used and esteemed in this Church, no man shall be accounted or taken to be a lawful Bishop, Priest, or Deacon, in this Church, or suffered to execute any of the said Functions, except he be called, tried, examined, and admitted thereunto, according to the Form hereafter following, or hath had Episcopal Consecration or Ordination.

> ¶ *And none shall be admitted a Deacon, Priest, or Bishop, except he be of the age which the Canon in that case provided may require.*
>
> ¶ *And the Bishop, knowing either by himself, or by sufficient testimony, any Person to be a man of virtuous conversation, and without crime; and, after examination and trial, finding him sufficiently instructed in the Holy Scripture, and otherwise learned as the Canons require, may, at the times appointed, or else, on urgent occasion, upon some other day, in the face of the Church, Limit him a Deacon, in such manner and form as followeth.*
>
> ¶ NOTE, *That in the discretion of the Bishop, the* PREFACE *or any portion thereof may be read before the Presentation of the Candidates at all Ordinations.*

The Litany and Suffrages for Ordinations

O GOD the Father,
Have mercy upon us.
O God the Son,

Have mercy upon us.
O God the Holy Ghost,
Have mercy upon us.
O holy Trinity, one God,
Have mercy upon us.

WE beseech thee to hear us, good Lord; and that it may please thee to grant peace to the whole world, and to thy Church;
We beseech thee to hear us, good Lord.

That it may please thee to sanctify and bless thy holy Church throughout the world;
We beseech thee to hear us, good Lord.

That it may please thee to inspire all Bishops, Priests, and Deacons, with love of thee and of thy truth;
We beseech thee to hear us, good Lord.

That it may please thee to endue all Ministers of thy Church with devotion to thy glory and to the salvation of souls;
We beseech thee to hear us, good Lord.

¶ *Here, at the Ordination of Deacons or of Priests shall be said,*

That it may please thee to bless these thy servants, now to be admitted to the Order of Deacons (or Priests), and to pour thy grace upon them; that they may duly execute their Office to the edifying of thy Church, and to the glory of thy holy Name;
We beseech thee to hear us, good Lord.

¶ *Here, at the Consecration of a Bishop shall be said,*

That it may please thee to bless this our Brother elected, and to send thy grace upon him, that he may duly execute the Office whereunto he is called, to the edifying of thy Church, and to the honour, praise, and glory of thy Name;
We beseech thee to hear us, good Lord.

That it may please thee to guide by thy indwelling Spirit those whom thou dost call to the Ministry of thy Church; that they may go forward with courage, and persevere unto the end;
We beseech thee to hear us, good Lord.

That it may please thee to increase the number of the Ministers of thy Church, that the Gospel may be preached to all people;
We beseech thee to hear us, good Lord.

That it may please thee to hasten the fulfilment of thy purpose, that thy Church may be one;
We beseech thee to hear us, good Lord.

That it may please thee to grant that we, with all thy saints, may be partakers of thy everlasting kingdom; We beseech thee to hear us, good Lord.

Hearken unto our voice, O Lord, when we cry unto thee;
Have mercy upon us and hear us.
O Lord, arise, help us;
And deliver us for thy Name's sake.
Let thy priests be clothed with righteousness;
And let thy saints sing with joyfulness.
Lord, hear our prayer;
And let our cry come unto thee.

Let us pray.

O GOD, who dost ever hallow and protect thy Church; Raise up therein, through thy Spirit, good and faithful stewards of the mysteries of Christ, that by their ministry and example thy people may abide in thy favour and be guided in the way of truth; through Jesus Christ our Lord, who liveth and reigneth with thee in the unity of the same Spirit ever, one God, world without end. *Amen.*

The Form and Manner of Ordaining Deacons

¶ *When the day appointed by the Bishop is come, there shall be a Sermon, or Exhortation, declaring the Duty and Office of such as come to be admitted Deacons; how necessary that Order is in the Church of Christ, and also, how the People ought to esteem them in their Office.*

¶ *The Sermon being ended, a Priest shall present unto the Bishop, sitting in his chair, such as desire to be ordained Deacons, each of them being vested in Surplice or Alb, and shall say,*

REVEREND Father in God, I present unto you this person present, to be admitted Deacon.

¶ *The Bishop.*

TAKE heed that the persons, whom ye present unto us, be apt and meet, for their learning and godly conversation, to exercise their Ministry duly, to the honour of God, and the edifying of his Church.

> ¶ *The Priest shall answer*

I HAVE inquired concerning him, and also examined him, and think him so to be.

> ¶ *Then the Bishop shall say unto the People,*

BRETHREN, if there be any of you who knoweth any Impediment, or notable Crime, in any of these persons presented to be ordered Deacons, for the which he ought not to be admitted to that Office, let him come forth in the Name of God, and show what the Crime or Impediment is.

> ¶ *And if any great Crime or Impediment be objected, the Bishop shall cease from Ordering that person, until such time as the party accused shall be found clear of that Crime.*

> ¶ *Then shall the Bishop require of him the following Promise of Conformity to the Doctrine, Discipline, and Worship of the Protestant Episcopal Church.*

I DO believe the Holy Scriptures of the Old and New Testaments to be the Word of God, and to contain all things necessary to salvation; and I do solemnly engage to conform to the Doctrine, Discipline, and Worship of the Protestant Episcopal Church in the United States of America.

> ¶ *Then shall be said the Liturgy with the following Collect, Epistle and Gospel.*

The Collect

ALMIGHTY God, who by thy divine providence hast appointed divers Orders of Ministers in thy Church, and didst inspire thine Apostles to choose into the Order of Deacons the first Martyr Saint Stephen, with others; Mercifully behold these thy servants now called to the like Office and Administration; and so replenish them with the truth of thy Doctrine, and endue them with innocency of life, that, both by word and good example, they may faithfully serve thee in this Office, to the glory of thy Name, and the edification of thy Church; through the merits of our Saviour Jesus Christ, who liveth and reigneth with thee and the Holy Ghost, now and for ever. Amen.

The Epistle. Acts vi. 2

THEN the twelve called the multitude of the disciples unto them, and said, It is not reason that we should leave the word of God, and serve tables.

Wherefore, brethren, look ye out among you seven men of honest report, full of the Holy Ghost and wisdom, whom we may appoint over this business. But we will give ourselves continually to prayer, and to the ministry of the word. And the saying pleased the whole multitude: and they chose Stephen, a man full of faith and of the Holy Ghost, and Philip, and Prochorus, and Nicanor, and Timon, and Parmenas, and Nicolas a proselyte of Antioch: whom they set before the apostles: and when they had prayed, they laid their hands on them. And the word of God increased; and the number of the disciples multiplied in Jerusalem greatly; and a great company of the priests were obedient to the faith.

¶ *Then the Bishop, commending such as shall be found meet to be Ordered, to the Prayers of the congregation, shall with the Clergy and People present, say the Litany for Ordinations.*

¶ *Then, the People being seated, the Bishop shall examine every one of those who are to be Ordered, in the presence of the People, after this manner following.*

DO you trust that you are inwardly moved by the Holy Ghost to take upon you this Office and Ministration, to serve God for the promoting of his glory, and the edifying of his people?

Answer. I do.

Bishop. Do you think that you are truly called, according to the will of our Lord Jesus Christ, and according to the Canons of this Church, to the Ministry of the same?

Answer. I do.

Bishop. Are you persuaded that the Holy Scriptures contain all Doctrine required as necessary for eternal salvation through faith in Jesus Christ?

Answer. I am.

Bishop. Will you diligently read the same unto the people assembled in the Church where you shall be appointed to serve?

Answer. I will.

Bishop. It appertaineth to the Office of a Deacon, in the Church where he shall be appointed to serve, to assist the Priest in Divine Service, and specially when he ministereth the Holy Communion, and to help him in the distribution thereof; and to read Holy Scriptures and Homilies in the Church; and to instruct the youth in the Catechism; in the absence of the Priest to baptize infants; and to preach, if he be admitted thereto by the Bishop. And furthermore, it is his Office, where provision is so made, to search for the sick, poor, and impotent people of the Parish, that they may be relieved with the alms of the Parishioners, or others. Will you do this gladly and willingly?

Answer. I will, by the help of God.

Bishop. Will you apply all your diligence to frame and fashion your own lives, and the lives of your families, according to the Doctrine of Christ; and to make both yourselves and them, as much as in you lieth, wholesome examples of the flock of Christ?

Answer. I will, the Lord being my helper.

Bishop. Will you reverently obey your Bishop, and other chief Ministers, who, according to the Canons of the Church, may have the charge and government over you; following with a glad mind and will their godly admonitions?

Answer. I will, the Lord being my helper.

¶ *Then the People standing, the Bishop shall proceed, saying,*

Bishop. The Lord be with you.
Answer. And with thy spirit.
Bishop. Lift up your hearts.
Answer. We lift them up unto the Lord.
Bishop. Let us give thanks unto our Lord God.
Answer. It is meet and right so to do.

¶ *Then the Bishop shall say,*

IT is very meet, right, and our bounden duty, that we should at all times, and in all places give thanks unto thee, O Lord, Holy Father, Almighty, Everlasting God; and especially are we bound to praise thee, because of thy great goodness thou dost send forth labourers into thy harvest, and hast vouchsafed to call these thy servants into the Order of Deacons in thy Church. Fill them, we beseech thee, with the Holy Ghost, that, enabled by the manifold gifts of His grace, they may be faithful to their promises, modest, humble, and constant in their ministration, and may have a ready will to observe all spiritual discipline; that, having always the testimony of a good conscience, they may continue ever stable and strong in thy Son Jesus Christ; to whom with thee and the same Holy Ghost be honour and glory, world without end. *Amen.*

¶ *Then the Bishop shall lay his Hands severally upon the Head of every one to be made Deacon, humbly kneeling before him, and shall say,*

TAKE thou Authority to execute the Office of a Deacon in the Church of God committed unto thee; In the Name of the Father, and of the Son, and of the Holy Ghost. *Amen.*

¶ *Then shall the Bishop deliver to every one of them the New Testament, saying,*

TAKE thou Authority to read the Gospel in the Church of God, and to preach the same, if thou be thereto licensed by the Bishop.

¶ *Then each of those ordained Deacon shall have a stole placed over his left shoulder.*

¶ *Then one of them, appointed by the Bishop, shall read the Gospel.*

The Gospel. St. Luke xii.35

LET your loins be girded about, and your lights burning; and ye yourselves like unto men that wait for their lord, when he will return from the wedding; that when he cometh and knocketh, they may open unto him immediately. Blessed are those servants, whom the lord when he cometh shall find watching: verily I say unto you, that he shall gird himself, and make them to sit down to meat, and will come forth and serve them. And if he shall come in the second watch, or come in the third watch, and find them so, blessed are those servants.

¶ *Then shall the Bishop proceed in the Liturgy.*

The Form and Manner of Ordaining Priests

¶ *When the day appointed by the Bishop is come, there shall be a Sermon, or Exhortation, declaring the Duty and Office of such as come to be admitted Priests; how necessary that Order is in the Church of Christ, and also, how the People ought to esteem them in their Office. A Priest shall present unto the Bishop, sitting in his chair, all those who are to receive the Order of Priesthood that day, each of them being vested in a Surplice or Alb with a Stole over the left shoulder, and shall say,*

REVEREND Father in God, I present unto you this person present, to be admitted to the Order of Priesthood.

¶ *The Bishop.*

TAKE heed that the persons, whom ye present unto us, be apt and meet, for their learning and godly conversation, to exercise their Ministry duly, to the honour of God, and the edifying of his Church.

¶ *The Priest shall answer,*

I HAVE inquired concerning him, and also examined him, and think him so to be.

¶ *Then the Bishop shall say unto the People.*

GOOD People, these are they whom we purpose, God willing, to receive this day unto the holy Office of Priesthood; for, after due examination, we find not to the contrary, but that they are lawfully called to their Function and Ministry, and that they are persons meet for the same. But yet, if there be any of you who knoweth any Impediment, or notable Crime, in any of them, for the which he ought not to be received into this holy Ministry, let him come forth in the Name of God, and show what the Impediment, or notable Crime is.

¶ And if any Impediment, or notable Crime be objected, the Bishop shall cease from Ordering that person, until such time as the party accused shall be found clear of that Crime.

¶ Then the Bishop shall require that he read aloud the following Promise of Conformity to the Doctrine, Discipline, and Worship of the Protestant Episcopal Church.

I DO believe the Holy Scriptures of the Old and New Testaments to be the Word of God, and to contain all things necessary to salvation; and I do solemnly engage to conform to the Doctrine, Discipline, and Worship of the Protestant Episcopal Church in the United States of America.

¶ Then shall be said the Liturgy with the following Collect, Epistle, and Gospel.

The Collect

ALMIGHTY God, giver of all good things, who by thy Holy Spirit hast appointed divers Orders of Ministers in thy Church; Mercifully behold these thy servants now called to the Office of Priesthood; and so replenish them with the truth of thy Doctrine, and endue them with innocency of life, that, both by word and good example, they may faithfully serve thee in this Office, to the glory of thy Name, and the edification of thy Church; through the merits of our Saviour Jesus Christ, who liveth and reigneth with thee and the same Holy Spirit, world without end. *Amen.*

The Epistle. Ephesians iv. 7

UNTO every one of us is given grace according to the measure of the gift of Christ. Wherefore he saith, When he ascended up upon high, he led captivity captive, and gave gifts unto men. (Now that he ascended, what is it but that he also descended first into the lower parts of the earth? He that descended is the same also that ascended up far above all heavens, that he might fill all things.) And he gave some, apostles; and some, prophets; and some, evangelists; and some, pastors and teachers; for the perfecting of the saints, for the work of the ministry, for the edifying of the body of Christ: till we all come in the unity of the faith, and of the knowledge of the Son of God, unto a perfect man, unto the measure of the stature of the fulness of Christ.

The Gospel. St. John x. 1

VERILY, verily, I say unto you, He that entereth not by the door into the sheepfold, but climbeth up some other way, the same is a thief and a robber. But he that entereth in by the door is the shepherd of the sheep. To him the porter openeth; and the sheep hear his voice: and he calleth his own sheep by name, and leadeth them out. And when he putteth forth his own sheep, he goeth before them, and the sheep follow him: for they know his voice. And a stranger will they not follow, but will flee from him: for they know not the voice of strangers. This parable spake Jesus unto them: but they understood not what things they were which he spake unto them. Then said Jesus unto them again, Verily, verily, I say unto you, I am the door of the sheep. All that ever came before me are thieves and robbers: but the sheep did not hear them. I am the door: by me if any man enter in, he shall be saved, and shall go in and out, and find pasture. The thief cometh not, but for to steal, and to kill, and to destroy: I am come that they might have life, and that they might have it more abundantly. I am the good shepherd: the good shepherd giveth his life for the sheep. But he that is an hireling, and not the shepherd, whose own the sheep are not, seeth the wolf coming, and leaveth the sheep, and fleeth: and the wolf catcheth them, and scattereth the sheep. The hireling fleeth, because he is an hireling, and careth not for the sheep. I am the good shepherd; and know my sheep, and am known of mine, even as the Father knoweth me, and I know the Father; and I lay down my life for the sheep. And other sheep I have, which are not of this fold: them also I must bring, and they shall hear my voice; and there shall be one flock, and one shepherd.

> ¶ *Then the Bishop, commending such as shall be found meet to be Ordered, to the Prayers of the congregation, shall with the Clergy and People present, say the Litany for Ordinations.*

> ¶ *Then the People being seated, the Bishop shall say to those who are to be ordained Priests as follows.*

YE have heard, Brethren, in the exhortation which was now made to you, and in the holy Lessons taken out of the Gospel, and the writings of the Apostles, of what dignity, and of how great importance this Order is, whereunto ye are called. And now again we exhort you, in the Name of our Lord Jesus Christ, that ye have in remembrance, into how high a Dignity, and to how weighty an Office and Charge ye are called: that is to say, to be Messengers, Watchmen, and Stewards of the Lord; to teach, and to premonish, to feed and provide for the Lord's family; to seek for Christ's sheep that are dispersed abroad, and for his children who are in the midst of this naughty world, that they may be saved through Christ for ever.

Have always therefore printed in your remembrance, how great a treasure is committed to your charge. For they are the sheep of Christ, which he bought with his death, and for whom he shed his blood. The Church and Congregation whom you must serve, is his Spouse, and his Body. And if it shall happen that the same Church, or any Member thereof, do take any hurt or hindrance by reason of your negligence, ye know the greatness of the fault, and also the horrible punishment that will ensue. Wherefore consider with yourselves the end of the Ministry towards the children of God, towards the Spouse and Body of Christ; and see that ye never cease your labour, your care and diligence, until ye have done all that lieth in you, according to your bounden duty, to bring all such as are or shall be committed to your charge, unto that agreement in the faith and knowledge of God, and to that ripeness and perfectness of age in Christ, that there be no place left among you, either for error in religion, or for viciousness in life.

Forasmuch then as your Office is both of so great excellency, and of so great difficulty, ye see with how great care and study ye ought to apply yourselves, as well to show yourselves dutiful and thankful unto that Lord, who hath placed you in so high a dignity; as also to beware that neither you yourselves offend, nor be occasion that others offend. Howbeit, ye cannot have a mind and will thereto of yourselves; for that will and ability is given of God alone: therefore ye ought, and have need, to pray earnestly for his Holy Spirit. And seeing that ye cannot by any other means compass the doing of so weighty a work, pertaining to the salvation of man, but with doctrine and exhortation taken out of the Holy Scriptures, and with a life agreeable to the same; consider how studious ye ought to be in reading and learning the Scriptures, and in framing the manners both of yourselves, and of them that specially pertain unto you, according to the rule of the same Scriptures; and for this self-same cause, how ye ought to forsake and set aside, as much as ye may, all worldly cares and studies.

We have good hope that ye have well weighed these things with yourselves, long before this time; and that ye have clearly determined, by God's grace, to give yourselves wholly to this Office, whereunto it hath pleased God to call you: so that, as much as lieth in you, ye will apply yourselves wholly to this one thing, and draw all your cares and studies this way; and that ye will continually pray to God the Father, by the mediation of our only Saviour Jesus Christ, for the heavenly assistance of the Holy Ghost; that, by daily reading and weighing the Scriptures, ye may wax riper and stronger in your Ministry; and that ye may so endeavour yourselves, from time to time, to sanctify the lives of you and yours, and to fashion them after the Rule and Doctrine of Christ, that ye may be wholesome and godly examples and patterns for the people to follow.

And now, that this present Congregation of Christ may also understand your minds and wills in these things, and that this your promise may the more move you to do your duties; ye shall answer plainly to these things, which we, in the Name of God, and of his Church, shall demand of you touching the same.

DO you believe in your heart, that you are truly called, according to the will of our Lord Jesus Christ, and according to the Canons of this Church, to the Order and Ministry of Priesthood?

> *Answer.* I do so believe.
>
> *Bishop.* Are you persuaded that the Holy Scriptures contain all Doctrine required as necessary for eternal salvation through faith in Jesus Christ? And are you determined, out of the said Scriptures to instruct the people committed to your charge; and to teach nothing, as necessary to eternal salvation, but that which you shall be persuaded may be concluded and proved by the Scripture?
>
> *Answer.* I am so persuaded, and have so determined, by God's grace.
>
> *Bishop.* Will you then give your faithful diligence always so to minister the Doctrine and Sacraments, and the Discipline of Christ, as the Lord hath commanded, and as this Church hath received the same, according to the Commandments of God; so that you may teach the people committed to your Cure and Charge with all diligence to keep and observe the same?
>
> *Answer.* I will, by the help of the Lord.
>
> *Bishop.* Will you be ready, with all faithful diligence, to banish and drive away from the Church all erroneous and strange doctrines contrary to God's Word; and to use both public and private admonitions and exhortations, as well to the sick as to the whole, within your Cures, as need shall require, and occasion shall be given?
>
> *Answer.* I will, the Lord being my helper.
>
> *Bishop.* Will you be diligent in Prayers, and in reading the Holy Scriptures, and in such studies as help to the knowledge of the same, laying aside the study of the world and the flesh?
>
> *Answer.* I will endeavour so to do, the Lord being my helper.
>
> *Bishop.* Will you be diligent to frame and fashion your own selves, and your families, according to the Doctrine of Christ; and to make both yourselves and them, as much as in you lieth, wholesome examples and patterns to the flock of Christ?
>
> *Answer.* I will apply myself thereto, the Lord being my helper.
>
> *Bishop.* Will you maintain and set forwards, as much as lieth in you, quietness, peace, and love, among all Christian people, and especially among them that are or shall be committed to your charge?
>
> *Answer.* I will so do, the Lord being my helper.

Bishop. Will you reverently obey your Bishop, and other chief Ministers, who, according to the Canons of the Church, may have the charge and government over you; following with a glad mind and will their godly admonitions, and submitting yourselves to their godly judgments?
Answer. I will so do, the Lord being my helper.

¶ Then, all standing, shall the Bishop say,

ALMIGHTY God, who hath given you this will to do all these things; Grant also unto you strength and power to perform the same, that he may accomplish his work which he hath begun in you; through Jesus Christ our Lord. Amen.

¶ After this, the Congregation shall be desired, secretly in their Prayers, to make their humble supplications to God for all these things; for the which Prayers there shall be silence kept for a space.

¶ After which, the Persons to be ordained Priests kneeling, and others standing, the Bishop shall sing or say the Veni, Creator Spiritus; the Bishop beginning, and the Priests, and others that are present, answering by verses, as followeth.

Veni, Creator Spiritus

COME, Holy Ghost, our souls inspire,
And lighten with celestial fire.
Thou the anointing Spirit art,
Who dost thy sevenfold gifts impart.

Thy blessed unction from above,
Is comfort, life, and fire of love.
Enable with perpetual light
The dulness of our blinded sight.

Anoint and cheer our soiled face
With the abundance of thy grace.
Keep far our foes, give peace at home;
Where thou art guide, no ill can come.

Teach us to know the Father, Son,
And thee, of both, to be but One;
That, through the ages all along,
This may be our endless song:
Praise to thy eternal merit,
Father, Son, and Holy Spirit.

Bishop. The Lord be with you.
Answer. And with thy spirit.
Bishop. Lift up your hearts.
Answer. We lift them up unto the Lord.
Bishop. Let us give thanks unto our Lord God.
Answer. It is meet and right so to do.

¶ *Then the Bishop shall say,*

IT is very meet, right, and our bounden duty, that we should give thanks unto thee, O Lord, Holy Father, Almighty, Everlasting God, who, of thine infinite love and goodness towards us, hast given to us thy only and most dearly beloved Son Jesus Christ, to be our Redeemer, and the Author of everlasting life; who, after he had made perfect our redemption by his death, and was ascended into heaven, sent abroad into the world his Apostles, Prophets, Evangelists, Pastors and Teachers; by whose labour and ministry he gathered together a great flock in all the parts of the world, to set forth the eternal praise of thy holy Name: For these so great benefits of thy eternal goodness, and for that thou hast vouchsafed to call these thy servants here present to the same Ministry, appointed for the salvation of mankind, we render unto thee most hearty thanks, we praise and worship thee; and we humbly beseech thee, by the same thy blessed Son, to grant unto all, which either here or elsewhere call upon thy holy Name, that we may continue to show ourselves thankful unto thee for these and all thy other benefits; and that we may daily increase and go forwards in the knowledge and faith of thee and thy Son, by the Holy Spirit. So that as well by these thy Ministers, as by them over whom they shall be appointed thy Ministers, thy holy Name may be for ever glorified, and thy blessed kingdom enlarged; through the same thy Son Jesus Christ our Lord, who liveth and reigneth with thee in the unity of the same Holy Spirit, world without end. *Amen.*

¶ *When this Prayer is done, the Bishop with the Priests present, shall lay their Hands severally upon the Head of every one that receiveth the Order of Priesthood; the Receivers humbly kneeling, and the Bishop saying,*

RECEIVE the Holy Ghost for the Office and Work of a Priest in the Church of God, now committed unto thee by the Imposition of our hands. Whose sins thou dost forgive, they are forgiven; and whose sins thou dost retain, they are retained. And be thou a faithful Dispenser of the Word of God, and of his holy Sacraments; In the Name of the Father, and of the Son, and of the Holy Ghost. Amen.

¶ *Then each of those ordained Priest shall have his stole placed over both shoulders.*

¶ Then the Bishop shall deliver to every one of them kneeling, the Bible into his hand, and he may deliver into the other hand; the Paten and Chalice, saying,

TAKE thou Authority to preach the Word of God, and to minister the holy Sacraments in the Congregation, where thou shalt be lawfully appointed thereunto.

¶ When this has been done, the Nicene Creed shall be said, and the Bishop shall continue with the Liturgy.

¶ All they who receive Orders shall remain in the same place where Hands were laid upon them, until they have received Holy Communion with the Bishop.

¶ And if, on the same day, the Order of Deacons be given to some, and the Order of Priesthood to others; the Deacons shall be first presented, and then the Priests; and it shall suffice that the Litany be once said for both. The Epistle shall be Ephesians iv. 7 to 13, as before in this Office. Immediately after which, they that are to be made Deacons, shall be examined and Ordained, as is above prescribed. Then one of them having read the Gospel, (which shall be Saint Luke xii. 35 to 38, as before in the Form for the Ordering of Deacons,) they that are to be made Priests shall likewise be examined and Ordained, as is in this Office before appointed. The Collect shall be as follows.

The Collect

ALMIGHTY God, giver of all good things, who by thy Holy Spirit hast appointed divers Orders of Ministers in thy Church; Mercifully behold these thy servants now called to the Office of Deacon and these thy servants now called to the Office of Priest; and so replenish them with the truth of thy Doctrine, and endue them with innocency of life, that, both by word and good example, they may faithfully serve thee in their Ministry, to the glory of thy Name, and the edification of thy Church; through the merits of our Saviour Jesus Christ, who liveth and reigneth with thee and the same Holy Spirit, world without end. Amen.

The Form of Ordaining or Consecrating a Bishop

¶ When all things are duly prepared in the Church, and set in order, the Presiding Bishop, or some other Bishop duly appointed, shall begin the Liturgy, in which this shall be

The Collect

ALMIGHTY God, who by thy Son Jesus Christ didst give to thy holy Apostles many excellent gifts, and didst charge them to feed thy flock; Give grace, we beseech thee, to all Bishops, the Pastors of thy Church, that they may diligently preach thy Word, and duly administer the godly Discipline thereof; and grant to the people, that they may obediently follow the same; that all may receive the crown of everlasting glory; through the same thy Son Jesus Christ our Lord. *Amen.*

¶ *And another Bishop shall read the Epistle.*

The Epistle. 1 Timothy iii.1

THIS is a true saying, If a man desire the office of a bishop, he desireth a good work. A bishop then must be blameless, the husband of one wife, vigilant, sober, of good behaviour, given to hospitality, apt to teach; not given to wine, no striker, not greedy of filthy lucre; but patient, not a brawler, not covetous; one that ruleth well his own house, having his children in subjection with all gravity; (for if a man know not how to rule his own house, how shall he take care of the church of God?) not a novice, lest being lifted up with pride he fall into the condemnation of the devil. Moreover he must have a good report of them which are without; lest he fall into reproach and the snare of the devil.

¶ *Or this.*

For the Epistle. Acts xx. 17

FROM Miletus Paul sent to Ephesus, and called the elders of the church. And when they were come to him, he said unto them, Ye know, from the first day that I came into Asia, after what manner I have been with you at all seasons, serving the Lord with all humility of mind, and with many tears, and temptations, which befell me by the lying in wait of the Jews: and how I kept back nothing that was profitable unto you, but have shewed you, and have taught you publickly, and from house to house, testifying both to the Jews, and also to the Greeks, repentance toward God, and faith toward our Lord Jesus Christ. And now, behold, I go bound in the spirit unto Jerusalem, not knowing the things that shall befall me there: save that the Holy Ghost witnesseth in every city, saying that bonds and afflictions abide me. But none of these things move me, neither count I my life dear unto myself, so that I might finish my course with joy, and the ministry, which I have received of the Lord Jesus, to testify the gospel of the grace of God. And now, behold, I know that ye all, among whom I have gone preaching the kingdom of God, shall see my face no more. Wherefore I take you to record this day, that I am pure from the blood of all men. For I have not shunned to declare unto you all the counsel of God. Take heed therefore unto yourselves, and to all the flock, over the which the Holy Ghost hath made you overseers, to feed the church of God, which he hath purchased with his own blood. For I know this, that after my departing shall grievous wolves enter in among you, not sparing the flock. Also of your own selves shall men arise, speaking perverse things, to draw away disciples after them. Therefore watch, and remember, that by the space of three years I ceased not to warn every one night and day with tears. And now, brethren, I commend you to God, and to the word of his grace, which is able to build you up, and to give you an inheritance among all them which are sanctified. I have coveted no man's silver, or gold, or apparel. Yea, ye yourselves know, that these hands have ministered unto my necessities, and to them that were with me. I have shewed you all things, how that so labouring ye ought to support the weak, and to remember the words of the Lord Jesus, how he said, It is more blessed to give than to receive.

¶ *Then another Bishop shall read the Gospel.*

The Gospel. St. John xxi. 15

JESUS saith to Simon Peter, Simon, son of Jonas, lovest thou me more than these? He saith unto him, Yea, Lord; thou knowest that I love thee. He saith unto him, Feed my lambs. He saith to him again the second time, Simon, son of Jonas, lovest thou me? He saith unto him, Yea, Lord; thou knowest that I love thee. He saith unto him, Feed my sheep. He saith unto him the third time, Simon, son of Jonas, lovest thou me? Peter was grieved because he said unto him the third time, Lovest thou me? And he said unto him, Lord, thou knowest all things; thou knowest that I love thee. Jesus saith unto him, Feed my sheep.

¶ *Or this.*

The Gospel. St. John xx. 19

THE same day at evening, being the first day of the week, when the doors were shut where the disciples were assembled for fear of the Jews, came Jesus, and stood in the midst, and saith unto them, Peace be unto you. And when he had so said, he shewed unto them his hands and his side. Then were the disciples glad, when they saw the Lord. Then saith Jesus to them again, Peace be unto you: as my Father hath sent me, even so send I you. And when he had said this, he breathed on them, and saith unto them, Receive ye the Holy Ghost; whose soever sins ye remit, they are remitted unto them; and whose soever sins ye retain, they are retained.

¶ *Or this.*

The Gospel. St. Matthew xxviii. 18

JESUS came and spake unto them, saying, All power is given unto me in heaven and in earth. Go yet therefore, and teach all nations, baptizing them in the name of the Father, and of the Son, and of the Holy Ghost: teaching them to observe all things whatsoever I have commanded you: and, lo, I am with you alway, even unto the end of the world.

¶ *Then shall follow the Nicene Creed, and after that the Sermon; which being ended, the Elected Bishop, vested with his Rochet, or with his Alb and Stole, shall be presented by two Bishops of this Church unto the Bishop Presiding, sitting in his chair; the Bishops who present him saying,*

REVEREND Father in God, we present unto you this godly and well-learned man, to be Ordained and Consecrated Bishop.

¶ *Then shall the Bishop Presiding demand Testimonials of the person presented for Consecration, and shall cause them to be read.*

¶ *He shall then require of him the following Promise of Conformity to the Doctrine, Discipline, and Worship of the Protestant Episcopal Church.*

IN the Name of God, Amen. I, *N.*, chosen Bishop in the Church of God in *N.*, do promise conformity and obedience to the Doctrine, Discipline, and Worship of the Protestant Episcopal Church in the United States of America. So help me God, through Jesus Christ.

¶ *Then the Bishop Presiding shall move the Congregation present to pray, saying thus to them:*

BRETHREN, it is written in the Gospel of Saint Luke, that our Saviour Christ continued the whole night in prayer, before he chose and sent forth his twelve Apostles. It is written also, that the holy Apostles prayed before they ordained Matthias to be of the number of the Twelve. Let us, therefore, following the example of our Saviour Christ, and his Apostles, offer up our prayers to Almighty God, before we admit and send forth this person presented unto us, to the work whereunto we trust the Holy Ghost hath called him.

¶ *And then shall be said the Litany for Ordinations.*

¶ *Then, the People being seated, the Bishop Presiding sitting in his chair, shall say to him that is to be Consecrated,*

BROTHER, forasmuch as the Holy Scripture and the ancient Canons command, that we should not be hasty in laying on hands, and admitting any person to Government in the Church of Christ, which he hath purchased with no less price than the effusion of his own blood; before we admit you to this Administration, we will examine you in certain Articles, to the end that the Congregation present may bear witness, how you are minded to behave yourself in the Church of God.

ARE you persuaded that you are truly called to this Ministration, according to the will of our Lord Jesus Christ, and the order of this Church?

Answer. I am so persuaded.

Bishop. Are you persuaded that the Holy Scriptures contain all Doctrine required as necessary for eternal salvation through faith in Jesus Christ? And are you determined out of the same Holy Scriptures to instruct the people committed to your charge; and to teach or maintain nothing, as necessary to eternal salvation, but that which you shall be persuaded may be concluded and proved by the same?

Answer. I am so persuaded, and determined, by God's grace.

Bishop. Will you then faithfully exercise yourself in the Holy Scriptures, and call upon God by prayer for the true understanding of the same; so that you may be able by them to teach and exhort with wholesome Doctrine, and to withstand and convince the gainsayers?

Answer. I will so do, by the help of God.

Bishop. Are you ready, with all faithful diligence, to banish and drive away from the Church all erroneous and strange doctrine contrary to God's Word; and both privately and openly to call upon and encourage others to the same?

Answer. I am ready, the Lord being my helper.

Bishop. Will you deny all ungodliness and worldly lusts, and live soberly, righteously, and godly in this present world; that you may show yourself in all things an example of good works unto others, that the adversary may be ashamed, having nothing to say against you?

Answer. I will so do, the Lord being my helper.

Bishop. Will you maintain and set forward, as much as shall lie in you, quietness, love, and peace among all men; and diligently exercise such discipline as by the authority of God's Word, and by the order of this Church, is committed to you?

Answer. I will so do, by the help of God.

Bishop. Will you be faithful in Ordaining, sending, or laying hands upon others?

Answer. I will so be, by the help of God.

Bishop. Will you show yourself gentle, and be merciful for Christ's sake to poor and needy people, and to all strangers destitute of help?

Answer. I will so show myself, by God's help.

¶ *Then, all standing, the Bishop Presiding shall say,*

ALMIGHTY God, our heavenly Father, who hath given you a good will to do all these things; Grant also unto you strength and power to perform the same; that, he accomplishing in you the good work which he hath begun, you may be found perfect and irreprehensible at the latter day; through Jesus Christ our Lord. *Amen.*

¶ *Then shall the Bishop elect kneel down; and the* Veni, Creator Spiritus *shall be said or sung; the Bishop Presiding shall begin, and the Bishops and the others that are present, standing, shall answer by verses, as follows.*

Veni, Creator Spiritus

COME, Holy Ghost, our souls inspire,
And lighten with celestial fire.
Thou the anointing Spirit art,
Who dost thy sevenfold gifts impart.

Thy blessed unction from above,
Is comfort, life, and fire of love.
Enable with perpetual light
The dulness of our blinded sight.

Anoint and cheer our soiled face
With the abundance of thy grace.
Keep far our foes, give peace at home;
Where thou art guide, no ill can come.

Teach us to know the Father, Son,
And thee, of both, to be but One;
That, through the ages all along,
This may be our endless song:
Praise to thy eternal merit,
Father, Son, and Holy Spirit.

¶ *Then the Bishop Presiding shall say*

Bishop. The Lord be with you.
Answer. And with thy spirit.
Bishop. Lift up your hearts.
Answer. We lift them up unto the Lord.

Bishop. Let us give thanks unto our Lord God.

Answer. It is meet and right so to do.

¶ *Then the Bishop Presiding shall say,*

IT is very meet, right and our bounden duty, that we should give thanks unto thee, O Lord, Holy Father, Almighty, Everlasting God, who, of thine infinite goodness toward us, halt given thy only Son Jesus Christ, to be our Redeemer and the Author of everlasting life; who, after that he had made perfect our redemption by his death, and was ascended into heaven, poured down his gifts abundantly upon men, making some Apostles, some Prophets, some Evangelists, some Pastors and Doctors, to the edifying and making perfect his Church; Grant, we beseech thee, to this thy servant, such grace, that he may evermore be ready to spread abroad thy Gospel, the glad tidings of reconciliation with thee; and use the authority given him, not to destruction, but to salvation; not to hurt, but to help: so that, as a wise and faithful servant, giving to thy family their portion in due season, he may at last be received into everlasting joy; through the same Jesus Christ our Lord, who, with thee and the Holy Ghost, liveth and reigneth, one God, world without end. *Amen.*

¶ *Then the Bishop Presiding and Bishops present shall lay their hands upon the head of the Elected Bishop, kneeling before them, the Bishop Presiding saying,*

RECEIVE the Holy Ghost for the Office and Work of a Bishop in the Church of God, now committed unto thee by the Imposition of our hands; In the Name of the Father, and of the Son, and of the Holy Ghost. Amen. And remember that thou stir up the grace of God, which is given thee by this Imposition of our hands; for God hath not given us the spirit of fear, but of power, and love, and discipline.

¶ *Then the Bishop Presiding shall deliver to him the Bible, and he may deliver to him the Pastoral Staff, saying,*

GIVE heed unto God's Word. Think upon the things contained in this Book. Safeguard the Gospel. Maintain and defend the Faith, that the increase coming thereby may be manifest to all men, for by so doing thou shalt save both thyself and them that hear thee. Make full proof of thy priesthood. Ordain and send forth men to preach the Gospel and to administer the Holy Sacraments. Confirm to the faithful the strengthening gifts of grace. Be to the flock of Christ a shepherd. Hold up the weak, heal the sick, bind up the broken, bring again the outcast, seek the lost. Be so merciful, that thou be not too remiss; so administer discipline, that thou forget not mercy; that when the Chief Shepherd shall appear, thou mayest receive the never-fading crown of glory; through Jesus Christ our Lord. *Amen.*

¶ *Then shall the newly consecrated Bishop be vested in the Episcopal habit.*

¶ *Then the Bishop Presiding shall proceed in the Liturgy; with whom the newly consecrated Bishop, with others, shall receive Holy Communion.*

PRAYER BOOK STUDIES IX: THE CALENDAR

The Standing Liturgical Commission
of the Protestant Episcopal Church in the
United States of America

1957

PREFACE

The last revision of our Prayer Book was brought to a rather abrupt conclusion in 1928. Consideration of it had preoccupied the time of General Convention ever since 1913. Everyone was weary of the long and ponderous legislative process, and desired to make the new Prayer Book available as soon as possible for the use of the Church.

But the work of revision, which sometimes has seemed difficult to start, in this case proved hard to stop. The years of debate had aroused widespread interest in the whole subject: and the mind of the Church was more receptive of suggestions for revision when the work was brought to an end than when it began. Moreover, the revision was actually closed to new action in 1925, in order that it might receive final adoption in 1928: so that it was not possible to give due consideration to a number of very desirable features in the English and Scottish revisions, which appeared simultaneously with our own. It was further realized that there were some rough edges in what had been done, as well as an unsatisfied demand for still further alterations.

The problem of defects in detail was met by continuing the Revision Commission, and giving it rather large 'editorial' powers (subject only to review by General Convention) to correct obvious errors in the text as adopted, in the publication of the new Prayer Book. Then, to deal with the constructive proposals for other changes which continued to be brought up in every General Convention, the Revision Commission was reconstituted as a Standing Liturgical Commission. To this body all matters concerning the Prayer Book were to be referred, for preservation in permanent files, and for continuing consideration, until such time as the accumulated matter was sufficient in amount and importance to justify proposing another Revision.

The number of such referrals by General Convention, of Memorials from Dioceses, and of suggestions made directly to the Commission from all regions and schools and parties in the Church, has now reached such a total that it is evident that there is a widespread and insistent demand for a general revision of the Prayer Book.

The Standing Liturgical Commission is not, however, proposing any immediate revision. On the contrary, we believe that there ought to be a period of study and discussion, to acquaint the Church at large with the principles and issues involved, in order that the eventual action may be taken intelligently, and if possible without consuming so much of the time of our supreme legislative synod.

Accordingly, the General Convention of 1949 signalized the Fourth Centennial Year of the First Book of Common Prayer in English by authorizing the Liturgical Commission to publish its findings, in the form of a series of *Prayer Book Studies*.

It must be emphasized that the liturgical forms presented in these *Studies* are not — and under our Constitution, cannot be — sanctioned for public use. They are submitted for free discussion. The Commission will be grateful for copies or articles, resolutions, and direct comment, for its consideration, that the mind of the Church may be fully known to the body charged with reporting it.

In this undertaking, we have endeavored to be objective and impartial. It is not possible to avoid every matter which may be thought by some to be controversial. Ideas which seem to be constructively valuable will be brought to the attention of the Church, without too much regard as to whether they may ultimately be judged to be expedient. We cannot undertake to eliminate every proposal to which anyone might conceivably object: to do so would be to admit that any constructive progress is impossible. What we can do is to be alert not to alter the present *balance* of expressed or implied doctrine of the Church. We can seek to counterbalance every proposal which might seem to favor some one party of opinion by some other change in the opposite direction. The goal we have constantly had in mind — however imperfectly we may have succeeded in attaining it — is the shaping of a future Prayer Book which *every* party might embrace with the well-founded conviction that therein its own position had been strengthened, its witness enhanced, and its devotions enriched.

The objective we have pursued is the same as that expressed by the Commission for the Revision of 1892: "*Resolved*, That this Committee, in all its suggestions and acts, be guided by those principles of liturgical construction and ritual use which have guided the compilation and amendments of the Book of Common Prayer, and have made it what it is."

THE STANDING LITURGICAL COMMISSION:

GOODRICH R. FENNER, *Chairman*
ARTHUR C. LICHTENBERGER
* BAYARD H. JONES, *Vice Chairman*
JOHN W. SUTER, *Custodian*
MASSEY H. SHEPHERD, JR.
CHARLES W. F. SMITH
FRANCIS B. SAYRE, JR.
BERTRAM L. SMITH
SPENCER ERVIN, *Secretary*
JOHN ASHTON
* Died, April 27, 1957

The Commission has been at work on this report since 1945. Throughout its preparation, the sub-committee responsible for the Calendar Study has consisted of Dr. Shepherd, Dr. Jones, and the Reverend Morton C. Stone. The Commission gratefully records that Dr. Jones' invaluable assistance in preparing materials for this Study continued with unabated energy and interest until his untimely death on April 27, 1957. He had been able to read and give his approval to most of the manuscript of this Study.

A companion Study to this volume will follow in due time, with proposals for the propers of the minor Holy Days — Collects, Epistles and Gospels.[1] Only those entries in the present proposed Calendar that are printed in italics will be provided with a full set of propers; the other Black Letter commemorations will have only a memorial Collect. In view of the length of the two Studies, it has seemed best to publish them as separate volumes.

MASSEY H. SHEPHERD, JR.

When this Study was in final stages of proof, the Commission received the Report of a Commission appointed by the Archbishop of Canterbury, preliminary to the Lambeth Conference of 1958, entitled *The Commemoration of Saints and Heroes of the Faith in the Anglican Communion* (London: S.P.C.K., 1957). The Commission regrets that it was not available in time for its study and use in the preparation of this book. But we commend it to the readers of this Study as a valuable supplement of comment and illustration upon the subject of Calendar revision.

---

1. Ed. Note: This would be printed as *Prayer Book Studies* XII which appears in Volume 3 of this edition along with issues X-XV.

The Proposed Calendar

		JANUARY
1	A	THE HOLY NAME OF OUR LORD JESUS CHRIST
2	b	
3	c	
4	d	
5	e	
6	f	THE EPIPHANY OF OUR LORD JESUS CHRIST
7	g	
8	A	
9	b	
10	c	William Laud, Archbishop of Canterbury, 1645
11	d	
12	e	
13	f	
14	g	*Hilary*, Bishop of Poitiers, 367
15	A	
16	b	
17	c	*Antony*, Abbot in Egypt, 356
18	d	
19	e	
20	f	
21	g	Agnes, Martyr at Rome, 304
22	A	Vincent, Deacon of Saragossa, and Martyr, 304
23	b	Phillips Brooks, Bishop of Massachusetts, 1893
24	c	*Saint Timothy*
25	d	THE CONVERSION OF SAINT PAUL THE APOSTLE
26	e	*Polycarp*, Bishop of Smyrna, and Martyr, 156
27	f	*John Chrysostom*, Bishop of Constantinople, 407
28	g	
29	A	
30	b	
31	c	

		FEBRUARY
1	d	*Ignatius*, Bishop of Antioch, and Martyr, c. 115
2	e	THE PRESENTATION OF OUR LORD JESUS CHRIST IN THE TEMPLE
3	f	Ansgarius, Archbishop of Hamburg, Missionary to Denmark and Sweden, 865
4	g	*Cornelius*, the Centurion
5	A	
6	b	*Saint Titus*
7	c	
8	d	
9	e	
10	f	
11	g	
12	A	
13	b	
14	c	
15	d	Thomas Bray, Priest and Missionary, 1730
16	e	
17	f	
18	g	
19	A	
20	b	
21	c	
22	d	
23	e	
24	f	SAINT MATTHIAS THE APOSTLE
25	g	
26	A	
27	b	George Herbert, Priest, 1633
28	c	
29		

			MARCH
	1	d	*David*, Bishop of Menevia, Wales, c. 544
	2	e	
	3	f	
	4	g	
	5	A	
	6	b	
	7	c	*Perpetua and her Companions*, Martyrs of Carthage,
	8	d	
	9	e	Thomas Aquinas, Friar, 1274
	10	f	
	11	g	
	12	A	*Gregory the Great*, Bishop of Rome, 604
	13	b	
	14	c	
	15	d	
	16	e	
	17	f	*Patrick*, Bishop and Missionary of Ireland, 461
	18	g	
	19	A	*Saint Joseph*
	20	b	Thomas Ken, Bishop of Bath and Wells, 1711
	21	c	
14	22	d	
3	23	e	Gregory the Illuminator, Bishop and Missionary of Armenia, c. 332
	24	f	
11	25	g	THE ANNUNCIATION OF THE BLESSED VIRGIN MARY
	26	A	
19	27	b	
8	28	c	
	29	d	John Keble, Priest, 1866
16	30	e	
5	31	f	

			APRIL
	1	g	John Frederick Denison Maurice, Priest, 1872
13	2	A	
2	3	b	
	4	c	*Ambrose*, Bishop of Milan, 397
10	5	d	
	6	e	William Law, Priest, 1761
18	7	f	
7	8	g	William Augustus Muhlenberg, Priest, 1877
	9	A	
15	10	b	
4	11	c	*Leo the Great*, Bishop of Rome, 461
	12	d	George Augustus Selwyn, Bishop of New Zealand, 1878
12	13	e	
1	14	f	*Justin*, Martyr at Rome, c. 167
	15	g	
9	16	A	
17	17	b	
6	18	c	
	19	d	
	20	e	
	21	f	*Anselm*, Archbishop of Canterbury, 1109
	22	g	
	23	A	
	24	b	
	25	c	SAINT MARK THE EVANGELIST
	26	d	
	27	e	
	28	f	
	29	g	
	30	A	

		MAY
1	b	SAINT PHILIP AND SAINT JAMES, APOSTLES
2	c	*Athanasius*, Bishop of Alexandria, 373
3	d	
4	e	Monnica, Mother of Augustine of Hippo, 387
5	f	
6	g	John of Damascus, Priest, c. 760
7	A	
8	b	
9	c	*Gregory of Nazianzus*, Bishop of Constantinople, 389
10	d	
11	e	Cyril and Methodius, Missionary Bishops to the Slavs, 869, 885
12	f	
13	g	
14	A	
15	b	
16	c	
17	d	
18	e	
19	f	Dunstan, Archbishop of Canterbury, 988
20	g	Alcuin, Deacon, and Abbot of Tours, 804
21	A	
22	b	
23	c	
24	d	Jackson Kemper, First Missionary Bishop in the United States, 1870
25	e	
26	f	*Augustine*, First Archbishop of Canterbury, 605
27	g	Bede, the Venerable, Priest, and Monk of Jarrow, 735
28	A	
29	b	
30	c	
31	d	

		JUNE
1	e	
2	f	The Martyrs of Lyons, 177
3	g	
4	A	
5	b	*Boniface*, Archbishop of Mainz, Missionary to Germany, Martyr, 754
6	c	
7	d	
8	e	
9	f	*The First Book of Common Prayer*, 1549
10	g	Columba, Abbot of Iona, 597
11	A	SAINT BARNABAS THE APOSTLE
12	b	
13	c	
14	d	*Basil the Great*, Bishop of Caesarea, 379
15	e	
16	f	Joseph Butler, Bishop of Durham, 1752
17	g	
18	A	Ephrem of Edessa, Syria, Deacon, 373
19	b	
20	c	
21	d	
22	e	*Alban*, First Martyr of Britain, c. 304
23	f	
24	g	THE NATIVITY OF SAINT JOHN BAPTIST
25	A	
26	b	
27	c	
28	d	*Irenaeus*, Bishop of Lyons, c. 202
29	e	SAINT PETER AND SAINT PAUL, APOSTLES
30	f	

		JULY
1	g	
2	A	*The Visitation of the Blessed Virgin Mary*
3	b	
4	c	INDEPENDENCE DAY
5	d	
6	e	
7	f	
8	g	
9	A	
10	b	
11	c	*Benedict of Nursia*, Abbot of Monte Cassino, c. 540
12	d	
13	e	
14	f	
15	g	
16	A	
17	b	William White, Bishop of Pennsylvania, 1836
18	c	
19	d	
20	e	
21	f	
22	g	*Saint Mary Magdalene*
23	A	
24	b	
25	c	SAINT JAMES THE APOSTLE
26	d	Thomas a Kempis, Priest, 1471
27	e	William Reed Huntington, Priest, 1909
28	f	
29	g	William Wilberforce, 1833
30	A	
31	b	

		AUGUST
1	c	
2	d	
3	e	
4	f	Dominic, Friar, 1221
5	g	
6	A	THE TRANSFIGURATION OF OUR LORD JESUS CHRIST
7	b	
8	c	
9	d	
10	e	Laurence, Deacon, and Martyr at Rome, 258
11	f	
12	g	
13	A	Hippolytus, Bishop, and Martyr, c. 235
14	b	Jeremy Taylor, Bishop of Down, Connor and Dromore, 1667
15	c	*Saint Mary the Virgin*, Mother of Our Lord Jesus Christ
16	d	
17	e	
18	f	
19	g	
20	A	*Bernard*, Abbot of Clairvaux, 1153
21	b	
22	c	
23	d	
24	e	SAINT BARTHOLOMEW THE APOSTLE
25	f	Louis, King of France, 1270
26	g	
27	A	
28	b	*Augustine*, Bishop of Hippo, 430
29	c	
30	d	
31	e	*Aidan*, Bishop of Lindisfarne, 651

SEPTEMBER		
1	f	
2	g	
3	A	
4	b	
5	c	
6	d	
7	e	
8	f	
9	g	
10	A	
11	b	
12	c	John Henry Hobart, Bishop of New York, 1830
13	d	*Cyprian*, Bishop of Carthage, and Martyr, 258
14	e	*The Exaltation of the Holy Cross*
15	f	
16	g	
17	A	
18	b	
19	c	*Theodore of Tarsus*, Archbishop of Canterbury, 690
20	d	John Coleridge Patteson, Bishop of Melanesia, and Martyr, 1871
21	e	SAINT MATTHEW, APOSTLE AND EVANGELIST
22	f	
23	g	
24	A	
25	b	Sergius, Abbot of Holy Trinity, Moscow, 1392
26	c	Lancelot Andrewes, Bishop of Winchester, 1626
27	d	
28	e	
29	f	SAINT MICHAEL AND ALL ANGELS
30	g	Jerome, Priest, and Monk of Bethlehem, 420

		OCTOBER
1	A	
2	b	
3	c	
4	d	*Francis of Assisi*, Friar, 1226
5	e	
6	f	William Tyndale, Priest, and Martyr, 1536
7	g	
8	A	
9	b	
10	c	
11	d	
12	e	
13	f	
14	g	
15	A	Samuel Isaac Joseph Schereschewsky, Bishop of Shanghai, 1906
16	b	Hugh Latimer and Nicholas Ridley, Bishops and Martyrs, 1555
17	c	
18	d	SAINT LUKE THE EVANGELIST
19	e	
20	f	
21	g	
22	A	
23	b	
24	c	
25	d	
26	e	*King Alfred the Great*, 899
27	f	
28	g	SAINT SIMON AND SAINT JUDE, APOSTLES
29	A	James Hannington and his Companions, Bishop and Martyrs of Uganda, 1885
30	b	
31	c	

NOVEMBER		
1	d	ALL SAINTS
2	e	
3	f	
4	g	
5	A	
6	b	
7	c	Willibrord, Archbishop of Utrecht, Missionary to Frisia, 738
8	d	
9	e	
10	f	
11	g	*Martin*, Bishop of Tours, 397
12	A	Charles Simeon, Priest, 1836
13	b	
14	c	*Consecration of Samuel Seabury*, First American Bishop, 1784
15	d	
16	e	Margaret, Queen of Scotland, 1093
17	f	Hilda, Abbess of Whitby, 680
18	g	
19	A	Elizabeth, Princess of Hungary, 1231
20	b	
21	c	
22	d	
23	e	Clement, Bishop of Rome, c. 100
24	f	
25	g	
26	A	
27	b	
28	c	
29	d	
30	e	SAINT ANDREW THE APOSTLE

		DECEMBER
1	f	
2	g	Channing More Williams, Missionary Bishop in China and Japan, 1910
3	A	
4	b	*Clement of Alexandria*, Priest, c. 210
5	c	
6	d	Nicholas, Bishop of Myra in Lycia, c. 342
7	e	
8	f	
9	g	
10	A	
11	b	
12	c	
13	d	
14	e	
15	f	
16	g	
17	A	
18	b	
19	c	
20	d	
21	e	SAINT THOMAS THE APOSTLE
22	f	
23	g	
24	A	
25	b	THE NATIVITY OF OUR LORD JESUS CHRIST
26	c	SAINT STEPHEN, DEACON AND MARTYR
27	d	SAINT JOHN, APOSTLE AND EVANGELIST
28	e	THE HOLY INNOCENTS
29	f	
30	g	
31	A	

Part One
The History of Prayer Book Calendar Revision

The Reformation

The compilers of the first two English Prayer Books, issued in the years 1549 and 1552 of the reign of Edward VI, put forth no explanation or apology of their treatment of the Calendar, whether by preservation or revision, that had come down to their times in the medieval Latin service-books. No major change was made at the Reformation in the cycle of the Church Year, the Sundays and seasons as they were ordered in relation to the pivotal days of Easter and Christmas. The seasonal Propers of the moveable feasts and fasts continued to be observed in the same manner that had been followed in the English Church since the days of the conversion of the English people by the Roman missionaries sent to them in the seventh century.

But the Reformers made a drastic reduction in the number of fixed holy days, particularly in the "Proper of Saints." Of the 175 or more entries in the Calendar of the Sarum Missal, exclusive of Octaves, and not counting separately the individual names of saints observed on the same day, the First Prayer Book of 1549 preserved only twenty-four. These twenty-four festivals were all devoted to our Lord, or to the Apostles and Evangelists, except four: St. Mary Magdalen, Michaelmas, All Saints, and St. Stephen.

It is not difficult, however, to reconstruct the principal reasons that guided the Reformers in their extensive excisions in the *Sanctorale*. Their action in this regard was not, at the times considered to be novel or arbitrary. Given the opportunity and means of reform, they were merely carrying out principles of Calendar revision that had been vigorously promoted both by ecclesiastical and by lay critics throughout the fourteenth and fifteenth centuries. The excessive number of holy days, many of which were also civil holidays, that had developed by the late Middle Ages had become a cause of scandal to devout minds, because of the disorderly behavior of so many of the people on these days of enforced idleness. And the disadvantages of so many holidays to the general economic welfare of society were apparent to employers and employees alike. The great increase in holy days had not contributed to the advancement of religion, but had only provided greater temptations to indecorous merry-making. The leisure provided by them had not been used to the profit either of men's spiritual or of their material well-being.

Church canons and conciliar decrees forbade all servile and commercial work on Sundays and major feasts, and enjoined all persons to attend Mass and otherwise engage themselves on these days in edifying pursuits of religious devotion. But neglect of these salutary admonitions was notorious; and often even the celebration of Mass was disturbed by riotous groups of disorderly idlers. Business men found ways and means of circumventing the laws against buying and selling; and farmers were many times forced to carry on their work, despite severe censures and penalties. Much confusion was added to the situation by the varying customs of local districts. There was much variation in medieval Calendars of holy days. Festivals and holidays were not uniformly observed from diocese to diocese, or even from parish to parish. Nor was there always agreement, even among Church authorities, as to what constituted servile or non-servile employment on feast days.

Protests against the multiplicity of festivals were voiced by late medieval churchmen of various standing and opinion, not only by extreme reformers such as Wyclif, but by moderate men such as Pierre d'Ailly and Nicolas de Clemanges, the former a Cardinal, the latter a professor at Paris. Another who shared their views was Jean Gerson, chancellor of the University of Paris and leader in the Conciliar Movement. The satire of Erasmus on this subject, in his colloquy, *The Rich Beggars*, is well-known. Little success, however, attended the efforts of these men to get either the great Councils or the Papacy to initiate reform or to restrict the canonization of new saints. At the Diet of Nuremberg, 1522-23, the lay powers presented the papal legate with a list of one hundred grievances, among which was a petition for the reduction of holy days. The grounds given were: 1) the farmers had difficulty in harvesting their crops because of the excessive number of holidays; and 2) these days were marked by "innumerable transgressions" so that it was doubtful if they redounded to the glory of God. Such grievances were not inspired entirely by the growing Lutheran movement.

Precedents for the English Reformers' revision of the Calendar were not lacking, among the schismatical groups that had already broken away from the papal obedience before the English Church severed its own ties with Rome. The followers of John Hus in Bohemia discarded the observance of saints' days. The extremer Waldensians also rejected them, though some of them saw no reason to oppose days in honor of the Virgin, and the Apostles and Evangelists. Luther's views, which were certainly well-known and influential among many of the English Reformers, had been stated as early as 1520, in his Open Letter to the Christian Nobility. "All festivals," he said, "should be abolished, and Sunday alone retained. If it were desired, however, to retain the festivals of Our Lady and of the greater saints, they should be transferred to Sunday, or observed only by a morning mass, after which all the rest of the day should be a working-day." His reasons are the customary ones: the current abuse of holy days by "drinking, gaming, idleness, and all manner of sins," and in addition to this "spiritual injury," the neglect of work and spending of money more than at other times, so that the layman "weakens his body and unfits it for work." Luther's principles were included in his reform of the Mass, the *Formula Missae* issued in 1523.

Luther never posed as a legislator in liturgical matters, but confined himself to outlining the broader principles upon which reform in worship should be based. His cardinal principle was conformity to Scriptural doctrine, and he was lenient towards practices that were traditional, even though they were not prescribed by Scripture. The various rites among the Lutherans were laid out in the Church Orders (*Kirchenordnungen*) of the several states and free cities that embraced the Lutheran reform. These Church Orders not only kept the Proper of Time, but generally included also feasts of our Lord, the Apostles and Evangelists, and a few other days such as Michaelmas and All Saints. There is a closer similarity between the Lutheran and Anglican Calendars than between those of any other Christian bodies; and the similarity is marked in the liturgical books of the two Communions to this day.

However much the English Reformers may have been influenced by the Lutheran experiments, they were also working, in their reform of the Calendar, within a framework of English precedent. Dr. F. E. Brightman, in his standard edition of *The English Rite* (Rivingtons, 1915), has noted that the feasts retained in the 1549 Prayer Book were fewer by twelve than the list of holy days prescribed by Archbishop Simon Mepham in 1332 to be kept by cessation from work, and fewer by nineteen than a similar list drawn up in 1400 by Archbishop Thomas Arundel. In 1532 the House of Commons petitioned the crown, doubtless under direction from the King himself, to reduce the number of holy days, especially those falling within the harvest season. A prompt rejoinder by the bishops, however, prevented any immediate action being taken upon this request. Four years later, however, after the break with the Roman See, King Henry moved to take action in the matter, first through a decree issued by Archbishop Cranmer with his consent and that of the clergy in Convocation, and then through his Royal Injunctions of 1536. The customary arguments against excessive holy days, observed as holidays, were brought forward: the disorderly behavior, economic disadvantages, and the general lack of religious effect and usefulness. All parishes were enjoined to keep the commemoration of their dedication on the first Sunday in October, rather than on the feast of their patron saint. During harvest and term-time at Westminster, only feasts of the Virgin, Apostles, and St. George were to be kept, unless a festival fell on a day when the king's court did not sit. Other feast days could, of course, be observed by a morning mass, provided that it was not celebrated with such solemnity as to suggest that the day was a holiday from work. Much resistance to these injunctions was encountered, both from the clergy and from the laity. But the measure revealed very clearly the way reform was moving.

Any evaluation of the drastic reduction of holy days made in the first Prayer Books must take account of a variety of motivations that are no longer relevant to modern circumstances. In an age when Church and nation were conceived as a single society, when legislation affecting the worship of Christians was the concern of the highest civil authorities of the realm, the promulgation of a religious holy day was equivalent to the establishment of a legal holiday. Hence the economic aspect loomed large in any consideration of the number of liturgical festivals. But religious and theological concerns were not overlooked. The leadership of the Church was genuinely alarmed at the lack of devotional effect produced by so many saints' days. And so many of the legends associated with the saints were not conducive to that Scriptural piety, shorn of superstition, that the Reformers felt to be so needed. The Calendar produced by the Reformers was by and large a Scriptural list of saints. One can judge the Scriptural rule of thumb exercised in their revision by study of the propers for the holy days that they kept in the Prayer Book. Whereas most of the old Collects for the Proper of Time were retained in the English liturgy, the Collects for Saints' Days were almost entirely new compositions, written anew so as to bring out the New Testament lesson about the life of the individual saint wherever possible. It may well be, too, that the retention of a day such as Michaelmas, apart from its time-honored associations with the terms of law courts and universities, was determined by the mention of St. Michael in the New Testament. The elimination of All Souls' Day immediately following All Saints' Day also shows how careful the Reformers were to return to the New Testament conception of "saints."

Red and Black Letter Days

The official copies of the English Prayer Book, both the manuscript *Book Annexed* and the *Sealed Books*, distinguish the days of the Calendar by the use of red and black ink. The terms "Red Letter" and "Black Letter" are popularly used to describe two types of days. The Red Letter Days of the Prayer Book are those which are "to be observed in the Church of England through the year," and are provided with a proper, *i.e.*, a Collect, Epistle and Gospel. The Black Letter Days, though listed in the Calendar, have no provision for liturgical observance. The distinction takes the place of the older classification of feasts in the medieval service books, in which the solemnity of the holy day was noted by the use of ranks such as greater doubles, doubles, semidoubles, simples, etc.

All of the holy days listed in the First Prayer Book of 1549 were "Red Letter" Days. All of them, too, are to be found on the same dates in the service books of the Sarum use. The Calendars in the manuscripts of the Sarum Missals generally classify them all among the greater feasts. But the *Sarum Directorium* (called the "Pie") makes more precise distinctions. The Principal and Greater Doubles include Christmas, Epiphany, Purification, Easter, Ascension, Whitsunday, Trinity Sunday, and All Saints. The other holy days of the 1549 Book appear in the Sarum directory as Lesser and Inferior Doubles, with the exception of the Conversion of St. Paul, St. Matthias, St. Barnabas, and St. Mary Magdalen. These four are classed as Simples. It may be noted also that the Sarum "Doubles" in Red and Black Letter Days include the Monday, Tuesday, and Wednesday of Easter Week and Whitsun Week, but not the other days of these weeks, though they were provided in the Missal with full propers. Two "Doubles" in the Sarum classification that were not included in the Prayer Book, though they have a Scriptural record, are the Visitation (July 2) and the Transfiguration (August 6). The omission of the latter was doubtless due to its recent institution by Pope Callistus III in 1457; and it had not found its way into all of the Sarum books. But the dropping of the Visitation cannot be explained.

The Second Prayer Book of 1552 retained all of the 1549 holy days except the feast of St. Mary Magdalen. The conjecture has been made that the reason for its omission was doubt regarding the identification of the saint with the woman who was "a sinner," whose story was recounted in the Gospel for the day (Luke 7:36 ff.). The Second Book also added to the Calendar a number of astronomical and legal notations, and four "Black Letter" Days: St. George (April 23), Lammas Day (August), St. Laurence (August 10), and St. Clement (November 23). No liturgical propers were provided for these four days. The reason for their insertion has never been satisfactorily explained. The same Calendar, with the four Black Letter Days, was reproduced in the Elizabethan Prayer Book of 1559.

A new Calendar was issued by Queen Elizabeth in 1561, with some revisions in the lectionary of the Daily Offices. It contained sixty-four Black Letter Days, but the basis of their selection has not been altogether clarified. It included such Biblical feasts as the Visitation and Transfiguration, two of the more ancient feasts of the Virgin, the Nativity and Conception, and a variety of the more popular saints of English tradition. The late W. H. Frere spoke of the list as "a not very discriminating adherence to the chief days of the familiar Sarum Kalendar." The 1561 Calendar was, in truth, an almanac, not an enrichment of the liturgy. It distinctly directed that the Red Letter Days already contained in the Prayer Book should be "observed for holy days, and none other," thereby ruling out all liturgical recognition of the new Black Letter listings.

It was contended by leading Anglican liturgiologists of the early eighteenth century, such as Nicholls and Wheatly, that the Black Letter Days of the 1561 Calendar had only a local and secular association, and that they were not intended to have any religious significance. Some modification of this extreme view is probably necessary, in view of the issuance in 1564, under royal authority, of a new Primer, the *Preces Privatae*. This book, which contains all the Black Letter Days of the 1561 Calendar and many more besides — there are only six days vacant in the whole year —, was certainly intended for devotional purposes. From its Calendar were drawn the three additions made to the 1561 list in later editions of the English Prayer Book. One of these appeared in the edition of 1604: St. Enurchus (September 7) — a mistaken spelling for Evurtius. The adoption of this obscure Gallican saint, who had no special connection with the history of the Church in England, has been explained by Vernon Staley as a cover to "mark the birthday of Queen Elizabeth as a holiday in the succeeding reign, without any intention of honouring the memory of the saint chosen." The other two additions, drawn from the *Preces Privatae*, appeared first in the Prayer Book of 1661, and are more definitely a mark of honor to traditional worthies: the Venerable Bede (May 27), and St. Alban (June 17).

One other feature of the Elizabethan Calendar of 1561 is of interest; namely, the introduction of the word "fast" before certain of the chief holy days. This occurs before the following: Purification, St. Matthias, Annunciation, Nativity of St. John Baptist, St. Peter, St. James, St. Bartholomew, St. Matthew, SS. Simon and Jude, All Saints, St. Andrew, St. Thomas, and Christmas Day. These "fasts" are nothing other than reminders of the Vigils that preceded the major feasts in the medieval Calendars. The principle of selection in the 1561 Calendar seems to have been to confine such Vigils to feasts of our Lord and the Apostles, with All Saints also, except during the seasons of Christmastide and Eastertide. Only some such principle can explain the omission of a "fast" before such days as SS. Philip and James (falling in Eastertide) and St. Luke (not an Apostle).

The Puritans, as might have been expected, were long and loud in their objections to saints' days, both of the Red Letter and of the Black Letter varieties. Their last stand on the subject was presented in the *Exceptions* against the Prayer Book at the Savoy Conference of 1661. Number VI of these "exceptions" reads as follows:

> That the religious observation of saints-days appointed to be kept as holy-days, and the vigils thereof, without any foundation (as we conceive) in Scripture, may be omitted. That if any be retained, they may be called festivals, and not holy-days, nor made equal with the Lord's-day, nor have any peculiar service appointed for them, nor the people be upon such days forced wholly to abstain from work, and that the names of all others now inserted in the Calendar which are not in the first and second books of Edward the Sixth, may be left out.

The *Answer of the Bishops* to the Puritans' request was a firm negative. Its importance lies in its character as a rationale of the classic Anglican position regarding the liturgy, and its appeal to the authority not of Scripture alone, but of the ancient Church:

> The observation of saints' days is not as of divine but ecclesiastical institution, and therefore it is not necessary that they should have any other ground in Scripture than all other institutions of the same nature, so that they be agreeable to the Scripture in the general end, for the promoting piety. And the observation of them was ancient, as appears by the rituals and liturgies, and by the joint consent of antiquity, and by the ancient translation of the Bible, as the Syriac and Ethiopic, where the lessons appointed for holydays are noted and set down; the former of which was made near the apostles' times. Besides our Saviour himself kept a feast of the churches institution, viz, the feast of the dedication (St. John x. 22). The chief end of these days being not feasting, but the exercise of holy

duties, they are fitter called holydays than festivals: and though they be all of like nature, it doth not follow that they are equal. The people may be dispensed with for their work after the service, as authority pleaseth. The other names are left in the calendar, not that they should be so kept as holydays, but they are useful for the preservation of their memories, and for other reasons, as for leases, law-days, etc.

Of particular interest in this answer, apart from its historical justification of the observance of holy days, are three points: 1) the admission that all holy days are not of equal importance; 2) the disassociation of the idea of a religious holy day from the notion of a civil or secular holiday; and 3) the clear distinction, as regards liturgical observance, of the Red Letter and Black Letter Days.

Recent Anglican Revisions

The Bishops' defense of the Calendar of 1661 did not lead to any notable interest in holy day celebrations in the succeeding generations of Anglicanism. For over two hundred years, liturgical concerns remained at a virtual standstill in the English Church. The only creative development, the researches and experiments of the Non-Jurors, was confined almost exclusively to the Eucharistic rite. There is no indication in the sources of liturgical exposition or practice during this period of any interest in the Black Letter Days. The first American Prayer Book of 1789 is an index of the general situation. It omitted from its Calendar any listing of the Black Letter Days, and added nothing to the Red Letter observances except a set of propers for Thanksgiving Day, a festival at was more a national celebration than an ecclesiastical holy day. The liturgical revival of the nineteenth century, however, produced an awakened zeal for the restoration of usages of past ages. Many factors contributed to this revival. The Romantic Movement cast a new glow of admiration upon the medieval "age of faith," to which the liturgical innovations incident upon the Tractarian discussions and controversies in Anglicanism responded with enthusiasm. A deepened and more extensive sacramental practice in Anglicanism provoked interest in liturgical enrichments, that included not only the revival of a more elaborate ceremonial, but also a keener appreciation of many traditional elements in the Church's liturgy that had been lost sight of in the Reformation and the ensuing struggle with Puritanism. Another factor of equal significance was the development in the later nineteenth century of new methodologies in Biblical and historical criticism and research. The sharp edge of distinction between the New Testament and succeeding ages of the Church's corporate life was considerably dulled, and a new perspective was gained upon the concepts of "development" and "continuity" in the history of the Church. The same period witnessed the expansion of Anglican missions to all corners of the earth, with the consequent problems of adapting its liturgical heritage to new cultural situations. The increasing detachment of independent, self-governing provinces of the Church from the mother Church of England gave a new freedom for liturgical experiments, uninhibited by the conservative restrictions of Parliamentary control.

It was the American revision, culminating in the 1892 Prayer Book, that first gave a hint of the new freedom and activity in liturgical revision. So far as the Calendar was concerned, the American revision was, to say the least, extremely cautious. The only enrichment made in the 1892 Book was the introduction of the feast of the Transfiguration as a Red Letter Day, with proper Collect, Epistle and Gospel. This single addition was largely due to the ardent promotion of the Reverend Dr. William Reed Huntington, the prime leader of the revision movement. But it should not be overlooked that the 1892 Book made numerous enrichments, through rubrical direction and new propers for the Daily Office, in the Proper of Time, not to speak of the provision for a second celebration of the Holy Communion at Christmas and Easter.

The full flowering of Anglican Prayer Book revisions came in the second decade of the present century, in the new Prayer Books proposed, and adopted with the exception of the Church in England, in the provinces of Canada (1922), Ireland (1927), England and the United States (1928), South Africa and Scotland (1929). Since then, the work of revision has proceeded in India, and proposals are currently before the Churches in Japan, the West Indies, and Canada. In nearly all of these revisions and proposals for revision, the Calendar has undergone expansions of considerable extent. A comparative Table of the Calendars in these books will be found in the Appendix. The addition of holy days range in extent from the modest increase of the Irish Book, the feasts of St. Patrick and the Transfiguration, to the 117 new holy days of the South African Book of 1954 and the 132 days proposed in the current Draft Prayer Book of the Church in Canada.

The American revision of 1913-28 did not result in so extensive an enlargement of the Calendar as was the case in the other Anglican reforms of the period (excepting the Irish Book). The Joint Commission of the Book of Common Prayer, appointed in 1913, proposed in its first report to General Convention (1916) the addition of 45 saints' days to the Calendar. This number was increased to 54 in its third report made in 1922. These days were not provided with special propers, but a common Collect, Epistle and Gospel for "A Saint's Day" was proposed. In addition Eucharistic propers were presented for the Feast of the Dedication of a Church, the Ember and Rogation Days, and Independence Day. The Convention failed to adopt the new Calendar, but it did approve the new propers.

Thus the American Book of 1928 was left with the anomaly of having a common proper for a Saint's Day, but without any directives regarding what saints would be appropriate for such liturgical observance. The initiative was therefore left to the parish priest to insert in the Collect for a Saint's Day (Prayer Book, page 258) whatever name he might see fit to commemorate.

The frequent use of the new propers for a Saint's Day and the Dedication of a Church, in all types of parishes and missions, has shown, at least, that the American Church is ready and desirous of a greater enrichment of its Calendar of saints' days and commemorations. In the absence of official guides, however, many of the clergy have followed the suggestions of calendars produced by various publishing houses. Others, despite canonical prohibitions to the contrary, have resorted to the use of numerous English and American Missals, designed to adapt the Prayer Book rites to the usages of medieval or of modern Roman books. The temptations to such breaches of canonical obedience are particularly strong in places where frequent week-day, or daily celebrations of the Holy Communion are customary. The repetition of the Sunday propers throughout the days of the week, or the constant use of a single common of saints throughout the year, is monotonous and not always conducive to a creative and vital spirit of devotion. Only a few dioceses and missionary jurisdictions have sought to meet this problem by official directives for the guidance of the clergy. The most notable example has been, to date, the *Service Book for the Diocese of New Jersey*, published in 1940, with the authorization of the diocesan Bishop, the late Rt. Rev. Wallace J. Gardiner. This book contains a Calendar with seventy-six entries additional to the holy days of the Prayer Book, with a limited selection of propers, for the most part of "common" classifications.[2] Though it may be objected that these commons of saints, and the other Collects, Epistles and Gospels for specified days, are in a strict sense illegal — in a way that the Calendar is not — it may at least be said that the doctrine of these propers conformable to the Prayer Book, an assertion that cannot be said of much of the material found in the Missals.

The construction of an enlarged Calendar for the American Church is no easy task, as the Liturgical Commission, even with its limited personnel, has found out during its deliberations on the problem for the past ten years. Prejudices and emotional feelings run very deep at the mere mention of certain worthies who have enjoyed a long and almost universal place in the Calendars of the Church prior to the Reformation. The fact of the matter is that the motivations that have led churchmen to cultivate the memories of the saints have undergone basic shifts of interest and emphasis in the course of the centuries. The modern Anglican, living in an age and environment of rationalistic and scientific criticism, is less inclined to be impressed by the miraculous and legendary elements in the lives of the saints that moved earlier generations to enthusiastic devotion. He is also much less aroused by the appeal to a purely Scriptural norm such as guided

---

2. Ed. Note: The *Service Book for the Diocese of New Jersey* contains a Common of Martyrs, a Common of Confessors and Doctors (with separate collects for Confessors, Evangelists, and Doctors), a Common of Bishops, a Common of Abbots, and a Common for Holy Women. It also includes propers for The Visitation of the Blessed Virgin Mary, St. Mary Magdalene, the Nativity of the Blessed Virgin Mary, Holy Cross Day, and the Feast of Christ the King.

the sixteenth-century Reformers. Though there remain among us still a host of traditionalists, romanticists, and even sentimentalists, the majority of the clergy and laity can be attracted to a conscious devotion to the saints only when the particular individual proposed for commemoration is shown, on good historical evidence, to have exhibited both distinguished service in the cause of Christ and exemplary personal holiness. Even in such cases, it is difficult for many persons to free themselves from the caprices of personal feelings and tastes.

Part Two
Principles of Calendar Construction

The Development of Saints' Days

If the widespread desire in the Church for an enrichment of its Calendar is not to be vitiated by the prejudices of individualistic *parti pris*, it will be necessary to establish some objective criteria for judgment upon particular proposals. To do this, the first step will properly be a consideration of the principles that have shaped the historical development of the Calendar, as it has come down to us, with successive modifications, from the earliest days of the Church. The appeal to historical tradition is, of course, not the only, nor the final, arbiter in the matter. But in a Christian Communion such as ours, which stresses the continuity of its worship with that of the historic Catholic Church of Christ, the reference to antiquity and subsequent historical development is an obvious basis for beginning our search for fundamental principles.

We are not concerned here to trace the history of the Christian Year and the major seasons that are pivoted about the principal feasts of Easter and Christmas. There is no desire in any quarter to change or modify the basic, seasonal framework in which the liturgy is set. Our main concern in this Study is with the fixed holy days that commemorate a "saint" or a few of the more notable events in the historic life of the Church. It will soon be evident, however, to any serious student of the development of the Calendar that the primary significance of all the fixed holy days is rooted in the meaning of Easter and, to a much lesser degree, in the festivals of our Lord's Nativity.

In the earliest days of the Church, the only festivals observed were the fifty-day period from the Pascha to Pentecost, and Sundays. Christian worship in its primitive and most essential forms was completely dominated by the memorial of the Lord's Passion and Resurrection, the Gift of the Spirit, and the expectation of His Second Coming. During the second century, penitential and disciplinary devotions began to be observed on Wednesdays and Fridays, and the beginnings of a "Lenten" fast preparatory to Easter made an appearance. But these days were integrated into the Sunday and Easter cycles, and had no significance apart from the festivals to which they were directed.

The oldest record that has come down to us of a commemoration of a Christian "saint" by official action of a church, through a celebration of the liturgy, is contained in the *Martyrdom of Polycarp*, composed in the year 155 or 156. The Christians of Smyrna, in writing to their fellow believers at Philomelium about the valiant witness of their aged and beloved bishop, gave the following record:

> We later took up his bones, more precious than costly stones and more valuable than gold, and laid them away in a suitable place. There the Lord will permit us, so far as possible, to gather together in joy and gladness to celebrate the day of his martyrdom as a birthday, in memory of those athletes who have gone before, and to train and make ready those who are to come hereafter.

Whether Polycarp was the first Christian so honored, we do not know. But from this time onwards, the evidence accumulates of the custom in the various churches of the Roman Empire to observe annually the anniversaries of their martyrs by a celebration of the Eucharist, if possible, near the place of their burial. In every case, the anniversary date is the day of death, called significantly by the early Christians the "birthday," the day on which the martyr fulfilled in his own life the self-offering of His Lord and entered into His rest. This fact is of fundamental importance for any understanding of the Church's observance of saints' days, and distinguishes the practice of Christianity from that of all its pagan rivals in the ancient world. The anniversaries of the triumphs of the martyrs were celebrated by the churches in the same manner as Sundays: namely, as a recalling and renewal of the Easter faith. The Church paid no attention in its cult to the natural birthdays of its members — unlike the pagan religions which dutifully observed the birthdays of its heroes, emperors, and notable leaders. To the Christian mind, the only birthday of any significant religious meaning was "death and resurrection," effectually promised in Baptism, effectively realized in departure from this world. Even in the private and familial observances of Christians of their beloved departed — those who were not distinguished by a liturgical gathering of the Church — the anniversaries remembered and celebrated were the death-days, the "birthdays" into eternal life.

Each local church developed its own Calendar of anniversaries. The list of saints' days kept in any one church was different from that in any other, though sometimes a church borrowed an anniversary from a sister community, particularly when some relic of a martyr was sent as a gift of love and devotion. After the peace of the Church under Constantine, the cult of the martyrs was pursued with an even greater degree of enthusiasm. The discovery (technically known as the "invention") and the identification of relics, long unknown or forgotten, were avidly promoted. There was an increasing tendency to exchange relics, or to transfer them to splendid edifices built in their honor. Indeed, with the breakdown of order and security in many provinces of the Empire, the bishops ordered the removal of the more highly prized relics from cemeteries outside the walls of their cities to churches within the bulwarks, where they would not only be safe from barbarian depredations but more easily accessible to the throngs that crowded to honor them. Thus the local Calendars of the churches were continuously expanded by additions to the anniversaries of death-days: namely, the anniversaries of "inventions," of "translations" of relics, of dedications of edifices in honor of the saints, or of altars erected over their bodily remains.

The fourth century also witnessed the beginning of cult offered to distinguished churchmen who were not martyrs, but whose lives were outstanding examples of courageous witness for the faith against heresy, of monastic virtues of worldly renunciation, or of conspicuous charity and service. Such holy men and women were treated in the same way as the martyrs, and their relics also were "translated" to fitting resting places in churches and chapels where they could be accessible to the devotion of the faithful. Thus, by the close of the ancient period of the Church's history, the Calendars of the several churches contained a variety of types of commemoration, of which the chief ones were these:

1. Anniversaries of the death of martyrs.
2. Anniversaries of the death of saints, not martyrs.
3. Dates of the translation of relics of martyrs and saints.
4. Dates of the dedication of churches and edifices of cult in honor of martyrs and saints.
5. Dates of the invention of relics of martyrs and saints (including the Apostles and Evangelists).

Yet in all this elaboration of the cult of saints, one basic principle unites all its varied forms of commemoration. It was the celebration of the fulfillment of a holy life, not its temporal beginning, but its earthly end. The conception of "death and resurrection" was inherent in all of these anniversaries.

The institution of Christmas Day in the early fourth century, with the somewhat older feast of the Epiphany, provided a second major focus for the development of the Calendar. Unlike Easter, these feasts were fixed dates, related to the winter equinox as then reckoned, and they were celebrations which were deliberately set over against concurrent pagan festivals of the "birthday" of a divine being. Whatever other motivations and purposes these Incarnation feasts may have fulfilled, the idea of such feasts was not a primitive element in the Christian tradition, but the result, in part at least, of influences from the Church's Gentile environment. It is all the more significant, therefore, that the holy days that developed in association with these feasts never expanded beyond certain clearly defined limits. They did not lead to any celebration of the birthdays into time of any Christian saint, with but two exceptions: John the Baptist and the Virgin Mary, the two figures of major significance in the Gospel story of the birth of our Lord. The date chosen for the feast of the Nativity of John the Baptist was in direct relation with the date of Christmas. The feast of the Nativity of the Virgin was part of a wider cycle of feasts, based upon legendary traditions of her life, which included the commemoration of her Conception and Presentation, as well as the days in her honor that were also feasts of the Lord, the Annunciation and Purification. At the same time, both the Baptist and the Virgin came to be honored on days of their death, as was the case with other saints of the New Testament.

The medieval Church built its Calendars upon the basic principles of the earlier period. Martyrdom was still the supreme testimony to sanctity, though the occasion for such testimony was not so constant. Particularly notable in the medieval outlook was the emphasis upon the miraculous as evidence of a holy life. The early Church, of course, had not overlooked this aspect of supernatural grace in the lives of the saints. But the medieval churchmen came to regard miracles as the primary proof of sanctity — whether the miracles were performed during the course of the saint's earthly life, or after his death. This emphasis upon miracles still obtains in the Latin Church's weighing of evidence for official canonization.

The medievalists were not, however, so superstitious about the miraculous as to forget the importance of character, or the variety of ways whereby the grace of sanctity was made effectual in the Church. The roster of medieval saints includes all kinds of distinguished service: missionaries and founders of churches and monasteries, eminent scholars and theologians, masters of the discipline of contemplation and life of prayer, and ministers of charity and works of mercy. Special mention should also be made of the deep impression made upon the medieval mind by unselfish, Christian statesmanship in the arena of politics. It has been said that medieval saints tend to fall into one of three categories: royal, episcopal, or monastic, But these were precisely the chief avenues, given the structure of medieval society, by which men and women were drawn into ways of constructive and outstanding leadership, paths that tested to the full the qualities of humility, courage and charity.

There was no uniformity in the Calendars of medieval times. The ancient privilege of Bishops in authorizing the cult of saints in their dioceses obtained throughout the Middle Ages. Yet even within the boundaries of a diocese, there was variation in the veneration of saints, due to local or popular circumstances. After the reform of Charlemagne, which introduced the Roman rite throughout most of Western Christendom, the Calendar of the church in Rome was gradually diffused and became the basis of most medieval observances. But the Roman Calendar was constantly modified or increased by the names of saints who enjoyed local or regional fame. Many of these non-Roman worthies were accepted at Rome itself, with the result that by the close of the medieval period the Calendars of the churches, however varied in details, had something of an international character.

Beginning with the reform movement of the twelfth century, the Papacy sought to place some control upon the process of canonization. But it never succeeded in obtaining a complete authority over the promulgation of new saints. It was not until the year 1634 that Pope Urban VIII was able to bring an end to the older liberty and confine the machinery of canonization to the authorities of the papal Curia. This, it will be noted, was a century after the Reformation. Undoubtedly papal canonization in the Middle Ages added enormously to the prestige of the cult of a saint, and those whose veneration was accepted by the Papacy enjoyed a far wider devotion than others. But the mere fact that the Pope had canonized a saint did not necessarily mean adoption of the name in all and sundry Calendars of the dioceses or monastic Orders. Even today, a certain number of holy days are recognized by the Papacy only in a limited area or sphere of observance.

One other element in medieval Calendar-making deserves mention: the erection of festivals in honor of specific doctrines or devotions. The earliest example of a feast of this kind was the Feast of the Holy Trinity, on the Sunday after Pentecost, first instituted in Liège in the early years of the tenth century. The Papacy resisted for several centuries any recognition of this feast, though it became immensely popular in northern Europe, and especially in England through the efforts of Thomas Becket. Another noteworthy example, also promoted originally in Liege, but adopted more readily by the Papacy, was the thirteenth century institution of the Feast of Corpus Christi. In modern times, the Latin Church has shown a greater readiness to promote this type of festival, among which may be noted the Sacred Heart, the Precious Blood, and the Feast of Christ the King.

We have already noted the radical alterations made by the Reformers of the sixteenth century in the traditional Calendars of the Church, and the reasons, theological, moral, and political, that motivated their revision. Though they remained generally conservative in theology, they were all sufficiently influenced by the outlook of the new Humanism to be highly critical of the miraculous and legendary aspects associated with so much of medieval devotion to the saints. Yet their exclusion from the Calendar of the great Fathers of the ancient Church, to whom they so often appealed in their writings of theological controversy, can only be explained by the rigidity with which they applied the Scriptural norm to the Calendar. It must be admitted that in the matter of holy days the Reformers set up a new principle of selection, unknown hitherto in the tradition of the Church. They were not so radical, however, as to change the accustomed dates of the festivals that they did retain.

The Reformation also introduced a new basis of authority for the observance of holy days. The older liberty of diocesans in instituting new feasts gave way to the principle of uniformity of observance throughout the national Church. The tendency towards uniformity was, of course, characteristic of the times. It was already strongly at work within the Latin Church. The invention of printing made it not only possible, but probable. But the greater power of the State, at least in England, to enforce its will made uniformity in the liturgy an actuality. Once established, the principle of uniformity has operated as a strong cohesive force to the Anglican Reformation settlement, though it met with stout resistance and has probably never been completely effected. In recent generations, it has tended to break down with the relaxing or removal of pressure from the civil power. Where all legal connection between the Church and the State has been dissolved, as in most provinces of Anglicanism today, the maintenance of uniformity is obtained only by the force of popular opinion within the Church, the powers of moral persuasion by the Church's leadership, and the conscience of ministers in regard to canonical obedience.

The Problem of Modern Reconstruction

The sole authority in the American Church for revising the Prayer Book Calendar resides in the General Convention, acting under the specific directives of the Constitution and Canons. This obvious truism is mentioned here as a reminder, first of all, of the very practical necessities confronting the Church with respect to the modification or enrichment of any part of its inherited liturgy. Despite the numerous criticisms, some of them well-considered, some of them captious, that are voiced regarding the constitution and machinery of the General Convention, it is nonetheless in its present embodiment representative by and large of the varied outlooks and interests of the Church as a whole. A revision of the Prayer Book Calendar, that has any chance of being adopted by the General Convention, must be based upon principles that are consistent with and agreeable to the various perspectives on the problem that are widely held throughout the Church. On the one hand, the approach to the problem by a large segment of the Church's membership is mainly influenced by tradition. Its immediate reaction to any specific holy day proposed for inclusion in the Calendar is to apply the tests of antiquity, universality, and authoritative usage in the past, especially in the generations before the breakup of the unity of Western Christendom. This group is not primarily interested in the older canons of judgment upon sanctity insofar as they involve miraculous and legendary elements. But it treasures the heritage of prayer and devotion in the corporate worship of the Church through the ages that has surrounded the memory of saints, even in certain instances where little of an authentic, historical tradition has survived concerning their life and witness. To the common reputation for sanctity it would insist upon a certain reputation for orthodoxy. The outlook of this group is not averse to the inclusion of some of the saints of the Eastern Church, who never found a place in Western Calendars, or even to a limited acceptance of some of the post-Reformation worthies of "Catholic" Communions. By and large, however, it would build the Church's Calendar upon the basis of those holy days that were of widespread observance in the Western Church at the time of the Reformation.

The strength of this point of view is obvious. It reminds us of the continuity of the Church's corporate life of worship, and the need of loyalty to it. It provides, at least, some objective criteria of judgment in its appeal to the testimony of an undivided Church. It is less likely to accept or to reject the memorial of a particular saint on the mere basis of individualistic and personal feelings.

There is, on the other hand, another approach to the question, also very widespread in the Church, that is less moved by considerations of tradition, than by the evaluations of modern historiography. These persons do not, of course, reject the principle of traditional authority and usage, though they are less likely to make this principle a decisive norm. They would see the Calendar in terms of its teaching value, a list of heroes in the long life of the Church, whose lives and accomplishments continue to be a living inspiration to modern churchmen. Not only would they stress the importance of authentic information about the life and death of each saint commemorated — that is, a "true story" that is inspiring and edifying but they would be "ecumenical" in selection. Less concerned with the orthodoxy of the saint, they are more interested in his achievement and his impact upon the on-going life of Christendom. In between these two major points of view there are many varying shades of interest and perspective. Certain concerns are held in common, however, by all parties interested in revision of the Calendar. Neither the pre-Reformation test of miracle nor the Reformation norm of Scripture carries much weight in the Church any longer. The common basis of all judgment is the effect upon edification, the moral and spiritual influence of devotion to the memory of the saints. This is, in effect, a pragmatic norm, and difficult to apply with assured objectivity. It is undoubtedly colored by our unconsciously "American" way of evaluating heroism in all spheres of life. It is our way of knowing men "by their fruits." It is unlikely that any saint will be admitted to the Calendar of the American Church, by vote of General Convention, unless it can be shown that the candidate for such an honor is "worthy" of emulation by his life and example, irrespective of his ancient record of cult in the Calendars of past generations. By the same token, it is unlikely that any saint will be "canonized" by the General Convention, without considerable evidence, by official cult or otherwise, of widespread agreement as to his merits.

During the process of Prayer Book revisions made throughout Anglicanism in the 1920's, one of the most influential discussions of the Calendar and its problems was contained in the late Bishop W. H. Frere's book, *Some Principles of Liturgical Reform* (London: John Murray, 1911). Dr. Frere laid out two principles of Calendar construction that mediate between the main schools of thought on the problem: "first, whether there is sufficient historical justification for the inclusion of the candidate in any Kalendar; and secondly, whether it can command sufficient interest to make it suitable to the Kalendar of any particular Church" (page 22). In regard to the second proposition, Dr. Frere gave much attention to the popularity of certain saints as evidenced in church dedications. This aspect of the question should not be overlooked, and with it the popularity of certain saints as patrons of parish guilds, church societies, and church schools and institutions. Obviously, the situation is different in England, to which he particularly addressed his discussion, than it is in America, since so many English parishes were founded by or named for pre-Reformation saints.

In the American scene, the dedications of churches and institutions have been, until fairly recent times, largely confined to saints and feasts included in the Prayer Book Calendar, or to titles of our Lord and incidents in His life. The use of non-Prayer Book saints' names first became popular among us for designating voluntary guilds and societies, and then for the titles of secondary schools for boys and girls. But in late years, there has been an extensive growth of parish dedications to saints who are not commemorated in the Prayer Book. This tendency appears to be on the increase. A good example of the trend is provided by one of our larger American dioceses that embraces various types of "churchmanship" (as it is curiously called) among its parishes. This diocese is neither one of the oldest, nor one of the most recent, of the Church; but it is a diocese which is growing rapidly in the number of new parishes and missions. There are at present (1956) ninety-six parishes and missions in union with the diocesan convention. Of these, seventy are dedicated to a "saint" — the others being denominated as Christ, Grace, Trinity, Epiphany, etc. Of these seventy dedications to a saint, nineteen, or over one-fourth, are under the patronage of saints not listed in the Prayer Book. Fourteen different names are used for these nineteen parishes and missions: Aidan, Alban, All Souls, Augustine, Clement, Columba, Cuthbert, Cyprian, David, Elizabeth, Francis, George, Patrick, and Timothy. One may easily check the general popularity of these names, and others, by reference to the table of church' dedications usually included in The Episcopal Church Annual.

It would make an interesting study if one were to make research into the reasons for the sudden development of popularity for non-Prayer Book saints in church dedications, or, for that matter, the principal reasons why names of all kinds are selected by parishes. They are doubtless many, nor are they always carefully considered. Sometimes it is due to the personal interest of a priest or layman, or to a desire to relate the name to that of a "mother" parish. The continuing influence of English church dedications is still very strong. And there are ethnic and regional influences that play a part, not to speak of the natural human disposition to be different. Whatever the reason, the weight of popularity evidenced by the choice of "patrons" cannot be ignored in any consideration of the Church's Calendar.

Recent Anglican Calendars

It is to be expected that the various independent provinces of the Anglican Communion, as they shape their inherited Prayer Book tradition to the needs and circumstances of their own country and mission, will produce divergent Calendars. The several revision committees of the different provinces try to keep in touch with one another's work, and they always consider carefully the proposals made or adopted by one another. But final decisions are the prerogative of each province. Anyone who takes the trouble to examine the various Calendar schedules now obtaining in Anglican Prayer Books, or in proposals for their revision, cannot be insensitive to the large degree of common material found among them all. The principal differences have to do with the proportion of entries of purely local or national interest. This is particularly evident if one compares the Calendars of the English Proposed Book of 1928 and the Scottish Book of 1929.

It may be useful, as a background for the proposals of this present Study, to point out some of the characteristics of recent Anglican revisions. No attention will be paid to Red Letter Days, since these have been retained unchanged in all the Anglican Prayer Books, but with the addition of a few additional ones in some of them. For example, the Transfiguration on August 6, first adopted by the American Church in 1892, has been taken up into every one of the modern Anglican Prayer Books that have been revised. St. Mary Magdalen, on July 22, has been restored to Red Letter eminence, as in the first Prayer Book of 1549, in all the revisions except the American, Irish, and Canadian. But the current Draft Prayer Book in Canada has followed the trend. The Irish and Scottish Books have made St. Patrick's Day, March 17, a Red Letter feast; and the Scottish Book has in addition given the same rank to St. Columba, June 9, and St. Ninian, September 16, the two "apostles" of Christianity in Scotland. There has been no movement in the modern Anglican revisions to overwhelm the major distinction given by the Reformers to the New Testament saints and holy days. This fact, in itself, shows how strongly the Prayer Book tradition, as set by the sixteenth-century Reformers, continues to be maintained.

It is clear that the fundamental list of Black Letter Days used by all the revision committees at work in the first quarter of this century has been the Calendar of the English Book of 1661, with its sixty-seven notations of commemorations. A breakdown of these sixty-seven Black Letter Days reveals the following classification:

- 19 are martyrs of the early Church, chiefly Roman, but not exclusively so.
- 9 are leading Fathers and Bishops of the ancient Church.
- 18 are saints and missionaries of the early period of the evangelization of the British Isles.

- 8 are ancient Gallican saints, most of whom had a cult in the medieval English Church.
- 13 are festivals of the ancient Church of various types: of the Virgin, Holy Cross, New Testament worthies, etc.

Every one of these sixty-seven days were observed in the Church, whether in England or on the Continent, before the Norman Conquest, except four. Of these four, two, the Transfiguration and the Name of Jesus (August 7), were introduced in the late Middle Ages; the other two were Richard of Chichester (d. 1253) and Hugh of Lincoln (d. 1200). None of the Anglican Prayer Books, issued in the 1920's, retained the entire list of these Black Letter Days.

The English Proposed Book of 1928 omitted sixteen of the old Black Letter Days, and added twenty-seven new ones. Eleven of the new days were drawn from the Sarum Calendar. Of the remaining sixteen, six were names of early Fathers of the Church, all of whom except Clement of Alexandria have an honored place in the Roman Calendar; six were noted leaders in the early days of the Christian mission in England; and four were medieval saints (Anskar, Anselm, Bernard, and Catherine of Siena), one of whom was an Archbishop of Canterbury. There were no entries of Reformation or post-Reformation figures.

More extensive was the new listing of the Scottish Book of 1929. It contains in sum 109 Black Letter Days, including only forty-nine of the sixty-seven days of the 1661 Calendar. There are fewer early English saints than in the English Book of 1928; but there are thirty-four Celtic saints, not counting the four that were made Red Letter observances (Patrick, Columba, Ninian, and Queen Margaret). The Scottish Calendar includes a few notable persons not found in the English Book, such as St. Joseph, the Church Fathers Justin Martyr, Cyril of Jerusalem, and Gregory Nazianzen, and the medieval theologian Thomas Aquinas. The Scottish Book like the English, however, contains no saints since the time of the Reformation; but Bishops are given authority to license other saints of local interest.

The English and Scottish Books naturally carried much weight in other provinces of the Anglican Communion, and all the Prayer Books of the other provinces reveal their influence. But neither the English nor the Scottish Books were slavishly followed. The Canadian Book of 1922 contained only sixty-eight Black Letter entries, all but six being in agreement with the English. Of these six, one, St. Valentine, was contained in the 1661 Black Letter Days, but omitted in the English Book of 1928. The other five were: St. Joseph, Justin Martyr, Gregory Nazianzen, Paulinus, the first Archbishop of York, and Thomas Becket.

The South African Calendar has an interest all its own, both by reason of its more eclectic character, and by its initiative in including memorial Collects for Post-Reformation worthies. It omits twelve of the Black Letter Days of the 1661 Book; but of its additions, twenty-four are absent from the English 1928 Book, and seventeen from the 1929 Scottish Book. Six of the new names are drawn from the New Testament: Timothy, Joseph, Silas, Mary and Martha, Philip the Deacon, and James, the brother of the Lord. There are six early English leaders, not found in the English Book of 1928, and two unusual medieval English churchmen, St. Gilbert of Sempringham and St. Osmund of Salisbury. Four other medieval saints are listed: Thomas Aquinas, Joan of Arc, Dominic, and Elizabeth of Hungary, in addition to those contained in the English Book. Many of the distinctive features of the South African Calendar were derived from the list suggested by Bishop Frere, in his work cited above.

In a separate listing, the South African Book names seventeen worthies, for whom a memorial Collect is provided. Of these, all are post-Reformation Anglicans except one, King Alfred the Great. Four of them are martyrs and leaders of the Church's mission in Africa. The South African example has been taken up in the current Draft Prayer Book before the Church in Canada. The Calendar of this Book has 119 Black Letter Days, of which twenty-four of them are Anglican — three of them associated with the Canadian Church — and one, David Livingstone, though not an Anglican, most certainly belongs to the company of the elect. The Canadian list is of unusual interest because of its diverse and eclectic character. It retains, although often bracketed, a number of the 1661 Black Letter entries that have dropped out of other Anglican Books. It memorializes medieval churchmen who never received a cult, such as Archbishop Stephen Langton and Bishop Grosseteste of Lincoln. Both Thomas More and Thomas Cranmer are included, as are Thomas Becket, John Wyclif and the Wesley brothers.

Much more modest is the Calendar in the Proposed Prayer Book of the Church of India, Pakistan, Burma, and Ceylon (1951). There are sixty-two Black Letter Days, mostly made up of martyrs and Fathers of the early Church, and the leading figures of early Christianity in Britain. Among the Fathers, one notes the appearance of Pantaenus (December 9), whom early tradition made a missionary in India before he established the great Christian School in Alexandria. Of the medieval saints included, perhaps the most striking are the Jesuits, Ignatius Loyola and Francis Xavier. Their inclusion is of interest, of course, for the early Jesuit missions in the Far East. The Indian Book contains no Anglicans, but Bishops are allowed to authorize other saints' days.

There remains to say a word about the list of Black Letter Days proposed in connection with the American revision of 1913-28. A full schedule of the names may be found in the Third Report of the Joint Commission, prepared for the 1922 General Convention. This Calendar never received much attention or interest, and it failed to be ratified. There are fifty-four names, most of which appear in the lists of the other Anglican revisions of the time. But there are several peculiarities about the selection. The number of early martyrs is very slight only those whose names occur frequently as patrons of church guilds and societies; Agnes, Vincent, and Cecilia. Particular emphasis is given to the "apostles" and "patrons" of the nations or ethnic groups, in view of the variegated ethnic make-up of the American people. This circumstance explains the entry of Cyril and Methodius, "Apostles of the Slavs" (May 11), Ansgarius, "Apostle of Denmark and Sweden" (February 3), Patrick, "Apostle and Patron of Ireland" (March 17), and similar citations. Even the mythical St. George is introduced, not as a martyr, but with the description "Patron of England." This ethnic interest accounts also for the inclusion of the "Martyrs of China, 1900." And St. Nicholas of Myra receives the title of "Patron of Children." Two rather singular entries are Botolf (June 17) and Teresa (October 15). The former appears in no modern Anglican list. One suspects at this point a local interest of Boston, Massachusetts![3] St. Teresa has the distinction of being the only person on the list who is post-Reformation.[4] Her name appears, however, in Dr. Frere's book, in his suggested Calendar. Full details of this proposed American Calendar will be found in the comparative tables in the Appendix.

Certain general characteristics concerning all the recent Anglican Calendars can be summarized:

1. The distinction of Red Letter and Black Letter Days is clearly marked in all revisions. In all the Prayer Books, only the Red Letter Days are required to be observed. The Black Letter Days are optional. None of the Prayer Books provide a complete schedule of propers for each of the Black Letter Days, but only a few selected propers with a number of "commons." The variations may be tabulated as follows:

	Special Propers	Commons
English 1928	9 (with duplications)	8
Scottish 1929	11 (with duplications)	4
South African	14	8
Indian	14	11 (also a Patronal festival)
Canadian 1955	8 (with duplications)	8

In each of the several Prayer Books, the propers provided for the Black Letter Days are in a section by themselves, and not scattered through the propers for the Red Letter Days.

---

3. Ed. Note: Botolf is the Latinization of St. Botwulf of Thorney, an English abbot who died in 680, a patron saint of farmers and travellers. He is mentioned in both the *Anglo-Saxon Chronicle* and the *Life of Ceolfrith* (often attributed to Bede). The English contraction of "Botwulf's-town" is "Boston" and the city in Massachusetts commemorates his name with a famous private club, a street in the Back Bay area, and Boston College's President's house.

4. Ed. Note: This St. Teresa is Teresa of Avila, the Spanish mystic, reformer, and Doctor of the Church.

2. There is greater agreement among the Prayer Books respecting the names of saints of the ancient Church than of medieval times. Certain early figures of the period of the conversion of the British Isles are found in all the Calendars; but there is great variation in the number of saints included from that period.
3. In certain cases there is no agreement as to date. For example, Titus is commemorated in some on January 4, in others on February 6; Ignatius of Antioch appears in some on February 1, in others on December 17. In nearly every case of this kind, the reason for disagreement lies in the absence of the name from early English or Sarum Calendars. The choice of date, therefore, is made with reference either to the date in the Roman Calendar or to the date in Calendars of the Eastern Church. Occasionally the date chosen is derived from a Martyrology. In a few cases, choices have been made between the traditional date of the saint's death, or the date of a later "translation."
4. Most of the Anglican Calendars avoid more than one entry on a single day. The exceptions are the Scottish Book and the Canadian Draft Book of 1955. In no case, however, is a Black Letter commemoration included on a Red Letter Day.
5. All of the Calendars provide descriptive notes, identifying the rank of the saint, the place of his principal activity, and, where known, the date of his death.

Part Three
Proposals for Revision

Principles of the Present Proposals

For the past ten years, the Standing Liturgical Commission has devoted time at each of its meetings in discussing the materials of this Study. With each change in personnel of the Commission the tentative list of Calendar changes, first drawn up in 1945, has been reviewed and revised. Many suggestions sent in to the Commission have all been given consideration, and close study has been made of the Calendars adopted in other Prayer Books of the Anglican Communion. The changes and additions herewith proposed have with but few exceptions been unanimously approved throughout the long period of study and discussion. Where the Commission has been sharply divided over particular proposals for inclusion, and has been unable to come to a solution satisfactory to most, if not all, of the members, the proposed entry has been omitted. Thus some of the most prolonged and difficult work of the Commission on this Calendar has led, seemingly, to negative results. But the Commission believes that the energy spent on these disputed and unresolved problems has by no means been wasted.

We believe that the concrete result of our labors probably represents the type of Calendar that will be acceptable to the vast majority of the Church's membership.

No doubt every person will find missing on this Calendar one or more names that he would wish to see there; and contrarily, there may be a few names in the present proposals that do not strike an enthusiastic response in the hearts of some believers. We remind the readers of this Study once again of what was said above about the difficulty of establishing objective criteria in a matter of this kind. The Commission believes, however, that historical honesty is a *sine qua non* requirement in a task of this nature. The achievements of modern historical criticism within the past hundred years, to which members of our own Communion have made rich contributions, have made very questionable some of the standards of evaluation employed by the ancient and medieval Church in developing the Calendar. This is no criticism of the past. The Church of an earlier age was honest in its own methods. But the same methods are not always honest for a modern churchman.

Not only are many of the most popular and widely commemorated saints of both the Eastern and the Western Churches of dubious historical authenticity; but, if their historicity is beyond reasonable doubt, there is no certain knowledge or information about their lives and character. It is impossible, for example, to establish the historical existence of St. George. The fact that he has become a patron saint of England does not make him any the more real; nor does it necessitate making him a saint of the American Church. Fairy-book tales may indeed be edifying. When they become part of the folklore and tradition of a great nation they can become stirring symbols. But it is asking too much of the majority of our American Church membership, who have no such traditional and patriotic associations with the name, to respond with mature devotion to a saint of whom it can only be said, "He may have existed, sometime, somewhere." There are innumerable saints, many of them martyrs for the Faith, who deserve the thankful remembrance of the Church, but for whom the accidents of history have left no certain testimony. For these holy men and women whose memory might otherwise be forgotten by the faithful the Church provides the common feast of All Saints with its Octave. Where church dedications or other circumstances have left the memorial of saints who are scarcely recorded in the annals of history, the Prayer Book already provides two sets of propers for their commemoration: the Feast of the Dedication of a Church, and A Saint's Day. These propers should give adequate coverage and usefulness for such occasions as may be desired by local parishes or parish groups.

The choice of commemorations in the proposed Calendar of this Study has been made primarily on the basis of selecting men and women of outstanding holiness, heroism, and teaching in the cause of Christ, whose lives and deaths have been a continuing, conscious influence upon the on-going life of the Church in notable and well-recognized ways. There are included martyrs, theologians, statesmen, missionaries, reformers, mystics, and exemplars of prayer and charitable service. In every instance care has been taken to list persons whose life and work are capable of interpretation in terms morally and spiritually edifying to the Church of our own generation. In addition, a few festivals commemorating events of particular importance in the heritage of our own Communion have been included, such as the memorial of the First Prayer Book and the bestowal of the American Episcopate.

The list is representative of all periods of the Church's history, and of various peoples and races. It is only natural that the predominant number of names belongs to the tradition of Western Christianity, with especial emphasis upon the Church in England. For the period since the Reformation, the list is confined to Anglican worthies only, both English and American. The Commission does not mean to suggest thereby any disparagement of the saints of other Christian Communions in modern times, many of whom have had a thankworthy influence upon our own tradition. But we believe that at the present time sufficient unanimity is lacking among our people regarding proper criteria for their selection. The Commission does believe very strongly, however, that any extension of the present Prayer Book Calendar should give recognition to the fact that our Anglican tradition has produced, and continues to produce saintliness. If we criticize the Reformers' schedule of saints for restricting commemorations of this kind to the New Testament period, the same basis of criticism can be equally applied to an arbitrary line drawn through the sixteenth century, as a time when "sainthood" ceased in the Church.

In drawing up the present schedule, constant recourse has been made to the Catholic Calendars of both the Eastern and the Western Church, no less than to the Calendars of other Anglican Prayer Books. Due consideration has also been given to the names of saints to whom churches are dedicated in America. But in no case have legendary or apocryphal figures been included, or names of purely local significance and interest. A few worthies of pre-Reformation times have been added, whose names never appeared on the Calendar of any Church until recent times. In such instances there has been a careful weighing of claims for such commemoration in the Church in the light of the best judgments of modern historical criticism.

The enlargement of the Calendar necessarily complicates the matter of the precedence of festivals. An attempt has been made to give directions regarding the classification and use of the new days, without disturbing in the least the principles laid down in the Tables of Precedence in the preface of the present Prayer Book. It should be carefully noted that *the Commission recommends that all of the proposed Black Letter Days be occasions of optional observance.*

It has often been remarked that the Prayer Book provides the parish priest with an excellent teaching manual for the study of the Bible, the doctrine and ethics of the Church, and, of course, the principles and practice of worship and prayer. It has lacked but one thing, an adequate instrument for teaching the history of the Church. The present proposal should do much to meet this need. With the names on this Calendar arranged in a historical, or topical, order, the parish priest or teacher will have a convenient guide and outline of Church History from its beginnings to the present time. Such a study should greatly reinforce the other teachings of the Prayer Book, as they are exemplified in the lives of the saints.

Changes Proposed in the Red Letter Days

The Commission does not recommend that any of the present Red Letter Days in our Calendar be either omitted or reduced from the rank of major feasts that are to be regularly observed in the Church. Nor does it recommend that any new feasts be added to the present number of Red Letter Days of required commemoration. We have already made certain proposals regarding the alteration of Epistles and Gospels for some of these days in our Prayer Book Study, Number II, *The Eucharistic Lectionary* (1950). In connection with that Study, and in discussions respecting the present proposed Calendar, the Commission does believe that two changes are desirable in the title and emphasis of two of the present Red Letter Days of the Calendar. We recommend, first, that the feast of the Circumcision of Christ on January 1 be given a new title: The Holy Name of our Lord Jesus Christ; and, secondly, that the commemoration of St. Paul be restored to its original association with St. Peter on June 29.

The Holy Name of our Lord Jesus Christ. Originally, January 1 was celebrated in the Latin Church as the Octave of Christmas, with propers especially appointed in honor of our Lord's Mother. It was the Gallican Church that first changed the emphasis to the gospel story of our Lord's Circumcision, and gave the day a quasi-penitential character by way of opposition to the pagan festivities that were associated in ancient times with New Year's Day. The Roman Church adopted the changed emphasis only in the ninth century.

At the time of the Reformation a new Collect was provided for the day, based upon one in the Westminster Missal and the teaching of the Epistle, that further strengthened the theme of commemoration of our Lord's Circumcision. But the Epistle itself was new; instead of the older Christmas Epistle, Titus 2:11-15, a lesson from Romans 4:8-14 was chosen. The total effect of these changes was to make the day, as Dr. F. E. Brightman keenly observed, actually "a commemoration of circumcision, rather than of the Circumcision of our Lord, not to edification" (*The English Rite*, I, xcv). A definite move away from this unbalanced proportion of things was made in the 1928 revision of the American Book, when a new Epistle was appointed for the day, from Philippians 2:9-13. The new selection contains no reference to circumcision at all, but calls attention to the Name of Jesus to which "every knee should bow." This new Epistle, together with the

Gospel (with its story not only of the circumcizing of our Lord but also of His naming), very definitely shifted devotional attention to the wondrous Name of Jesus — "for there is none other name under heaven given among men, whereby we must be saved" (Acts 4:12).

The other Anglican Prayer Books, in their recent revisions, have also shown dissatisfaction with the Reformation appointments for the day. The Irish Book of 1927, the most conservative of all the modern revisions, added a second Collect in honor of the Name, and altered the Epistle to Ephesians 2:11-18. The English 1928, the Scottish, the South African, and the Indian Books have the same alteration in the Epistle; and all four Books, except the Scottish, added a "New Year's" Collect to the propers, though the Scottish Book included two New Year's Collects among the occasional Prayers. The new Draft Book of the Canadian Church has gone further. It has given a new major title to the day: The Octave of Christmas, and placed the Circumcision in a sub-title. The Collect for Christmas Day is used as the principal Collect, but two others are added: one for the Circumcision and one for the New Year. This evidence is enough to show the direction in which Anglican revisions are moving in regard to January 1. It may also be noted that the Roman Church observes a feast of the Holy Name on January 2, or, when there is such a Sunday in the year, on the Second Sunday after Christmas.

In making its recommendation for a new title for January 1, the Commission does not imply that it rejects any religious significance to the fact that our Lord was circumcized, thereby fulfilling the commandments of the old Law, and being in all things a dutiful "member incorporate" in the covenant of the old Israel. But we believe that this theme should be subsidiary. The sign of the new Israel, of which we are members, is not circumcision, but the name of Christian which we bear by the salvation wrought for us in the Name of Jesus Christ. The new emphasis would more vividly call to mind our Baptism, in which we received our Christian name. It would point also to the coming celebration in the liturgy of our Lord's Baptism, during the Epiphany season.

The Feast of SS. Peter and Paul, June 29. The joint commemoration of the martyrdom of the two chief apostles was instituted at Rome in the year 258, during the Valerian persecution. So far as the records go, it is the earliest saints' day commemoration in the Roman liturgy. The joint feast is still a feature of the Roman, as it is of the Lutheran, Calendar, though it is only fair to say that Roman usage has developed in a way that emphasizes the commemoration of Peter on June 29, with an additional, special commemoration of Paul on June 30. At the Reformation in England, the association of Paul with Peter on June 29 was dropped, thus leaving the Anglican Calendar without special observance of the martyrdom of the Apostle of the Gentiles.

We can only surmise the reasons that induced the Reformers to omit Paul from the June 29 (or June 30) commemoration. Probably the principal factor was the retention of the Conversion festival on January 25 — with its Scriptural narrative — and the desire not to give more than one commemoration to any of the Apostles. The propers for Sexagesima Sunday, also, are anciently associated with St. Paul, because on that day the papal mass was celebrated in St. Paul's Basilica, and both the Collect and the Epistle were commemorations of the Apostle. Whatever the reason, it is no less anomalous that the Church should not memorialize the martyrdom of St. Paul, since his death for the faith is as strongly attested in the New Testament as is that of St. Peter.

There is, of course, no certain tradition as to the date of either St. Peter's or St. Paul's martyrdom; nor do we know for certain that the two apostles were martyred at the same time. Only the fact of their martyrdom at Rome, during the reign of Nero, appears to be sufficiently authentic, both in the tradition of the Western Church and in the light of archaeological evidence. The Commission does not believe that any value would accrue from selecting, arbitrarily, a separate date for St. Paul, but that it is better to restore the time-honored tradition of associating the two chief apostles together on the same day.

Notes on the Black Letter Days

The several paragraphs on each of the Black Letter Days proposed for inclusion in the Calendar are not intended to be biographies, but only suggestions, made as succinctly as possible, of the principal reasons that have led to the Commission's agreement concerning the selection. In each case, brief indications are given as to the appearance of the names in other Calendars and the reasons for the choice of dates. A convenient check on this information may be found in Appendix : Comparative Tables of Anglican Calendars.

The Commission recognizes that there will not be a general unanimity among readers of this Study about some of the names proposed. It does hope, however, that those who take the trouble to consider this Study will check the natural tendency to hasty or subjective judgment. To assist the reader to make an impartial assessment of the proposals here made, a Bibliography is appended where sufficient references may be found to more detailed biographical materials. It is likely that a readier agreement to these proposals will be forthcoming with respect to the pre-Reformation names than to the more modern entries. Once more, however, the Commission wishes to emphasize the fact that all of the Black Letter Days are designed to be optional, in the observances of any particular church or chapel. For a large number of the names, it is intended only that a memorial Collect be provided, not a full set of propers. This applies to all the post-Reformation entries, and to a number of the pre-Reformation worthies as well. If, in such cases, a full set of propers is desired, this can be provided by use of suitable "commons."

January

10. WILLIAM LAUD, *Archbishop of Canterbury, 1645*

Born at Reading, Oct. 7, 1573; Bishop of St. David's 1621-26, Bath and Wells, 1626-28, London, 1628-33; Archbishop of Canterbury, 1633-45; executed on a charge of treason, Oct. 10, 1645. The South African and Canadian Draft Books list his name.

The circumstance that Laud's name appears first among the Black Letter Days may cause surprise and dismay among some churchmen; for he continues to arouse strong feelings of distaste and even today. A militant champion of the principles of Anglicanism, against both Romanism and Puritanism, and a stern disciplinarian in enforcing the canons and rubrics of the Church no less than its moral standards, Laud provoked the deepest antagonisms and equally devoted loyalties. Accounted a traitor by his enemies and a martyr by his supporters, he remains a controversial figure in the history of the Church. His devotion to duty, his inner integrity, his sincere attachment to the faith and worship of the Church, his lack of self-regard, and his patience and courage in his final downfall, cannot be questioned. The chief gravamen against him is the harshness and rigor of the policies and methods he pursued against the Puritans, which was not tempered by any outward tenderness of manner. He was, however, tolerant and generous to churchmen of opposing views who remained loyal to the Church and Crown. His methods were in principle those of his age; and the period of the Commonwealth that followed his death and that of King Charles showed that his enemies were even more ruthless in the pursuit of their ideals. It is not fair to charge Laud with the major blame for the break-up of the unity of the Church in England. His ideals largely shaped the policies by which his disciples rebuilt the Church's order and life at the Restoration of Charles II. For succeeding generations, his works have been a primary source of apology for Anglicanism as both a reformed and Catholic expression of Christianity. The Prayer for Congress in the Prayer Book (page 35) is based upon a prayer written by Laud for "the High Court of Parliament."

14. HILARY, *Bishop of Poitiers, 367*

Born in Aquitaine in the second decade of the fourth century; Bishop of Poitiers, ca. 355-67. His death occurred on January 13, and he is commemorated on that day in the Sarum and the Prayer Book Calendars. The modern Roman Calendar has transferred the date to the 14th, and the present proposal does the same, to avoid a concurrence with the Octave of the Epiphany.

Hilary is one of the principal Fathers and theologians of the Western Church. An ardent defender of the Nicene faith, he was one of the few Latin Bishops in the fourth century who resisted the Arianizing policies of the Emperor

Constantius and in consequence suffered four years of exile (356-60) from his home and see. He took advantage of this period of exile, however, to acquaint himself thoroughly with the theological and political issues that were convulsing the Church. His works *On the Trinity* and *On the Synods* are fundamental expositions and apologies for the orthodox Christian faith, and the earliest Latin writings in defense of the Nicene theology. Other extant works include several Biblical commentaries and a few poems and hymns. Among his friends and proteges was Martin of Tours (see November 11), whom Hilary encouraged in his endeavors to develop the monastic life in the Western Church.

17. ANTONY, *Abbot in Egypt, 356*

Born ca. 250 in Heracleopolis, a village of Middle Egypt; died at the "Inner Mountain" (Dêr Mar Antonios), in the desert of Egypt, 356. Antony is commemorated on this date in the Eastern Church, and in the Sarum and Roman Calendars. He is also included in the English 1928, Scottish, South African, and Indian Calendars.

Known as the "Father of Monasticism," Antony is one of the most unique and astonishing persons in the history of the Church. At the age of about twenty he embraced the ascetic life, inspired by the Gospel lesson (Matthew 19:21) which he heard read in church. His rigor in ascetic discipline increased with the years, as he sought ever more barren and solitary places for his meditations. His fame brought him many disciples and encouraged many imitators. Though a recluse, Antony kept himself informed of affairs in the Church. He was a vigorous supporter and warm friend of Athanasius (see May 2) in the latter's arduous struggle with the Arian heresy; and it is to Athanasius that we owe a lively and moving Life of the saint. This biography of itself had a great influence in spreading the monastic movement; and we have the personal testimony of St. Augustine that it contributed to his own conversion. Antony's courage was unfailing. At the height of the last great persecution, he journeyed from his desert retreat to Alexandria to encourage the martyrs and confessors. When almost ninety years of age, he made the same trip to welcome Athanasius home from exile and to contend against the Arian heretics.

21. AGNES, *Martyr at Rome, 304*

A child of twelve or thirteen years, Agnes was martyred at Rome during the Diocletian persecution in 304. She appears in the earliest Calendar of the Roman Church, that of 354, and in all later medieval Calendars influenced by the Roman, including that of Sarum. She is listed in all the Prayer Book Calendars of Black Letter Days. The tradition of Agnes' martyrdom, though mixed with legendary elements, is sufficiently trustworthy. In the attempt to force her to deny her faith she was subjected to vicious outrages upon her person. She was beheaded for her steadfast refusal to offer worship to the heathen gods. The Emperor Constantine ordered a basilica in her honor erected over her tomb on the Via Nomentana. The church was reconstructed and adorned magnificently under Pope Honorius I (625-38). Visitors may still see her tomb there, and the splendid mosaic portrait of Agnes on the wall of the apse, as well as the neighboring catacomb that is named for her. The saint was eulogized by the leading Latin Fathers, Ambrose, Jerome, Augustine, and in the poetry of Prudentius.

22. VINCENT, *Deacon of Saragossa, and Martyr, 304*

A Deacon of the church in Saragossa, Spain, Vincent was arrested, with his Bishop, during the Diocletian persecution, and taken to Valencia, where he was martyred in 304. His cult was known at Rome in the sixth century, and he had an honored place in medieval Calendars, including Sarum. He is listed in all the modern Anglican Calendars except the Indian. Our knowledge of Vincent is based chiefly upon sermons of St. Augustine and a poem by Prudentius.

23. PHILLIPS BROOKS, *Bishop of Massachusetts, 1893*

Born in Boston, Mass., Dec. 13, 1835; Rector of the Church of the Advent, Philadelphia, 1859-62, Holy Trinity, Philadelphia, 1862-69, Trinity, Boston, 1869-91; Bishop of Massachusetts, 1891-93.

Brooks' reputation as the greatest preacher in the history of the American Church has never been challenged. But his character was even nobler than his eloquence. His pastoral ministry to all sorts and conditions of men was full of tenderness, understanding, and warm friendliness. He inspired many men to seek the Ministry, and taught many of them the art of preaching. His sermons are still considered classics, but do not glow with the warmth of his personal vitality that so impressed his hearers. He was generally accounted a leader in the "Liberal" circles of the Church, but in fact he was conservative and orthodox in theology. His liberalism was of the heart, and sprang from his deep personal loyalty to his Lord. His influence has been great outside the bounds of the Episcopal Church, and his fame has become international. Thousands who have never heard his voice, or read any of his sermons, know by heart his Christmas carol, "O little town of Bethlehem."

24. ST. TIMOTHY

The convert, companion, and faithful helper of St. Paul, Timothy's life and labors after the Apostle's death are not certainly known. The commemoration does not occur in medieval English Calendars or in Sarum. The date is taken from the Roman Martyrology and Calendar, and is due undoubtedly to a desire to place it in close proximity to a feast of St. Paul. The Scottish, South African, Indian, and

Canadian Draft Calendars have included this commemoration. Church dedications to St. Timothy have been very popular in the American Church.

26. POLYCARP, *Bishop of Smyrna, and Martyr,* 156

The *Martyrdom of Polycarp*, an eye-witness account and the oldest narrative of a Christian martyrdom outside the pages of the New Testament, places Polycarp's death on February 23. The year is not given, but it was either 155 or 156. The Eastern Churches still commemorate Polycarp on February 23; but Roman Martyrologies and Calendars since the eighth century have listed him on January 26, and this date was taken up in late Sarum Calendars. All the modern Anglican Prayer Books place him on the Western date.

Polycarp's sanctity and fame are amply attested not only by the account of his martyrdom, but by Ignatius (see February 1) and Irenaeus (see June 28), the latter of whom was his disciple and protege. According to Irenaeus, Polycarp was a pupil of John, the disciple of the Lord, and was appointed a Bishop by "apostles in Asia." A letter of Polycarp is extant, addressed To the Philippians; this letter, with the Martyrdom, are included in all modern editions of "The Apostolic Fathers."

27. JOHN CHRYSOSTOM, *Bishop of Constantinople,* 407

Born in Antioch, ca. 350; ordained Deacon, 381, and Priest, 386; consecrated Bishop of Constantinople, 398; sent into exile, 404, and died, from harsh treatment, Sept. 14, 407. The date of January 27 marks the day, in the year 438, when Chrysostom's remains were brought back to Constantinople and buried in the Church of the Holy Apostles. It is this date that was taken up in the Roman Martyrology and Calendar, since September 14 (Holy Cross Day) was already a major feast of the Church. All the modern Anglican Calendars adopt this date.

John, popularly called Chrysostom ("the Mouth of Gold"), is one of the greatest Fathers of the Church. He is commonly reputed to be the most eminent preacher in the whole history of the Church. In addition to his sermons, his exegetical works still rank among the finest commentaries on Holy Scripture ever produced. They are still useful to modern Biblical study, since Chrysostom was a literal, rather than an allegorical interpreter. His theological and pastoral works, including his best-known book, On the Priesthood, are with his sermons and commentaries distinguished for the clarity and correctness of his orthodox faith, the intense moral earnestness that consumed his energy, and the rhetorical grace of his style. The rectitude of his personal life, rigorous in its ascetic discipline, and the fire of his eloquence brought him a tremendous popular following. But it was his tragedy to have been placed in turbulent times in the administration of one of the largest and most important sees of Christendom, an office to which he was unsuited by training and temperament. His unsparing criticism of luxury and laxity in high places, and his naiveté in ecclesiastical politics led to his undoing, through the machinations of the imperial court and his unscrupulous episcopal rival, Theophilus of Alexandria. In popular estimation, Chrysostom died a martyr. It is to the credit of the Western Church that it never accepted the formal deposition of Chrysostom, and held firm his memory in reverence until the imperial court gave way and allowed his mortal remains to be buried in honor and his name restored in the prayers of the Church.

February

1. IGNATIUS, *Bishop of Antioch, and Martyr, ca. 115*

The martyrdom of Ignatius at Rome took place, according to Eusebius in the reign of Trajan (98-117). The later Acts of his martyrdom are legendary and utterly untrustworthy. But there survives the priceless collection of seven letters written by the Bishop-Martyr during his dolorous journey from Antioch to Rome, as a prisoner awaiting death for his faith in the amphitheatre. The Syrian Martyrology commemorates him on October 17. The Roman Martyrology and Calendar place his death on February 1; the translation of his body to Antioch, on December 17. The medieval English Calendars do not contain the memorial. All of the modern Anglican Calendars list him on December 17, except the Canadian Book of 1922, which adopts the present date. The Canadian Draft Book, however, has moved the date to December 17. Our Commission proposes to keep the February date, not only because it is in line with Western observance, but because there is greater historical evidence for the martyrdom than for the translation.

Ignatius' letters are contained in the collection known as "The Apostolic Fathers," and are contemporary with some of the later books of the New Testament. He is a link between the apostolic and post-apostolic ages. His letters are concerned in the main with two issues: the defense of the faith against those heretics who would deny the real humanity of our Lord, and his strong support of episcopal authority. His writing glows with an intense inner fire and mystic experience. It is a revelation, too, of the passionate devotion of the martyr to be united with the witness unto death of his Lord.

3. ANSGARIUS, *Archbishop of Hamburg, and Missionary to Denmark and Sweden, 865*

Born in 801, near the monastery of Corbie, where he was educated and professed as a monk, of Saxon parentage; later transferred to New Corvey, on the Weser River; first visit to Denmark, with King Harald, in 826, followed a few years later by a first visit to Sweden; consecrated Archbishop of Hamburg, 831, and appointed papal legate for the Danes, Swedes, and Slavs; in 848, made Bishop of Bremen also; died at Bremen, Feb. 3, 865.

It has been claimed that Ansgarius was canonized by Pope Nicholas I; but this cannot be substantiated, and there is no commemoration of him in the Roman Calendar. His successor and biographer speaks of him as being venerated as a saint, and there is evidence that for a period his "translation" was observed at Bremen on Sept. 9. He does not appear in medieval English Calendars. Ansgarius (Anglicized as Anskar) is listed in the English 1928, the South African, and the Canadian Draft Calendars.

Ansgarius is accounted by the Scandinavians as their "apostle," though he actually did little missionary work himself in Denmark and Sweden. His primary work was to lay the foundations for others, and particularly to train men for missionary work at his base sees in Germany. He did participate in the consecration of the first Bishop for Sweden. The disturbed political conditions in Scandinavia, no less than the ecclesiastical rivalries of sister sees in Germany did much to slacken the progress of his work. Like so much pioneering, the material results of his labors may seem small, but in spiritual fruits there is no means of measurement.

The relations between the English Church and the Churches of Scandinavia, especially the Church of Sweden, have always been cordial and intimate. In America, the two famous "Old Swedes" parishes in Wilmington, Delaware, and in Philadelphia have been for many years Episcopalian. The first Swedish parish of the Episcopal Church, founded in Chicago in 1848, was named St. Ansgarius. Its first rector, the Rev. Gustaf Unonius, was the first graduate of Nashotah House, and the first Swedish clergyman of the American Episcopal Church.

4. CORNELIUS, the Centurion

All that is known of Cornelius is contained in the Book of Acts, chapters 10-11. He was the first Gentile to be converted to the Christian faith. Even before his response to St. Peter's preaching and his baptism, "with all his house," he is described by the Evangelist as "a devout man, and one that feared God." In the fourth century, Christian tradition had made him the first Bishop of Caesarea in Palestine; and he appears in the Eastern Martyrology on September 2, in the Roman Martyrology on February 2. He is not listed in any medieval or Anglican Calendars. He was first proposed for this honor in the Calendar presented during the American revision of 1913-28. The date is based upon the Roman Martyrology, but transferred by two days because of the Purification, and the proposed addition of Ansgarius.

6. ST. TITUS

The status of Titus is much the same as that of Timothy (see January 24). All that is certainly known of his life and labors, as an assistant of St. Paul, is contained in the New Testament. The date is chosen from that assigned in the Roman Calendar. The Calendars of the Scottish and Indian Prayer Books place him on this day; but the South African, and the American proposals for the 1928 Book listed him on January 4.

15. THOMAS BRAY, *Priest and Missionary*, 1730

Born at Marton, Shropshire, and baptized on May 2, 1658; ordained in 1681; Rector of Sheldon, 1690-96; Commissary for the Bishop of London to Maryland, 1696-1703; Founder of the S.P.C.K., 1699, and of the S.P.G., 1701, and of "Dr. Bray's Associates for founding clerical libraries and supporting Negro schools," 1723; Rector of St. Botolph's, Aldgate, 1706-30; died in London, Feb. 15, 1730. This present Study is the first proposal of Thomas Bray's name for a Prayer Book Calendar.

Few men can claim so fruitful a ministry as Thomas Bray. He was an indefatigable worker for the improvement of learning among the clergy, for humanitarian projects of all kinds, and for the awakening of the Church of England to its missionary responsibilities. At the same time he was a faithful pastor and a man of exemplary devotion. Though he only spent two and a half months in Maryland during the period when he held the position of Commissary for the Bishop of London, his visitation was remarkably effective — including the establishment of the Church in the colony. The other years of his Commissariat were given over to the larger ventures of founding the two Societies that are his lasting monument. Both the S.P.C.K., through its publications, and the S.P.G., through its missionary endeavors, have kept the highest standards of learning and zeal before the Church, and have been a blessing to the entire Anglican Communion.

27. GEORGE HERBERT, *Priest*, 1633

Born at Montgomery Castle, April 3, 1593; prebend of Leighton Bromswold, Hunts, 1626-30; Rector of Fugglestone with Bemerton, near Salisbury, 1630-33. The South African and Canadian Draft Calendars contain his commemoration.

The saintly life of George Herbert is written in every line of his prose manual, *A Priest to the Temple, or The Country Parson, His Character, and Rule of Life*, and in his collection of religious poems, *The Temple*. Both works were published many years after his untimely death. They are not only classics of devotion, they are classics of English literature. Several of his poems have found their way into the Hymnals of the Church, notably, "Let all the world in every corner sing," and "Teach me, my God and King." A magnificent testimony to Herbert's life and ministry is recorded in the biography of him written by Isaak Walton, and published in 1670, where it is told how many of his parishioners, at the daily sound of the church bell, "let their plough rest when Mr. Herbert's saints-bell rung to prayers, that they might also offer their devotions to God with him."

March

1. DAVID, Bishop of Menevia, Wales, ca. 544

Born in Wales; abbot-bishop of Menevia, later the see of the Welsh diocese named for him; died, ca. 544 (some authorities place it in 601).

The only Welsh saint canonized by the papacy, David is listed in the Sarum Calendar, and in all modern Anglican Calendars. He is commonly called the "Patron of Wales." Nearly all that is known of David (Welsh, Dewi) is contained in a Life, written about 1090, by a Bishop of St. David's named Ricemarchus. Its traditions are good, but mixed with legends in the interest of the see of St. David's. David's life was typical of the best traditions of Celtic Christianity. Besides laying the foundations of much of the spread of Christianity in Wales, David was also sought out as a teacher by many Irish scholars and saints. He was not a diocesan in the later sense, but an abbot of a monastery, who also had episcopal orders. His tomb is in the choir of the present cathedral at St. David's.

7. PERPETUA AND HER COMPANIONS, Martyrs of Carthage, 202

Perpetua was a matron of twenty-two years, who with her slave Felicitas, and three catechumens, was martyred at Carthage. They were among the earliest martyrs to receive a cultus in the Western Church, and their date of martyrdom appears in all Western Calendars.

The Acts of their martyrdom, based upon a diary of Perpetua, is one of the most primitive monuments of Latin Christian literature. Many attribute the work to the Church Father Tertullian. It ranks with the *Martyrdom of Polycarp* as a moving and edifying, eye-witness story of the sufferings of these valiant Christians for their faith. Of especial interest are the visions of Perpetua, which she had during her time in prison; they introduce us into the heart of early Christian devotion and piety.

8. THOMAS AQUINAS, Friar, 1274

Born near Aquino, southern Italy, 1225; admitted to the Dominican Order of Preachers, 1244; taught in Paris, Rome, and Naples; died at the monastery of

Fossanuova, near Terracina, March 7, 1274; canonized by Pope John XXII, 1323. Listed in the Scottish, South African, and Indian Calendars.

Thomas Aquinas ranks with Augustine of Hippo in pre-eminence among the theologians and apologists of the Western Church, and, like Augustine, he is today one of the major influences in theological thought and discussion. Accounted a bold and daring thinker in his own generation, and suspected by his Franciscan rivals of unorthodoxy, Thomas's *Summae* actually saved Christian doctrine from the corroding effects of pagan philosophy so popular among the schoolmen of his time. His intellectual genius, in which critical reason is the handmaid of faith, was matched by the purity of his inner spirit and the humble devotion of his heart. He sought truth with a passion rarely equalled and never excelled. His deep piety may be judged from the propers which he composed for the Feast of Corpus Christi in 1263. Several of his Eucharistic hymns, taken from these propers (such as "O Saving Victim," and "Now my tongue the mystery telling"), are among the best known and beloved ones of the Hymnal.

12. GREGORY THE GREAT, *Bishop of Rome, 604*

Born in Rome, ca. 540; Prefect of the city, 573; founder, in his home, of the Benedictine monastery of St. Andrew, 574; papal ambassador to Constantinople, 579-85; Bishop of Rome, 590-604; founder and organizer of the mission to the English people, 596. The Council of the English Church held at Clovesho, held in 746, decreed his festival to be observed throughout England as a holy day of obligation. He is commemorated in all Western Calendars.

The Venerable Bede calls Pope Gregory the "apostle" of the English people, a title justly deserved. This alone would qualify him for continual remembrance by all churchmen who owe their faith to the tradition of English Christianity. But Gregory was a statesman and bulwark of the whole Western Church at one of the most critical times in its history. His writings, though unoriginal in thought, were principal textbooks of the faith in the Middle Ages, and his *Pastoral Care* still ranks among the finest works on the Christian Ministry. He was the definitive organizer of the Roman liturgy, and much of the structure of our Prayer Book — its seasons and days, its collects and lessons — are directly derived from his liturgical work. He has therefore had a larger part in molding the liturgical piety of the Church than any other single person. Through his efforts also, the magnificent corpus of liturgical plainchant was organized and handed on to the Church. He was the humblest of men, and exercised the authority of his great office, never for self-seeking, but always for the good of the Church and the cause of genuine religion. His life was a true witness to the title he assumed for his exalted office: "Servant of the Servants of God."

17. PATRICK, Bishop and Missionary of Ireland, 461

Born in an unknown town of Roman Britain, ca. 385; consecrated a missionary Bishop for Ireland, 432; died at Saul, in Ulster, March 17, 461. He is commemorated in the Sarum Calendar and in all modern Anglican Calendars. By common acclaim he is the "Apostle and Patron of Ireland."

The spirit of missionary and pastoral devotion that consumed Patrick's life can best be judged from the two writings of his that have providentially come down to us, his *Confession* and the *Letter to Coroticus*. Captured as a youth of sixteen, he served for six years as a slave in Ireland, during which time he appears to have undergone a conversion experience. Later restored to his family and friends, Patrick received a call to return to the land of his bondage as a missionary. After long years of preparation, enduring several heartbreaking disappointments, he was at long last sent forth on his mission. His work laid the foundations of Christianity in Ireland, though he was constantly beset by physical danger and harried by unfair criticism. His life story is one of the most heroic in the annals of Christian missions; and the passionate devotion of the Irish people to his memory is every whit deserved. The stirring *Lorica*, or Breastplate ("I bind unto myself today ") cannot be certainly ascribed to Patrick, but it expresses no less the faith and devotion of the man and the ancient Church that he brought into being in Ireland.

19. ST. JOSEPH

No defense is needed for the devotion of the Church to the memory of our Lord's foster-father. Only in modern times, however, has his feast become prominent in the Western Church. All the modern English Calendars list this date (from the Roman Calendar), with the exception of the English Book of 1928.

20. THOMAS KEN, Bishop of Bath and Wells, 1711

Born at Little Berkhampstead, Berks, in July, 1637; prebendary of Winchester, 1669-79; chaplain to Princess Mary (later Queen), 1679-80; Bishop of Bath and Wells, 1685-91; deprived of his see, with other "Non-Jurors," for his refusal to take the oath to William and Mary; declined restoration to his see, offered by Queen Anne in 1703, but later reconciled from the Non-Juring schism; died at Longleat, March 19, 1711. The South African and Canadian Draft Calendars list his name on the 19th; but the present Study proposes the 20th, to avoid concurrence with St. Joseph.

Bishop Ken is best known for his morning and evening hymns, and the famous Doxology, "Praise God from whom all blessings flow." These were written for his scholars at Winchester College, along with his *Manual of Prayers*. A man of pure life and self-effacing manners, Ken was also possessed of unusual courage. He did not flinch from showing his displeasure of sin in high places, and though a severe critic of King Charles II's morals, he did not disdain to attend him on his deathbed. Ken never went against his conscience, and this quality brought about his involvement in the Non-Juring schism. But it was with great reluctance that he consented to assist in the perpetuation of the episcopate among the Non-Jurors; and in later years he did all he could to heal the tragic division.

23. GREGORY, *The Illuminator, Bishop and Missionary in Armenia, ca. 332*

Born ca. 257; consecrated *Catholicos* of Armenia, ca. 300. He is commemorated by the Armenian Church on March 23rd, by the Greek Church on September 9th, by the Latin Church on October 1st. The present Study is the first proposal of his name on an Anglican Calendar.

Gregory's life, and the story of the conversion of Armenia in the time of King Tiridates, is known to us from a contemporary named Agathangelos, who was secretary to the king. The murder of Tiridates' father by Gregory's father was the occasion of vengeance upon Gregory's family. Only Gregory, as a small infant, was saved. He was brought up as a Christian in Caesarea (of Cappadocia); but returned to his native land in the 280's. Apprehended by Tiridates, he was imprisoned and subjected to tortures for over ten years; he succeeded ultimately, however, in converting the king and laying the foundations for the evangelization of the country. He was consecrated in Caesarea about 300 as the first Bishop or *Catholicos* of the Armenian Church. The last few years of his life were spent in retirement, after he had consecrated his son as his successor. There is no record of Gregory having attended the Council of Nicaea in 325, and some authorities believe he had died before the Council met. The dates of his life are very uncertain. Gregory is accounted the "Apostle" of Armenia, and, through his mission work, Armenia became the first nation to embrace Christianity as its national religion. The close friendship of the Episcopal Church with the Armenian Church in the United States makes this commemoration of the Armenian "Apostle" a bond of fellowship between the two Churches.

29. JOHN KEBLE, *Priest, 1866*

Born at Fairford, Glos, April 25, 1792; ordained Deacon, 1815, Priest, 1816; professor of Poetry, Oxford, 1831-41; Vicar of Hursley, near Winchester, 1836-66; died at Bournemouth, Mar. 29, 1866. Keble is commemorated in the South African and Canadian Draft Calendars.

Cardinal Newman called Keble "the true and primary author of the Oxford Movement"; and the inception of this revival in the Church is generally dated from Keble's Assize Sermon, preached at Oxford, July 14, 1833, entitled "National Apostasy." He was already famous for his volume of religious poetry, *The Christian Year*, published in 1827, one of the classics of English devotional verse, several of which poems have become popular hymns. The College which bears his name at Oxford was opened in 1870. In the bitter controversies that surrounded his work, Keble never gave in to bitterness or to cant. He had a childlike freshness and simplicity about him, and a sense of naturalness in his religious devotion and love of his Lord. He was particularly gifted as a spiritual counsellor and confessor, as may be seen in his *Letters of Spiritual Counsel*, published after his death. Despite many rebuffs and reproaches from his ecclesiastical superiors, Keble remained loyal to the English Church and never wavered in his conviction of its inherent catholicity.

April

2. JOHN FREDERICK DENISON MAURICE, *Priest, 1872*

Born at Normanston, Suffolk, Aug. 29, 1805; ordained, 2834; professor of English Literature, 1840-53, and of Theology, 1846-53, King's College; founder and first principal of the Working Men's College, 1854; rector, St. Peter's, Vere Street, 1860-69; professor of Moral Philosophy, Cambridge, 1866-72; rector of St. Edward's, Cambridge, 1870-72; died at Cambridge, April 1, 2872. The present Study is the first proposal of Maurice's name for a place in the Calendar.

Maurice's thought and work is still a keenly felt influence in the whole of the Anglican Communion. All parties of churchmanship claim him; but he cannot be easily classified, as his influence did much to liberalize the Oxford Movement and to give orthodox direction to the Church's liberal theologians. Of his many books, *The Kingdom of Christ* (1837) is perhaps his best known, and the key to his theological position. It is a classic defense of Anglicanism. But his *Theological Essays* (1853) were considered so "liberal" at the time that he was dismissed from his professorship at King's College. Maurice was also a pioneer, with Charles Kingsley, in the application of the gospel to social problems, and he did valiant service in awakening the Church of England to concern for the material and spiritual well-being of the working classes. His work had a particularly profound impact upon the American Church, especially upon William Augustus Muhlenberg (see April 8). In later years of his life, friend and foe alike honored him for the beauty of his character, the passionate and singleminded devotion of his ministry to truth, and the wide reach of his charity. The Anglican Communion will never be the same because of the witness of this man.

4. AMBROSE, *Bishop of Milan, 397*

Born in Rome, 339, of a distinguished family both in Church and State; elected Bishop of Milan by acclamation, 373, though as yet unbaptized, and at the time serving as governor of Aemilia-Liguria, and consecrated on December 7; died at Milan on Easter Even, April 4, 397. Ambrose, accounted one of the greatest

Fathers of the Church, is commemorated in all Latin Calendars, and in all Anglican Prayer Books.

The inclusion of Ambrose in the Calendar needs no defense. An intrepid defender of the faith and moral standards of the Church, a primary theological teacher of the Western Church, a preacher of pre-eminence and a devoted pastor of souls, the full weight of Ambrose's many titles to remembrance is inestimable. Not least was his contribution to the worship of the Church, through his introduction of antiphonal psalmody in the Western liturgy and his noble hymns. His preaching was an important factor in the conversion of St. Augustine, whom Ambrose baptized in Milan in 387.

6. WILLIAM LAW, Priest, 1761

Born at King's Cliffe, Northamptonshire, 1686; ordained, 1711; became a Non-Juror, for refusal to take oath to George I, 1714; tutor in the household of Edward Gibbon, father of the historian, 1727-37; retired to his native village, 1740, where he died, April 6, 1761. The South African Calendar includes his name.

William Law was an astute controversialist against the leading spirits of the Deistic philosophy of his time. But he is chiefly remembered for his mystical and devotional writings, notably the *Serious Call to a Devout and Holy Life* (1728), which have a place among the finest classics of devotion. Though often accounted a "high churchman" for his vigorous defense of Anglican principles, Law had great influence upon the leaders of the evangelical revival, notably the Wesley brothers. Even the caustic historian, Gibbon, praised his writing and his character. During the years of his retirement, Law was also active in founding schools and almshouses. His personal life was one of utmost simplicity and ascetic discipline. Though a Non-Juror for conscience' sake, Law was not a fomentor of schism; it is not certain that he ever officiated in church services after becoming a Non-Juror. The passage of time has not dulled the continuing spiritual effect of his example of life and the deep piety of his writings.

8. WILLIAM AUGUSTUS MUHLENBERG, Priest, 1877

Born in Philadelphia, Sept. 16, 1796; ordained, 1817, by Bishop White, under whom he served as curate until 1820; Rector of St. James' Church, Lancaster, Pa., 1820-26; Rector of St. George's, Flushing, N.Y., 1827, and founder of the Flushing Institute, 1828, later called St. Paul's College; Rector of the Church of the Holy Communion, New York City, 1846-60; founder of St. Luke's Hospital, New York City, 1850, and of the Sisterhood of the Holy Communion, 1852; founder of the community of St. Johnland, Long Island, 1866; died in New York City, April 8, 1877. This is the first proposal of his name for the Church's Calendar.

The ministry of Dr. Muhlenberg marked a turning point in the history of the Episcopal Church. A pioneer and innovator in Christian education, liturgy, humanitarian work, and pastoral care, Muhlenberg gave a magnificent vision to the Church of how it might truly minister to all sorts and conditions of men. He was greatly influenced by F. D. Maurice (see April 1), and called himself, with considerable appropriateness, an "Evangelical Catholic." Like Maurice, all parties in the Church claim him, but as he belonged to none, he influenced them all. Out of his ministry came the inspiration for the establishment of Church schools and hospitals, for a greater flexibility and enrichment of the Church's worship, leading ultimately to Prayer Book revision, and for a greater concern for the unity of the Church and the Church's ministry to working men. There was not a significant area of the Church's life, during his ministry, that he did not elevate and strengthen by the pureness of his life and the vigor of his consecrated imagination. Many account him the greatest "saint" in the history of the Episcopal Church in the United States.

11. LEO THE GREAT, *Bishop of Rome*, 461

Born, probably at Volterra, near the close of the fourth century; ordained Deacon at Rome, before 429; unanimously elected Bishop of Rome, and consecrated, Sept. 29, 440; died at Rome, Nov. to, 461, and buried in St. Peter's Basilica. The date of April 11 occurs in ancient martyrologies, and found its way into the Roman Calendar; it may commemorate the day of translation of his remains in 688, though this is also ascribed to June 28, the date of commemoration in the Sarum Calendar. All the modern Anglican Calendars adopt April 11, except the Canadian, 1922, which omits his name altogether.

Leo is one of two popes whom popular tradition has called "the Great." His personal influence has been credited with saving Italy from devastation by the Huns. But his chief fame rests in his decisive defense of the orthodox doctrine of the Person of Christ, written in his famous *Tome* and confirmed by the ecumenical Council of Chalcedon in 451. His sermons and letters are our principal sources for the measure of the man, as a pastor, teacher, and administrator. His pontificate is a model to all who have come after him for devotion to duty, indomitable courage, and unswerving honesty and rectitude.

12. GEORGE AUGUSTUS SELWYN, *Bishop of New Zealand*, 1878

Born at Hampstead, London, April 5, 1809; ordained, 1833; consecrated first Bishop of New Zealand, Oct. 27, 1841; translated to the see of Lichfield, England, 1867; died, April, 1878. Selwyn College, Cambridge, founded 1882, is named for him. The South African Calendar commemorates him on the 11th; the date is here transferred, to avoid the date assigned to Leo.

Selwyn's name ranks high among the great missionaries of the nineteenth century, for he laid the foundations of the Church not only in New Zealand, but in Melanesia. The martyr Patteson (see September 20) was among his disciples and helpers. It was with great reluctance that Selwyn, under pressure from the Prime Minister and Queen Victoria, left his work in New Zealand to accept the see of Lichfield. His grave in the cathedral close of Lichfield has ever been a place of pilgrimage for the Maoris, to whom he first brought the light of the gospel. His courage was matched only by his devotion to duty. During the tragic war of ten years between the English and the native Maoris in New Zealand, Selwyn was able to minister to both sides, and to keep the affection and admiration of colonists and natives. He twice visited the Church in America, where he was honored as a true hero of Christ.

14. JUSTIN, *Martyr at Rome, ca. 167*

A native of Samaria, in Palestine, converted to Christianity in Ephesus, Justin came to Rome sometime before 150, where he opened a school for the propagation of Christianity. He was martyred during the prefecture of Junius Rusticus (163-67). The Roman Calendar observes Justin's memory on this date, as do the South African and Indian Calendars. The Scottish Book places him on April 13; the Canadian on June 1 (the date in the Eastern Church's Calendar). The *Acts* of Justin's martyrdom, with that of several of his pupils, is authentic, but gives no clear indication of a date.

Justin's apologetic writings for the Christian faith, though not the first of their kind, were among the most influential upon later Christian theology. Though not an original thinker, he laid out the lines upon which later Catholic theology was to develop. The story of his life and conversion is given in his own words in his *Dialogue*, an apologetic work against Judaism. The *Acts* of his martyrdom testify to his character, to his effectiveness as a teacher and his devotion as a friend.

21. ANSELM, *Archbishop of Canterbury, 1109*

Born in Aosta, *ca.* 1033; took vows as Benedictine monk at Bec, Normandy, 1060, and made prior, 1063; invested as Archbishop of Canterbury, 1093, succeeding his former prior at Bec, Lanfranc; died, April 21, 1109; canonized by the pope, 1494. Though canonized too late to appear in the Sarum Calendar, Anselm's name appears in all the modern Anglican Calendars.

Anselm is chiefly remembered for his theological writings, which mark him out as one of the first and ablest of the scholastic theologians. Throughout his writing, however, there breathes a deep piety. His subtle reasonings for the faith were the fruit of prayer. As archbishop, his life was stormy and in constant conflict with King William Rufus. He has been charged with being an overly ardent papalist, and therefore a champion of Romish tyranny over the Church in

England. But such a judgment is anachronistic. Anselm's appeals to papal support were designed to free the Church from excessive interference from the Crown. In his later years he lived on good terms with King Henry I, and showed himself a true man of peace and reconciliation to his former enemies.

May

2. ATHANASIUS, *Bishop of Alexandria, 373*

Born in Alexandria, ca. 293; ordained Deacon, ca. 320; consecrated Bishop of Alexandria, June 8, 328; died at Alexandria, May 2, 373. This date is observed in the Roman Calendar, and in all the modern Anglican Calendars.

The militant champion of the Nicene faith, Athanasius is the outstanding figure of the Church's history in the fourth century. Five times sent into exile by Roman emperors, he never lost heart or gave up the fight against the Arian heresy that would have destroyed the Christian religion as a revelation of God in the Person of Jesus Christ. His theological writings are of the greatest significance, and still remain the clearest, as they are the most forceful, expositions of the doctrine of the Godhead. Athanasius was also a devoted bishop to his flock, and a warm supporter of the monastic movement.

4. MONNICA, *Mother of Saint Augustine, 387*

Born in North Africa, ca. 331; died at Ostia, May 4, 387. The original tomb of Monnica has recently been found in the excavations at Ostia; but her remains were transferred to the Church of St. Augustine in Rome in 1430. The Roman Calendar commemorates her on May 4, as do all the modern Anglican Calendars, except the Canadian, 1922.

The story of this consecrated Christian wife and mother is forever enshrined in the pages of St. Augustine's *Confessions* above all the matchless mystic experience which the saint shared with his mother shortly before her death. In Augustine's pages, we are enabled, too, to trace her spiritual growth. In her earlier years she was not without worldly ambitions and tastes. But the passionate devotion of the woman to the conversion of her family, and her ever-deepening life of prayer, gradually effaced from her spirit all self-regarding concern.

6. JOHN OF DAMASCUS, *Priest. ca. 760*

Born at Damascus, date unknown; monk and priest of monastery of St. Sabas near Jerusalem, before 726; died ca. 760, or somewhat earlier. The Greek Church commemorates him on December 4. The Roman Martyrology places his death on May 6. In 1890, Pope Leo XIII placed his feast on March 27. He does not appear in any Anglican Calendars.

John of Damascus was the last "Father" of the Eastern Church. His theological writings are generally accounted as definitive expositions of the faith by Orthodox Christians. The Seventh, and last, of the Ecumenical Councils, 787, venerated his memory, in particular his great witness to orthodoxy in the iconoclastic controversy. Five of his hymns are in the Hymnal 1940, of which the most popular is the Easter hymn, "Come, ye faithful, raise the strain." He is credited with having done much for the organization of the chants in the Eastern liturgy.

9. GREGORY OF NAZIANZUS, *Bishop of Constantinople, 389*

Born near Nazianzus, a village of Cappadocia, ca. 329; baptized ca. 357, and ordained Priest, ca. 363; consecrated Bishop of Sasima, 372, but never officiated in the see; made Bishop of Constantinople, 380, but retired shortly after the Second Ecumenical Council, held in Constantinople in 381; died in his native place in 389 or 390. The Greek Church commemorates him on January 25, the Latin Church on May 9. His name is listed in the Canadian, Scottish, and South African Calendars.

Gregory is called by the Greeks "the Theologian," and is accounted one of the chief orthodox Fathers of the Church. His name and work are closely associated with two other "Cappadocian Fathers," Basil of Caesarea (see June 14) and Gregory of Nyssa. To these three men, after Athanasius (see May 2), is given credit for the triumph of the Nicene faith in the Church against the Arian heresy. Gregory was also one of the ablest preachers in a generation of great pulpit orators. Most notable are his five *Theological Orations*, as they are called, on the Trinity. His heart was in the ascetic life, however, and it was with great diffidence that he was drawn into episcopal duties most of which were spent as assistant to his father, who was Bishop of Nazianzus. He had no taste for the ecclesiastical politics that were a passion of the age, and retired from the great see of Constantinople rather than be an object of contention over his right to this position of eminence.

11. CYRIL AND METHODIUS, *Missionary Bishops to the Slavs, 869, 885*

Cyril, also named Constantine, was born in Thessalonica, 827; became professor of philosophy at Constantinople, ca. 850, and shortly afterwards professed the monastic life; sent to the Khazars, a Tatar people northeast of the Black Sea, ca. 860; sent with his brother Methodius to evangelize Moravia, 863; ordained at Rome by Pope Hadrian II, but died there, February 14, 869.

Methodius, older brother of Cyril, after a distinguished secular career, embraced monasticism; sent with Cyril to Moravia, 863; consecrated Archbishop of Sirmium by Pope Hadrian II, 869; died at Hardisch, April 6, 885. The Greek Church commemorates Cyril on February 14, and Methodius on May 11. The Roman Church canonized them in 1881 and observes their memory on March 9.

The Canadian Draft Book of 1955 has introduced their commemoration. It was first proposed in the American Church for the 1928 Book.

Popularly known as the "Apostles of the Slavs," these two Greek monks laid foundations for the Church in the Balkans through their translations of the Gospels and the liturgy into Slavonic. Indeed, Cyril was the inventor of the old Slavonic alphabet. Their work was greatly hindered by the ecclesiastical rivalries between the sees of Rome and Constantinople for control of the new churches arising among the Slavs, and also by the jealousy of the German bishops, who likewise desired to extend their jurisdiction into the newly Christianized areas. Neither Cyril nor Methodius were partisans, and took whatever help they could for their work from East or West indifferently, though they valiantly defended their "vernacular" liturgy against the attempts of the Roman see to Latinize the Slavic churches. Methodius suffered much persecution from the German bishops, and only the support of the pope prevented the complete collapse of his missionary efforts.

19. DUNSTAN, *Archbishop of Canterbury*, 988

Born in Wessex, ca. 909; became a monk at Glastonbury, ca. 936, and abbot, 943-56; in exile at St. Peter's, Ghent, 956-59; Bishop of Worcester and of London, 957 and 959; Archbishop of Canterbury, 960-88; died at Canterbury, May 19, 988. King Knut made his feast obligatory in England. Dunstan's name is on all medieval English and modern Anglican Calendars.

The Viking incursions in Britain in the early ninth century were disastrous to the political and spiritual stability of England. Only the heroic efforts of the little kingdom of Wessex succeeded in stemming the tide of destruction. Two revival movements were necessary to restore once more the healthy state of the Church in England. The first, under the leadership of King Alfred (see October 26), was concerned for the most part with the education of the parish clergy. The second, led by Dunstan and his friends Aethelwold of Winchester and Oswald of Worcester, revived Benedictine monasticism, with its fine tradition of Christian culture and learning. Their efforts made it possible for England to withstand the second wave of Viking invasions without such ill effects. Dunstan was, throughout his mature years, the leading spiritual leader of the English people. He was also an accomplished man of culture, in music and the arts.

20. ALCUIN, *Deacon, and Abbot of Tours*, 804

Born near York, ca. 730-35; ordained Deacon, ca. 770, and placed in charge of the school at York; made head of the Palace School of Charlemagne, 782; Abbot of Tours, 796-804; died at Tours, May 19, 804, and buried in the Church of St. Martin. He was never canonized, despite his great reputation of character and learning. This is the first proposal to place his name on the Calendar — transferred one day, so as not to concur with the commemoration of Dunstan.

Alcuin inherited by blood and training the finest traditions of the early English Church. He was a relative of Willibrord (see November 7), the missionary to the Netherlands, and a pupil of Archbishop Egbert, who had been a pupil of Bede (see May 27). Because of his eminence in learning, as well as his personal charm and character, Charlemagne made him virtually "Prime Minister" of his vast kingdom, with especial responsibility for the revival of education. More than any other single individual Alcuin is responsible for the preservation of the classical heritage of Western Christendom. He is also worthy of remembrance for his work in editing the Latin service books brought by Charlemagne from Rome for use throughout his dominions. After Gregory the Great, Alcuin is the chief architect of the liturgy of the West.

24. JACKSON KEMPER, *First Missionary Bishop in the United States, 1870*

Born in Pleasant Valley, N.Y., Dec. 24, 1789; ordained Deacon, 1811, and Priest, 1814, by Bishop White of Pennsylvania, and assistant to the Bishop at Christ Church, Philadelphia, 181131; Rector of St. Paul's Church, Norwalk, Conn., 1831-35; consecrated first missionary Bishop of the American Church, with assignment to Missouri and Indiana, Sept. 25, 1835; in addition to these two states, Kemper laid the foundations of the Church in Iowa, Wisconsin, Minnesota, Nebraska, and Kansas; he also made extensive missionary tours in the South and Southwest; Bishop of Wisconsin, 1859-70; one of founders of Nashotah House, 1842; died at Delafield, Wis., May 24, 1870.

Though Bishop Philander Chase did valiant pioneer work in establishing the dioceses of Ohio and Illinois, it is Bishop Kemper who deserves the major credit for the foundation work of the Episcopal Church in the dioceses that now comprise the Province of the Midwest. Kemper's missionary enthusiasm was a life-time passion. It was under his inspiration, for example, that the aged Bishop White was induced to make his first (and only) visitation of western Pennsylvania. While serving under White, Kemper was active in founding the Episcopal Missionary Society of Philadelphia. It was Kemper who won James Lloyd Breck and his companions to come west and help him found Nashotah House — and later, the Seabury Divinity School at Faribault, Minnesota. Kemper was the first Bishop sent out by the American Church as a whole, organized at the General Convention of 1835 as the Domestic and Foreign Missionary Society of the Protestant Episcopal Church.

26. AUGUSTINE, First Archbishop of Canterbury, 605

Benedictine prior of St. Andrew's monastery, Rome, when sent by Pope Gregory the Great to head mission to the English people, 596; consecrated Archbishop of Canterbury, Nov., 597, in Arles; died May 26, 605, and buried in Cathedral Church of SS. Peter and Paul, Canterbury. Canonized by English Council of Clovesho, 746, Augustine appears in all medieval English and modern Anglican Calendars.

All that is known of Augustine's labors to establish Christianity among the English people is contained in the *Ecclesiastical History* of Bede (see May 27). Though not an imaginative man, Augustine performed his assigned task — and by no means an easy one — faithfully and devotedly. With the advice, encouragement and support of Pope Gregory (see March 12), Augustine laid firm foundations for the Church in England, despite temporary set-backs, and such discouragement that at one time he came near to abandoning the venture altogether.

27. BEDE, THE VENERABLE, Priest, and Monk of Jarrow, 735

Born near Jarrow, 673; at age of seven became a member of the monastic community of Jarrow, and remained so until his death on the Eve of the Ascension, May 25, 735; about 1020 his remains were taken to Durham, and buried in the Galilee of the Cathedral. His cult was popular in the north of England during the Middle Ages, on May 27, and this date became fixed in the Prayer Book of 1661. In 1899, Pope Leo XIII proclaimed his cult throughout the Roman Church. All modern Anglican Calendars include his name. The title "Venerable" was popularly given for his sanctity.

Bede was the greatest scholar of the early English Church, and his writings were primary texts throughout the Middle Ages. His *Ecclesiastical History* still ranks among the finest works of historical scholarship ever written. He was an exemplary monk, an ardent churchman, zealous for the good of religion, and a man of unusually pure and winsome character.

June

2. THE MARTYRS OF LYONS, 177

The *Acts* of the martyrs of Lyons is preserved in Eusebius' *Church History*, Book V, Chapters 1-3. It is the oldest testimony of Christianity in Gaul, and one of the most moving witnesses to the faith of the early Christians. The South African Calendar contains this entry.

5. BONIFACE, Archbishop of Mainz, Missionary to Germany, Martyr, 754

Born in Devonshire, ca. 675, and named Winifrid; educated at Exeter and Nursling, near Winchester; professed a monk at Nursling, and ordained Priest; first missionary journey to Frisia, 716-17, and a second, 719-22; commissioned by Pope Gregory II for missionary work in Germany, and given name of Boniface, 719; missionary work in Germany, 723-54; made Archbishop, 732, with see at Mainz, 743; presided over reform councils of Frankish Church, 742, 744, 745; anointed Pepin, King of the Franks, 752; founded the monastery of Fulda, 744; resigned his see, 753, and returned to missionary work in Frisia; martyred at Dokkum, June 5, 754, while awaiting a group of converts to be confirmed. Boniface is honored in all medieval Latin Calendars, and in all modern Anglican Calendars.

The achievement of Boniface only becomes the more amazing in the perspective of the centuries. He laid the foundations of Christianity in Germany, reformed the Church in France and thereby prepared the way for the great revival under Pepin and Charlemagne of church life in western Europe, and brought back to Continental Christendom the rich culture of Anglo-Saxon Christianity. The German Church hails him as their "Apostle." The universal Church acclaims him as a martyr.

9. THE FIRST BOOK OF COMMON PRAYER, 1549

The first Prayer Book, prepared by a commission headed by Archbishop Thomas Cranmer, was authorized by Parliament in an Act of Uniformity, passed January 2i, 1549. It was ordered to come into exclusive use in the Church of England on Whitsunday, which was June 9. In the year 1949 the entire Anglican Communion observed the four hundredth anniversary of its liturgy by appropriate commemorations. The Commission recommends that this observance become an annual commemoration in the Church.

10. COLUMBA, Abbot of Iona, 597

Born in County Donegal, Ireland, ca. 521; educated and ordained Deacon at monastery of Moville, and ordained Priest at monastery of Glasnevin, near Dublin; founded monasteries of Derry and Durrow; left Ireland ca. 561, and founded the monastery of Iona, whence he carried on the evangelization of Scotland; died at Iona, June 9, 597. Columba is the Patron saint of Scotland. He is commemorated in all modern Anglican Calendars on the 9th. The present Study proposes transferring the date to the 10th, to avoid concurrence with the Prayer Book anniversary.

Columba's foundation at Iona is to the Scottish Church what Canterbury is to the English — its mother shrine. Yet Columba was already famous as a scholar and monastic founder in Ireland, and he was not the first to preach the gospel in Scotland. He is largely responsible, however, for the conversion of the Pictish peoples of the Highlands. An impressive man, physically and spiritually, and a stern ascetic, Columba was not without gentleness and sweetness. His courage was undaunting. From his monastery at Iona were to come many of the best missionaries to the English (see Aidan, August 31).

14. BASIL THE GREAT, *Bishop of Caesarea*, 379

Born at Caesarea in Cappadocia, 329; baptized, ca. 357, and ordained Deacon shortly thereafter; founded monastery at Annesi, Pontus, 358; ordained Priest, 364; Bishop of Caesarea in Cappadocia, 370-79; died, January 1, 379. The Eastern Churches commemorate him on January 1; the Latin Church, since the ninth century, observes his memory on June 14. He appears in the Sarum, and in the modern Anglican Calendars.

Basil has three principal claims to fame. With his friend, Gregory Nazianzen (see May 9), and his brother, Gregory of Nyssa, he led the later phases of the orthodox reaction against Arianism. Though he did not live to see the triumph of the Nicene faith at the Second Ecumenical Council of 381, his efforts and writings did much to bring this great victory of orthodoxy to fulfillment. Basil is also accounted the Father of Eastern monasticism. His rules and ascetical writings are still the primary sources for the organization and ideals of the Greek monks. In particular, Basil gave to monasticism a sense of responsibility for leadership in the Church's life, and because of this emphasis, it has become traditional in the Orthodox Churches to draw most of their episcopal leaders from the monasteries. Finally, Basil did much to develop the liturgical life of the Greek Church. It is now generally accepted that the Liturgy of St. Basil, still used in the Orthodox Church, is of his authorship. It may well have been taken to Constantinople and introduced there by Gregory Nazianzen.

16. JOSEPH BUTLER, *Bishop of Durham*, 1752

Born at Wantage, Berks, May 18, 1692; preacher at the Rolls Chapel, 1718-26; rector of Houghton-le-Skerne, 1722-25, and of Stanhope, 1725-40; prebend of Rochester, 1736-38; Bishop of Bristol, 1738-50, and of Durham, 1750-52; died, June 16, 1752. Butler's name is included in the Calendar of the Canadian Draft Book of 1955.

The fame of Bishop Butler rests on the *Fifteen Sermons* published in 1726 and *The Analogy of Religion* produced ten years later. They mark him out as the most distinguished theologian of the English Church in the eighteenth century and one of the great apologists of Christianity of any generation. He is credited with breaking the force of Deistic thought in England. His masterpiece is still accounted one of the most reasoned and convincing defenses of Christian faith and ethic. Though not a warm supporter of the Wesleyan revival, he was himself a man of deep personal piety, and his practices of devotion brought upon him a strange charge of being a crypto-papist. His friend, Archbishop Secker of Canterbury, stoutly defended his reputation. The stature of Butler increases with the years. He stands out as a man of strong religion, both intellectually and spiritually, in an age marked by much arid rationalism. In ways quite different from the Wesleys, he contributed much to the restoration of a sound faith and piety in English religion.

18. EPHREM OF EDESSA, *Syria, Deacon, 373*

Born ca. 306, probably at Nisibis, and ordained Deacon there before 338; left Nisibis for Edessa in 363, where he became head of the "School of the Persians"; died, June 18 or 19, 373. The Syrians commemorate him on January 28; the Roman Martyrology, on February 1. In 1920, the Roman Church gave him the rank of "Doctor of the Church." He does not appear on any of the Anglican Calendars of other provinces.

Ephrem Syrus has always been accounted one of the chief Fathers of the Syrian Church, but he has not received until recently the honor due him by Western Christians. Yet his commentaries, homilies, and especially his hymns, marked him out as one of the great defenders of Nicene orthodoxy as well as a Christian of great holiness and beauty of life. Many of his hymns and selections from his sermons found a place in the liturgy of the Syrian Church.

22. ALBAN, *First Martyr of Britain, ca. 304*

The story of the martyrdom of St. Alban and his companions, preserved in Bede's *Ecclesiastical History* I, 7, is the earliest authentic document of the history of Christianity in Britain. Bede dates the martyrdom in the reign of Diocletian; but some modern scholars believe it to have happened, with greater probability, in the reign of Decius, A.D. 250-51. The present city and see of St. Albans is located slightly to the northeast of Verulamium, the Roman city where St. Alban's martyrdom took place. Devotion to St. Alban's memory has always been constant in English Christianity. His name appears in the Sarum and in all Prayer Book Calendars, and is popular in church dedications throughout the Anglican Communion.

28. IRENAEUS, *Bishop of Lyons, ca. 202*

A pupil of St. Polycarp (see January 26), Irenaeus was born and reared in Smyrna, but at an early age moved to Lyons in Gaul, after a possible period of study in Rome. After the persecution that broke out in the city in 177 (see The Martyrs of Lyons, June 2), he was selected Bishop of the see in succession to the aged

Pothinus, who had died in prison during the crisis. Irenaeus' fame rests in the main upon his great apologetic work, *Refutation of Knowledge Falsely So-Called*, commonly known as the *Against Heresies*. It was the most effective answer ever written against Gnosticism. But more than that, the work laid solid foundations for Catholic doctrine, both in the Eastern and Western Churches. There has also come to light in modern times a smaller work, *The Demonstration of Apostolic Preaching*, a brief summary of Christian teaching. Some of his letters are preserved in Eusebius' *Ecclesiastical History*. Irenaeus has always been accounted one of the most eminent Fathers of the Church. His sincere devotion to truth, his humble piety nurtured in all the Scriptures, and his missionary zeal, evident in every page that he wrote, make up for our lack of detailed information about his career. There is no authentic tradition that he died a martyr, but the Western martyrologies are the basis of fixing his commemoration on June 28. His name appears on this date in the Roman, though not in the Sarum, Calendar, and in the English 1928, Scottish, South African, Indian, and Canadian 1955 lists, and in the proposed calendar for the American 1928 Book.

July

2. THE VISITATION OF THE BLESSED VIRGIN MARY

This feast belongs to the "Christmas cycle" of festivals, coming in chronological succession to the Nativity of St. John the Baptist. Its basis is Luke 1:39-47. It was first instituted by Pope Urban VI in 1389, and within the next century found its way into the Sarum Calendar. It has appeared as a Black Letter Day in all Anglican Calendars, except the Irish and American, since Queen Elizabeth's Calendar of 1561. The propers of this feast bring into the Eucharistic lectionary the canticle *Magnificat*, in the same way that the Nativity of St. John Baptist includes the *Benedictus* and the Purification contains the *Nunc Dimittis*.

11. BENEDICT OF NURSIA, Abbot of Monte Cassino, ca. 540

The dates of Benedict's life can only be approximately determined: Born *ca.* 480 at Rome; founded monastery of Subiaco *ca.* 500; and of Monte Cassino, between 520 and 530, where he wrote the Rule; died after 540. The traditional day of his death is March 21, which is the date of commemoration in the Roman, Sarum, and modern Anglican Calendars. But he was also noted in medieval Calendars on July 11, the date of the translation of his relics to Fleury in 623. Archbishop Lanfranc of Canterbury favored the July date. The Commission also recommends this later date in order to avoid a frequent occurrence of the feast in Passiontide.

Though not the initiator, Benedict is the true Father of Western monasticism, since the constitution and customs of all Western monastic orders, both Roman and Anglican, have come to be founded upon his Rule. Our knowledge of

Benedict's saintly life is based mainly upon the biography contained in the second book of Pope Gregory the Great's *Dialogues*. The propriety of commemorating Benedict hardly needs to be argued, whether on the grounds of his own character or on the achievements of the great Order which he inspired and created. Most of the prominent leaders in the evangelization of England were Benedictine monks; see Gregory the Great (March 12), Augustine of Canterbury (May 26), Bede the Venerable (May 27). Other Benedictines in this proposed Calendar include: Anselm, Dunstan, Alcuin, Boniface, Bernard, Willibrord, and Hilda.

17. WILLIAM WHITE, *Bishop of Pennsylvania, 1836*

Born in Philadelphia, March 24, 1747; ordained Deacon, 1770, and Priest, 1772; assistant minister, 1772-79, and Rector, 1779-1836, of Christ Church and St. Peter's, Philadelphia; consecrated first Bishop of Pennsylvania, February 4, 1787; Presiding Bishop, 1795-1836; died in Philadelphia, July 17, 1836.

Bishop White was the primary constitutional architect of the American Church, and the wise overseer of its destiny during the first generation of its history as an independent, self-governing Church. Without his gifts of statesmanship and reconciling moderation it is hard to see how the American Church could have been launched so quickly and serenely after the American Revolution. His distinction in the Church was almost matched by his civic influence, both in his native city and in the nation. He was also a theologian of no mean ability. Among his proteges, in whose formation he had a large hand, were such leaders as Hobart, Kemper, and William Augustus Muhlenberg (all three of whom are listed in this proposed Calendar). To few men has the epithet "venerable" been more aptly applied than to William White.

22. SAINT MARY MAGDALENE

St. Mary Magdalene occurs in the Roman, Sarum, and all other Anglican Calendars. In the 1549 Prayer Book, her commemoration was a Red Letter Day. Though omitted from the 1552 Book, her name was restored as a Black Letter Day in Queen Elizabeth's Calendar of 1561. The English 1928, the South African, the Indian, and the Canadian 1955 Calendars have restored her festival to a Red Letter observance. Her place of honor rests chiefly upon the fact that she was a primary witness of our Lord's Resurrection.

26. THOMAS A KEMPIS, *Priest, 1471*

Born Thomas Hammerken, at Kempen in the Duchy of Cleves, ca. 1380; educated at Deventer, and received at the Augustinian convent of Mount St. Agnes, Zwolle, 1399, where he took his vows in 1407; ordained Priest, 1413, and made sub-prior, 1425; died July 25, 1471. Never canonized, Thomas a Kempis occurs on no church Calendar. This is the first proposal of his name for inclusion in the Prayer Book. The date is shifted from the 25th to the 26th of July to avoid concurrence with St. James' Day.[5]

The name of Thomas a Kempis is perhaps more widely known than that of any other Christian writer, for the *Imitation of Christ*, the devotional book upon which his fame rests, has been translated into more languages than any other book save the Holy Scriptures. In recent times his authorship of the *Imitation* has been questioned by many scholars, but without definitive success; and many who doubt that Thomas wrote much of the book admit that he was at least its compiler. Thomas wrote many other devotional and ascetical books and tracts, and he was also a noted copyist of manuscripts. But the *Imitation* alone is sufficient to establish his claim to remembrance. His saintliness is attested by the thousands, both Catholics and Protestants, who have found in his classic manual a treasured source of edification.

27. WILLIAM REED HUNTINGTON, Priest, 1909

Born at Lowell, Mass., September 20, 1838; ordained Deacon, October 1, 1861, and Priest, December 3, 1862; Rector of All Saints Church, Worcester, Mass., 1862-83, and of Grace Church, New York City, 1883-1909; died at Nahant, Mass., July 26, 1909. The date of the proposed commemoration is transferred one day, because of placing Thomas a Kempis on the 25th. His name does not occur in any previous Anglican Calendar.

Dr. Huntington shares with William Augustus Muhlenberg (see April 8) the honor of being one of the two most eminent presbyters in the history of the American Church. During his prime, Dr. Huntington was probably the most influential clergyman of the Church, and his leadership in the House of Deputies of thirteen consecutive General Conventions, from 1871 through 1907, left an enduring impress upon the larger life of the Church. Like Muhlenberg, Dr. Huntington belonged to no party in the Church; and though he was personally conservative in theological matters, he had a most profound understanding and vision of how truly a Catholic Church the Episcopal Church, with its comprehensiveness, might become in our national life. It should not be forgotten that Dr. Huntington was the original proponent of the Quadrilateral, which both the American House of Bishops and the Bishops of the entire Anglican Communion at the Lambeth Conference of 1888 adopted as a basis for negotiations with other Christian bodies in the interest of organic re-union. Dr. Huntington was also the primary instigator and guide of the American revision of the Prayer Book that culminated in 1892. Through this revision his ideals left a permanent mark upon the liturgical worship not only of the American Church but also of later revisions

---

[5]. The Commission wishes to express its gratitude to Professor Albert Hyma of the University of Michigan for his assistance in establishing the much-controverted date of Thomas' death. On all matters touching the history of the "New Devotion," Professor Hyma is an undisputed authority.

in other branches of Anglicanism. Another of his many notable services to the Church was his leadership in the revival of the Order of Deaconesses. Yet apart from these outstanding contributions to the larger life of the Church, Dr. Huntington's life and ministry would be worthy of remembrance for his example as a parish priest and pastor. Indeed, in all that he did and accomplished, his pastoral concern was always apparent and predominant.

29. WILLIAM WILBERFORCE, 1833

Born at Hull, August 24, 1759; member of the House of Commons, 1780-1825; died at London, July 29, 1833, and buried in Westminster Abbey. His name appears in the Calendar of the South African Book and the Canadian 1955 Draft Book.

The life of William Wilberforce is a stirring refutation of the all too common view that a politician cannot be a saintly Christian, dedicated solely to the service of his fellow men. Wilberforce's conversion to an evangelical Christian life occurred in 1784, several years after he had entered Parliament. Fortunately he was induced by friends not to abandon his political activities after this inward change in his life, but he steadfastly refused thereafter to accept office or a peerage. He gave himself unstintingly to the promotion of missions, popular education, and the reformation of public manners and morals. But above all, his fame rests upon his persistent, uncompromising, and single-minded crusade for the abolition of slavery. He died but one month before Parliament passed the Act that finally put an end to the sordid traffic. One of the last letters John Wesley ever wrote was addressed to Wilberforce, in which Wesley gave him his blessing in this noble enterprise. His eloquence as a speaker, his charm in personal address, and his profound religious spirit made him a formidable power for good. His countrymen came to recognize in him a greatness of heroic proportions.

August

4. DOMINIC, Friar, 1221

Born at Calaroga in Old Castile, 1170; Augustinian canon of the cathedral of Osma, 195; engaged in preaching in southern France, 1205-15; founder of the Order of Preachers, confirmed by bull of Pope Honorius III, December 22, 1216; died at Bologna, August 6, 1221 ; canonized in 1234. The Roman Calendar commemorates him on August 4th, as does the South African and Indian Prayer Books.

St. Dominic has never enjoyed the popularity of his contemporary Francis of Assisi, whom he admired and from whom he adopted the mendicant vow of poverty for his Order of Preachers. The valiant work of Dominic and his followers, both in preaching and in intellectual labor, did much to ward off the flood-tide of heresy that threatened to engulf the Church in the thirteenth century. Dominic's reputation has suffered from two false accusations; namely, that he was personally involved in the bloody repression of the Albigensian heretics of southern France, and that he was a founder of the Inquisition. His was a life of austere privation, zealous preaching and teaching, and devoted prayer. His ideal is summed up in the words of his Testament: "Have charity, serve humility, possess voluntary poverty."

10. LAURENCE, Deacon, and Martyr at Rome, 258

The martyrdom of Laurence on August 10th, four days after the similar fate of his Bishop, Xystus II, is attested by St. Cyprian. But no authentic acts of his passion have survived. According to tradition he was roasted over a fire, in view of the prefect's desire to extract from him, as a deacon, information about the Church's treasures. In antiquity, Laurence was the popular saint of the Roman church. Over his tomb on the Via Tiburtina stands a magnificent basilica, the foundations of which go back to Constantine. Two other basilicas of ancient date, within the city, are also dedicated to him. His name is recited in the Canon of the Roman Mass. His feast is marked in the Sarum and in all Anglican Calendars. Few of the martyrs of the ancient Church have been honored with so continuous and persistent devotion through the centuries.

13. HIPPOLYTUS, Bishop, and Martyr, ca. 235

St. Hippolytus of Rome has only come into his own in modern times, with the discovery of many of his works, notably the *Apostolic Tradition*, and a truer assessment of his great services to the Church. The details of his life remain obscure, except for his strenuous opposition to the doctrinal compromises of Pope Callistus (ca. 218-222). The view of modern critics that he was the first anti-pope is a conjecture. Of his martyrdom there is no reasonable doubt, and recent archaeological discoveries have identified his tomb in the catacomb at Rome that bears his name. An ancient statue of Hippolytus, found in 1551, that contains a list of his writings and a table for finding Easter Day that he compiled, may be seen in the Lateran Museum at Rome. He was the most eminent scholar of the Western Church in the early years of the third century, and ranks second to Origen of Alexandria among the Fathers of his time. His writings covered an enormous field of learning in exegesis, theology, history, liturgics, and apologetics. The *Apostolic Tradition* exhibits his importance for the future history of the liturgy both in the East and the West.

The date of Hippolytus is variously given in ancient Roman sources, the oldest being August 13th, which is the day of commemoration in the modern

Roman Missal. Various ancient listings give August 20th, 21st, and 22nd, among others. The Sarum and Canadian 1955 Calendars place him on the 13th.

14. JEREMY TAYLOR, *Bishop of Down, Connor and Dromore, 1667*

Born at Cambridge, and baptized there, August 15, 1613; ordained, 1633, and until 1645 held various positions as Fellow of Gonville and Caius and of All Souls Colleges, chaplain to Archbishop Laud and to King Charles I, and Rector of Uppingham and of Overstone; chaplain to the Earl of Carbery at Golden Grove, Carmarthenshire, 1645-55; Bishop of Down and Connor, 1661-67, to which was added administration of see of Dromore; died at Lisburn, August 13, 1667, and buried in cathedral of Dromore. His name occurs in the Canadian Draft Book Calendar of 1955. The date is transferred to avoid concurrence with Hippolytus in the 13th.

Jeremy Taylor has always been a favorite among the Caroline divines. The beauty of his style, his wide learning conjoined with a delightful wit, and the profound and subtle penetration of his insight into the heart of Christian devotion and conscience, are qualities that have endeared him to earnest seekers after truth and made him one of the creative molders of Anglican piety. A gentle spirit, he was never lacking in courage, and suffered imprisonment three times for his religious convictions. Though a prolific writer on theological, moral, and devotional subjects, his best-known works, *Holy Living* and *Holy Dying*, would alone give him a high place in the grateful remembrance of Christians. The prayer, adapted from the latter work, that appears in the Prayer Book, bottom of page 316, admirably summarizes his spirituality.[6]

15. SAINT MARY THE VIRGIN, *Mother of Our Lord Jesus Christ*

The feast of the Dormition (Falling Asleep) of the Blessed Virgin first appeared in the Eastern Church about 600 A.D., and was adopted by the Western Church, along with the Annunciation, Purification, and the Nativity of the Virgin, about a hundred years later. It has become a major festival of both the Orthodox and Roman Churches. The Scottish, South African, Indian, and Canadian 1955 Calendars include the festival.

Any fair listing of the saints of the Church would place the name of our Lord's mother first. In this primacy of honor to St. Mary both the Eastern and

---

[6]. Ed. Note: O GOD, whose days are without end, and whose mercies cannot be numbered; Make us, we beseech thee, deeply sensible of the shortness and uncertainty of human life; and let thy Holy Spirit lead us in holiness and righteousness, all our days: that, when we shall have served thee in our generation, we may be gathered unto our fathers, having the testimony of a good conscience; in the communion of the Catholic Church; in the confidence of a certain faith; in the comfort of a reasonable, religious, and holy hope; in favour with thee our God, and in perfect charity with the world. All which we ask through Jesus Christ our Lord. Amen.

Western Churches are unanimously in accord. The curious anomaly whereby she was deprived of any day especially her own in the several Prayer Books of our Communion is easily understood — it was a reaction of the Reformers to the exaggerations of Mariolatry in medieval piety. This prejudice has continued, of course, in view of the ever-increasing development of Marian devotion in the Roman Church, culminating in the proclamation by the Papacy in 1950 of the dogma of St. Mary's bodily assumption, associated with the festival of this date. Yet even so, St. Mary is the only saint commemorated by name in the heart of the Prayer Book liturgy. In the 1549 Book she was mentioned in the Prayer for the Church, and since 1552 her name has remained in the proper preface for Christmas Day. The festivals usually associated with her — the Annunciation and the Purification — are, however, specifically feasts of our Lord. She has always lacked in the Prayer Book a day of her own, in the manner of the apostles, evangelists, and other worthies of the New Testament. It is strange nonetheless that the Prayer Book should devote a day to St. Michael but none to St. Mary.

The ancient cycle of feasts of St. Mary rests so far as their dates are concerned upon no trustworthy historical tradition. But this is true also of most of the apostles' death-days, not to speak of the date of Christmas, the nativity of our Lord Himself. The Commission felt, however, that if any day was to be assigned to St. Mary as her own festival, it would be absurd to select one other than those associated with her memory in the unanimous tradition of the Eastern and Western Churches. The question was only that of which of the several commemorations to adopt: her Conception, Nativity, Presentation, or Falling Asleep. The New Testament and early tradition provide no account of these events of her life. Of these four, only two had a serious claim for adoption. The Nativity of the Virgin might be selected by analogy with the feast of the Nativity of St. John the Baptist. But in this case, such a festival would be in actuality an addition to the festival cycle of feasts of our Lord's Incarnation. (The same principle would apply essentially to such commemorations as that of her Conception and Presentation, as it does to the Annunciation, Visitation, and Purification.)

If St. Mary is to be commemorated, as other Christians, according to the ancient principle of observance, it would necessarily be the day associated with her death. Hence the only reasonable choice would seem to be August 15. The Commission is well aware of the prejudice that such a date may raise in the minds of many churchmen, in view of the Romish dogma of the Assumption. It should be borne in mind, however, that the Orthodox Churches have maintained this feast without any temptation to adopt the dogma, and several Anglican provinces have also admitted the day without compromising our inherited proportion of the faith. The ancient propers of the feast do not in any way foster a belief in the Romish doctrine.

20. BERNARD, Abbot of Clairvaux, 1153

Born at Fontaines-les-Dijon, 1090; professed as a monk at the Abbey of Citeaux, April; abbot of Clairvaux, 1115-53; died, August 20, 1153; canonized, January 18, 1174, and proclaimed a Doctor of the Church by Pius VIII, August 20, 1830. Bernard's commemoration occurs in the English 1928, Scottish, South African, Indian, and Canadian 1955 Calendars.

Though not so popular as St. Francis among all sorts of Christians, St. Bernard is without question the most characteristic saint of the medieval Church. In his person he combined, as it were miraculously, the loftiest ideal and manifestation of the active and contemplative life. Seldom has an individual so perfectly embodied the renunciation of self-will in devotion to the salvation of others and the good of the Church. At the height of his career he was in fact the most powerful influence in medieval Christendom and the arbiter of the Church's fortunes and destinies. At the same time he was a model of ascetic holiness and monastic virtue. His writings are the finest flowers of Christian mysticism, undergirded by a sturdy and orthodox faith. Many of the hymns which he wrote or inspired are a continuing, living enrichment of Christian devotion, such as the "Dulcis Jesu memoria" (*The Hymnal 1940*, No. 462) and *"Jesus dulcedo cordium"* (*The Hymnal 1940*, No. 485).

25. LOUIS, King of France, 1270

Born, April 25, 1214; crowned King of France at Reims, November 29, 1226; died at Carthage, August 25, 1270; canonized, 1297. Louis' name does not occur in the Sarum or in any Anglican Calendar.

Louis IX of France is not remembered by the faithful primarily as a Crusader, in which enterprise he accomplished little, but as a manly and devoted sovereign of unusual purity of life and manners. With Alfred of England he shares the honor of being in every way an exemplary Christian king. He was courageous and fearless in battle, patient and uncomplaining in adversity, and in all his administration and command of others an impartial and just ruler. From childhood his religious practice was intense, sincere, and uncommonly free of the bigotry of his age. He had an intelligent interest in the great theological issues of his time, and he put Christian ethics into concrete action in both his personal and public duties. The beautiful Sainte Chapelle in Paris, which he built to enshrine the relics of our Saviour's Passion, is in a very real sense a monument of his genuine piety and lovely character.

28. AUGUSTINE, Bishop of Hippo, 430

Born at Tagaste in North Africa, November 13, 354; baptized by St. Ambrose at Easter, 387; ordained Priest at Hippo, 391, and Bishop, 395; died at Hippo,

August 28, 430. His name is commemorated in the Roman, Sarum, and all modern Anglican lists.

No defense of proposing Augustine's name for the Church's Calendar is necessary. He is accounted by Catholics and Protestants alike the greatest of the Latin Fathers and the most influential theologian of Western Christendom. The continuing years only increase his fame and his ever-constant impact upon the thinking and piety of Christians. His theological perspectives are embedded in the prayers of the liturgy; his name is an authority unquestioned in the Prayer Book Articles. But the record of God's grace in his conversion, told in the pages of the *Confessions*, is alone sufficient for most Christians to account him among the saints; for it has been truly said of this work that, unlike so many imitations of it, the *Confessions* cannot be read without an edifying effect. His most monumental writing, the *City of God*, is without question the most influential theological work ever written since New Testament times.

31. AIDAN, *Bishop of Northumbria, 651*

Monk of Iona; consecrated Bishop for Northumbria, 634, with seat at the monastery of Lindisfarne; died at Bamborough, August 31, 651. His name has been added to all the recent Anglican Calendars.

The story of Aidan's life, recounted in Bede's *Ecclesiastical History*, opens to us one of the loveliest characters in all Church History. To him and to his pupils at Lindisfarne is due the evangelization of most of England north of the Thames, much less of the Humber. Bede said of him (III, 5): "it was the highest commendation of his teaching, with all men, that he taught no otherwise than he and his followers lived; for he neither sought nor loved anything of this world, but delighted in distributing immediately among the poor whatsoever was given him by the kings or rich men of the world." His work provided the link between the Roman and Celtic strains that produced the distinctive quality that marked out early English Christianity in its ascetic, missionary, and intellectual zeal.

September

12. JOHN HENRY HOBART, *Bishop of New York, 1830*

Born in Philadelphia, September 14, 1775; ordained Deacon, June 3, 1798, and Priest, April 5, 1801; in charge of Trinity, Oxford, and All Saints, Perkiomen, Pa., then of Christ Church, New Brunswick, N.J., and St. George's, Hempstead, Long Island; assistant minister, Trinity Church, New York City, 1800-16, and Rector, 1816-30; consecrated assistant Bishop of New York, May 29, 1811, becoming diocesan in 1816; died at Auburn, N.Y., September 12, 1830.

A man of undeviating principle and consuming energy, Bishop Hobart stands out pre-eminently among the leaders who revived the Episcopal Church after the period of "suspended animation" that marked its two decades of independent life after the American Revolution. Within four years he had doubled the number of clergy, quadrupled the number of missionaries in the state of New York, and before his death had planted the Church in almost every important town of the state. He was one of the founders of the General Theological Seminary, and the reviver of Geneva (now Hobart) College. He opened missionary work among the Oneida Indians. He also established the Bible and Common Prayer Book Society of New York, and was one of the first American churchmen to produce devotional manuals for the laity, and solid theological literature defending Episcopalian principles. Many consider him to have anticipated the teaching of the Tractarians. Though unbending in his doctrinal views, he was respected by his opponents for his devotion to what he considered to be just and right. In personal relations he was winning and charming, and he did not lack the virtue of humility.

13. CYPRIAN, *Bishop of Carthage, and Martyr, 258*

The martyrdom of Cyprian in the second year of the Valerian persecution occurred on September 14th. Together with Pope Cornelius he was commemorated on this day in the ancient Roman Calendars, and with Cornelius his name also appears in the saints named in the Roman Mass. The introduction of Holy Cross Day into the Western Calendar tended to supplant the older feast of the martyrs, as may be noted by its secondary rank on this day in the Sarum Calendar. The modern Roman Missal has transferred the observance of Cornelius and Cyprian to the 16th. Recent Anglican Calendars, with the exception of the one proposed for the American Book in 1928, have all shown a preference for anticipating Cyprian's commemoration on the 13th. He is listed in the English 1928, Scottish, South African, Indian, and Canadian 1955 Books, in every case without the addition of Pope Cornelius.

Cyprian stands next to Tertullian among the leading Latin Fathers of the Ante-Nicene period. His guidance of the Church during the difficult times of the first general persecutions was unexcelled in wisdom and effectiveness. His martyrdom made him the popular hero of North African Christianity. His theological writings, especially the treatise on the Unity of the Church, have exercised a constant influence, and not least upon our own Anglican tradition. At the present time, his name is one of the more popular of the non-Biblical saints for American church dedications.

14. THE EXALTATION OF THE HOLY CROSS

The festival of the Holy Cross, one of the major feasts of the Orthodox Churches, goes back to the dedication on this date at Jerusalem of the famous cathedral church founded by Constantine on the supposed sites of our Lord's crucifixion and burial. In the complex of structures built there was placed the relic of the true Cross, and over the tomb arose the magnificent shrine known as the *Anastasis* (Resurrection). Though much modified and rebuilt, the church survives today in Jerusalem as the Church of the Holy Sepulchre. Throughout the ages the site has been the most noted shrine of Christian pilgrimage. For its possession, the medieval Church launched the Crusades to win it back from the "infidel." Apart from the many romantic associations with this shrine in the history of the Church, the festival has become far more than the anniversary of dedication of one of the most famous and influential edifices in Christendom. In popular devotion it has been truly a festival in honor of our Lord's saving Cross and Passion, giving opportunity to a joyous commemoration of His redeeming death with a festal emphasis not possible or appropriate on Good Friday.

The feast is prominent in the Roman and Sarum Calendars, was admitted as a Black Letter Day in Queen Elizabeth's Calendar of 1561 and in the Prayer Book of 1661, and has found its way into all modern Prayer Book Calendars of a more extended listing. Our own Prayer Book recognizes the day, though not by name, in using it as a dating point for the autumnal Ember Days.

19. THEODORE OF TARSUS, Archbishop of Canterbury, 690

The biography of Theodore is given in Bede's *Ecclesiastical History*, Books IV and V (*passim*). A learned monk of the Eastern Church, living in exile in Rome, he was consecrated by Pope Vitalian as Archbishop of Canterbury on March 26, 668. He was the first archbishop, says Bede, whom all the English obeyed. His remarkable episcopate ended with his death at the age of eighty-eight on September 19, 690. Curiously, Theodore was not canonized by the medieval Church and does not appear in the Sarum Calendar. Nor are there any church dedications to him in England. His "sanctity" has been officially recognized only in modern Anglican Prayer Books: the English 1928, Scottish, South African, and Canadian. Yet his holiness of life, not to speak of his extraordinary learning and wisdom, is evident to any reader of Bede's history. Possibly to no other archbishop does English Christianity owe so much. He welded together the Roman and Celtic traditions in England into one united Church. He greatly extended the missionary and administrative effectiveness of the Church, and laid the foundations of the parochial organization that still obtains in England.

20. JOHN COLERIDGE PATTESON, *Bishop of Melanesia, and Martyr, 1871*

Born in London, April 1, 1827; ordained, 1853; missionary in Melanesia under Bishop G. A. Selwyn, 1855-61; consecrated Bishop of Melanesia, February 24, 1861; martyred on the island of Nikapu, September 20, 1871. Patteson is commemorated by the South African and Canadian Church Calendars.

The tragic death of Bishop Patteson and his companions by the Melanesian islanders whom he sought to protect from the slave-traders is one of the most glorious records in the annals of our Anglican Communion. It took this cost, all the more precious for its being a terrible mistake, to arouse the British government to take serious measures to prevent the piratical man-hunting among the South Sea peoples. The blood of these martyrs has indeed been a seed of the Church in Melanesia, to which many of our own countrymen can testify from their experiences in World War II in the Pacific area.

25. SERGIUS, *Abbot of Holy Trinity, Moscow, 1392*

Born at Rostov, ca. 1314; at age of twenty founded the monastery of the Holy Trinity at Radonezh, fifty miles north of Moscow; died, 1392.

To the Russian people St. Sergius is a national hero no less than an exemplary saint. His firm support of Prince Dmitri did more than anything else to encourage the Russians in their successful struggle to throw off the yoke of the Tatars and lay the foundations of their independent, national life. But the secret of his life lay in his utter simplicity, integrity, and faith. He remained throughout his mature life at his monastery, refusing greater honors and advancement. Not a learned theologian nor a writer, he seemed nonetheless able to inspire intense devotion to the orthodox Faith. Sergius' name is familiar to Anglicans from the Fellowship of St. Alban and St. Sergius, a society for the promotion of closer relations between the English and Russian Churches. Though not the "apostle" of the Russian people, Sergius is in a real sense their "patron," for his life and labors mark a turning point of revival in Russian Christianity. His monastery gave birth to some fifty new foundations, and it was also one of the most notable centers in later years of Russian Christian art.

26. LANCELOT ANDREWES, *Bishop of Winchester, 1626*

Born at Barking, London, 1555; ordained, 1580; vicar of St. Giles' Cripplegate, 1588, and prebendary of Southwell and of St. Paul's, London, 1589; prebendary of Westminster, 1597, and Dean of Westminster, 1601 ; Bishop of Chichester, 1605—o9, of Ely, 1609-19, and of Winchester, 1619-26; died at Southwark, September 25, 1626. He is commemorated on the 25th in the South African and

Canadian 1955 Calendars, but is transferred in this proposed Calendar to avoid concurrence with St. Sergius.

Among all the Caroline divines, Bishop Andrewes maintains a continuing popularity. The recurrent re-printing of his *Preces Privatae* is evidence of the enduring appeal of his personal devotions in their helpfulness to others. His sermons are also much admired, for their learning and subtlety, their balance of doctrine, and their literary grace. Though a favored court prelate in three reigns, Andrewes had little interest in politics and was a most unassuming and unworldly person of a self-denying spirit. In our American Prayer Book, the service for the Consecration of a Church is based upon a form that goes back to one composed by Bishop Andrewes. It is perhaps less remembered that he served on the committee of learned divines that prepared the Authorized Version of the Bible (1611).

30. JEROME, *Priest, and Monk of Bethlehem, 420*

Born at Stridon, Italy, ca. 347; ordained Priest at Antioch, 378; secretary of Pope Damasus, 383-384; founded monastery at Bethlehem, 386, where he died, September 30, 419 or 420. Accounted one of the four great Doctors of the Western Church, Jerome's name occurs on the Roman, Sarum, and all Anglican Calendars.

It is certain that St. Jerome's character and disposition are hardly worthy of emulation, nor can his extravagant promotion of the ascetical life be considered creditable. In short, he was not a very pleasant individual. But his enormous services to the Church make up for his obvious faults, and in view of them the Church cannot be mean enough to deny him a thankful remembrance. He was the greatest Biblical scholar of antiquity. His commentaries were invaluable resources to the Western Church for over a thousand years, and are still used by Bible students with profit. His Latin translation of the Bible, the Vulgate, would alone make him one of the immortals. He also performed good service in his valiant defense of the Church's faith, especially against the Pelagian heresy. Indefatigable in labor, St. Jerome for all his bitterness in controversy was never a self-seeking man; and there were times when he was candid enough to admit his failings. At least, he was never dull.

October

4. FRANCIS OF ASSISI, *Friar, 1226*

Born at Assisi, 1181 or 1182; converted to a life of poverty, 1206; primitive Rule of the Order of Friars Minor confirmed by Pope Innocent III, 1210; First Rule, 1221; Second Rule, confirmed by Pope Honorius III, November 25, 1223; died at Assisi, evening of October 3, 1226; canonized, July 16, 1228. Francis was not listed in the Sarum or Prayer Book of 1661 Calendars; but he has found a place in all recent Anglican revisions.

If a vote should be taken in the Church for names of saints to be added to the Prayer Book Calendar, undoubtedly Francis would lead the list, if not indeed be a unanimous choice. The appeal of this man, wedded to Lady Poverty, among all sorts of Christians in the modern world is phenomenal. We recognize in his life of utter self-renunciation the judgment upon all our material values. But above all else, Francis in his utter poverty of body and of spirit speaks to us as does no one else the unconquerable joy of the gospel. In his mortifications he sums up the piety of the medieval world; in his affirmation of God's goodness in creation he is the first modern saint.

6. WILLIAM TYNDALE, *Priest, and Martyr, 1536*

Born at Slymbridge, on the border of Wales, 1495; ordained ca. 1521; chaplain in household of Sir John Walsh, at Little Sodbury, Gloucestershire, and then of Humphrey Monmouth, alderman of London; left England for the Continent, 1524; executed at Brussels, October 6, 1536. The Canadian Book of 1955 lists Tyndale.

Tyndale was a man of one passion — to translate the Bible into English so that — as he said to a prominent churchman — "a boy that driveth the plough shall know more of the scripture than thou doest." His life reads like a mystery story. His glory is in his accomplished work. Of those portions of the Bible which he managed to translate before his betrayal and execution, eighty per cent survives in the language of our more familiar versions, the Authorized and Revised. He could be a bitter controversialist, as was the fashion of the time, but his loneliness and desperation in being hunted and hounded atone for it. In his personal life, he was amiable and self-denying. His last words were prophetic: "Lord, open the King of England's eyes."

15. SAMUEL ISAAC JOSEPH SCHERESCHEWSKY, *Bishop of Shanghai, 1906*

Born of Jewish parentage in Tauroggen, Russian Lithuania, May 6, 1831; came to America, 1854, and became a Christian the following year; ordained Deacon, July 7, 1859, and Priest, October 28, 1860; missionary in China, 1859-77; consecrated Bishop of Shanghai, October 31, 1877; resigned for reasons of health, 1883; died in Tokyo, October 15, 1906.

The career of Bishop Schereschewsky is unique, but in no case more so than its manifestation of how God gives strength out of weakness. His monuments are the foundation of St. John's University in Shanghai and the Chinese translation of the Bible. During the last third of his life Bishop Schereschewsky was an invalid, but he never stopped working. He was accounted one of the most eminent scholars in Oriental languages of his time. Yet he was so paralyzed that he typed the whole of his version of the Bible in Easy Wenli, some 2,000 pages, with the middle finger of his partially crippled right hand. His unconquerable spirit is best expressed in words spoken four years before his death: "I have sat in this chair for over twenty years. It seemed very hard at first. But God knew best. He kept me for the work for which I am best fitted."

16. HUGH LATIMER AND NICHOLAS RIDLEY, *Bishops and Martyrs, 1555*

Latimer: Born at Thurcaston, Leicestershire, *ca.* 1490; royal chaplain, 1530; Bishop of Worcester, 1535-39. Ridley: Born at Willemoteswick, Northumberland, *ca.* 1500; chaplain to Archbishop Cranmer, 1537, and vicar of Herne, Kent, 1538; Master of Pembroke, 1540, and chaplain to the King and Canon of Canterbury, 1541; Bishop of Rochester, 1547-50, and of London, 1550-53. The two men were burned at the stake at Oxford, October 16, 1555.

Latimer was the greatest preacher of the Reformation period in England; Ridley was more involved in theological and administrative work. Both men were avid proponents of the Reformation principles, and close friends and supporters of Archbishop Cranmer. They were undoubtedly Protestant in their convictions, firm in their adherence to the Edwardian settlement of religious affairs. This was their undoing, at the accession of Mary, and with Cranmer they became the primary victims of Mary's vengeance. In their deaths they were true martyrs for the freedom of the English Church. "Be of good comfort," said Latimer to his companion at the stake, "and play the man; we shall this day light such a candle by God's grace in England as (I trust) shall never be put out."

26. KING ALFRED THE GREAT, 899

Born at Wantage, Berkshire, 849; became King of Wessex, 871; died, October 26, 899, and buried in the Old Minster at Winchester. Alfred was never canonized. His name occurs in the English Proposed Book of 1928, and the Canadian Draft Book of 1955.

Both the opinion of scholars and the acclaim of popular devotion accord to Alfred the noblest character of any sovereign who ever reigned in England, and one of the purest natures in all Christian history. By his fearlessness and unquenchable faith he saved his country from destruction at the hands of the ruthless Vikings; yet he was generous to his foe and sought to win them to his own Christian faith. His successes in this latter endeavor were remarkable. His devotion to learning, and his labors to advance the education of the clergy place him in the front rank of the civilizing agents of the Middle Ages. The constant devotion of the English people to his memory has been more than deserved and has exercised an elevating influence in successive generations. In an age of crude and cruel manners, Alfred stands out as a Christian gentleman and a saint of manly virtues.

29. JAMES HANNINGTON AND HIS COMPANIONS, *Bishop and Martyrs of Uganda, 1885*

Born at Hurstpierpoint, Sussex, September 3, 1847; set out for missionary work in Africa, May 17, 1882; consecrated Bishop of Eastern Equatorial Africa, June, 1884; martyred near Victoria Nyanza, October 29, 1885. He is commemorated in the South African Book, and, on October 21st, in the Canadian Book of 1955.

Hannington's last words to his executioners were: "Go, tell Mwanga [the native king, who suspected him of seeking to enslave him] I have purchased the road to Uganda with my blood." The persecution of the Christians lasted for three years, and there still survive a few confessors from this bloody period among the native Christians. Today the diocese of Uganda alone counts some 125 native African clergy. In May 1955, the Archbishop of Canterbury consecrated at Namirembe four Africans as bishops for the various dioceses of East Africa and the Sudan, which shall shortly become an independent province of the Anglican Communion.

November

7. WILLIBRORD, *Archbishop of Utrecht, Missionary to Frisia, 738.*

Born, November 6, 658, in Northumbria; professed a monk at Ripon, *ca.* 753 [Ed.: sic]; in Ireland, 678-690; left for missionary work in Frisia, 690; consecrated Bishop of Utrecht at Rome by Pope Sergius, November 21, 695, and given the name of Clement; died, November 7, 739.

In addition to the brief notice in Bede's *Ecclesiastical History* (V, 10-11), we possess a fairly authentic life of Willibrord by his kinsman Alcuin. He was one of the most distinguished and successful missionaries sent out by the early Anglo-Saxon Church. In addition to his labors in the territory of the Frisians (now Holland), he also did work among the Danes and the Germans. Though not so eminent as his contemporary and friend, St. Boniface, Willibrord did much to prepare the way for Boniface's labors, especially in his cordial relations with the Frankish state and in his interest in having the Papacy sponsor and support his missionary work. Willibrord is commemorated in the South African and Canadian 1955 Calendars.

MARTIN, *Bishop of Tours, 397*

Born *ca.* 330 at Sabaria in Pannonia (Hungary), and brought up in Pavia, Italy; after a term of service in the army, he settled at Poitiers, where he was ordained by St. Hilary between 350 and 353, and soon founded a hermitage at Ligugé; consecrated Bishop of Tours, 372, but continued to live a monastic life at Marmoutier; died, November 11, *ca.* 397. His name appears in the Roman, Sarum, and all Anglican Calendars.

Martin's example, much enhanced by an able biographer, Sulpitius Severus, did a great deal to implant the monastic movement in the Western Church. His influence was particularly strong among the Celtic Christians of the British Isles. It is significant that the oldest church in Canterbury, which antedates the Anglo-Saxon settlement, is dedicated to him. His shrine at Tours was a major focus of pilgrimage down to its destruction in the eighteenth century. He is one of the patron saints of France. His virtues were not entirely monastic. He was a diligent missionary to the pagan peoples of the countrysides about his hermitages. And in the troublous affair of the Priscillianist heresy, Martin's was one of the few voices raised against its bloody repression. He was always the defender of the poor and helpless, and this reputation carried over after his death so as to make his shrine a potent sanctuary for those seeking justice.

12. CHARLES SIMEON, *Priest, 1836*

Born at Reading, September 24, 1759; ordained, 1782; Fellow of King's College from 1782, and vicar of Holy Trinity, Cambridge, from 1783 until his death, November 12, 1836. Simeon is commemorated in the South African and Canadian 1955 Calendars.

All of Simeon's ministry was in Cambridge, but its influence has reached throughout the Anglican world. His conversion was singular. Upon entering King's College in 1779, he discovered that he was required to receive Holy Communion. By his conscientious preparation for his act, his whole life was changed. Though a leader of the Evangelicals, Simeon was a staunch supporter of Anglican principles. The first ten years of his ministry were marked by much ridicule and abuse, but his steadfastness in his convictions and his unflagging zeal in the cause of true religion finally won all hearts. Simeon is a model of a faithful priest who follows duty and conscience irrespective of the world's opinion.

14. CONSECRATION OF SAMUEL SEABURY,
First American Bishop, 1784

It is entirely fitting that the American Church should commemorate the first major event that made possible its independent life as an episcopal Church after the American Revolution. Such a commemoration is also a fitting tribute to Bishop Seabury's own convictions, in which we all share, and in his labor and energy in obtaining for the American Church the apostolic succession. His consecration at the hands of the Scotch Non-Jurors, in the face of much adverse criticism, was itself a testimony to the catholicity of the Church and in particular to the steadfast way in which the Scottish episcopalians maintained their trust despite persecution. Seabury's consecration has given our Church a highly prized link of community with the Episcopal Church of Scotland, enriching and enlarging our ties with the mother Church of England. And not least, through his Concordat with the Scottish bishops who consecrated him, he brought to our American Church the magnificent liturgy of the Scottish tradition.

16. MARGARET, *Queen of Scotland, 1093*

Born *ca.* 1045, daughter of Edward Etheling, grand-daughter of Edmund Ironside; brought up at court of Edward the Confessor; married Malcolm III Canmore, King of Scotland, ca. 1067-68; died at Edinburgh, November 16, 1093; canonized, 1251. Her name appears in the Scottish Calendar.

From childhood Margaret's principal interests were religious, and had she not felt it her duty to bring England and Scotland closer together by marriage with Malcolm, she might well have ended her days in a convent. To her zeal is due the reform of the Scottish Church and its greater conformity to the larger life of the Western Church. Though Romanist in her background and sympathies, she rebuilt the Scottish shrine of Iona. Her personal asceticism was rigorous; her charities were generous.

17. HILDA, *Abbess of Whitby, 680*

Born, 614; died, November 17, 680. Hilda is commemorated in the English 1928, Scottish and South African Books on the 8th, to avoid concurrence with St. Hugh; in the Canadian Books on the 17th.

Most of what we know of Hilda comes from Bede's *Ecclesiastical History* (IV, 23-24). She was a potent leader at a critical time in the early history of the English Church, when Roman and Celtic traditions were in tension. Her monastery, a double house for men and women, was a civilizing force. It was there that the poet Caedmon was encouraged to compose his English verses. And it was at Whitby that the famous conference took place that determined the future destinies of the English Church. Hilda was a friend of both sides, devoted to the memory of St. Aidan, from whom she received the veil, but holding allegiance to the Roman customs that prevailed as a result of the conference.

19. ELIZABETH, *Princess of Hungary, 1231*

Born at Pressburg, 1207, daughter of King Andrew II of Hungary; married in 1221 to Louis IV, landgrave of Thuringia; died at Marburg, November 17, 1231; canonized, 1235. The Roman Calendar observes her memory on the 19th. Her name also appears on this date in the Indian Prayer Book.

St. Elizabeth's charity is fittingly remembered in countless hospitals that bear her name throughout the Christian world. After her husband's death, her life was full of tragedy, but she never thought of self, but only of the needs of others. She fulfilled in her short lifetime the "works of mercy," and there have been few who have so perfectly matched her love for even the least of Christ's brethren.

23. CLEMENT, Bishop of Rome, ca. 100

There are few authentic facts of Clement's life that can be documented, though many of the traditions about him seem plausible enough. He may have been a disciple of St. Peter, and the beautiful basilica named for him at Rome may well stand upon the site of his home. His name suggests an humble ancestry, and his family may have had some attachment to "Caesar's household." His fame rests upon the Epistle to the Corinthians, which he wrote in the name of the Roman Church about A.D. 95 — a document that was held in some ancient churches as canonical. It is the most significant writing of the post-apostolic age outside the later books of the New Testament, and deserves its honored place in the collection known as "The Apostolic Fathers." Later tradition accounted him a martyr, but there is no convincing proof of this.

December

2. CHANNING MOORE WILLIAMS, Missionary Bishop in China and Japan, 1910

Born in Richmond, Virginia, July 18, 1829; ordained Deacon, July 1, 1855, and Priest, January II, 1857; consecrated American Bishop in China, with jurisdiction in Japan, October 3, 1866; in 1874, his jurisdiction was divided, and he was named Bishop of Yedo, Japan; resigned, October 1889; died in Richmond, December 2, 1910.

Though he gave devoted service to China, Bishop Williams' name is chiefly associated with the laying of foundations in Japan. He was the first Anglican missionary to set foot in Japan, his first visit being in 1859. He founded St. Paul's University in Tokyo, and, in 1887, he brought together the American and English missions in the formation of the Nippon Sei Ko Kwai, the Holy Catholic Church of Japan. At the time, the Church in Japan numbered less than a thousand communicants. But Bishop Williams' vision and wisdom laid secure foundations. After his retirement he remained in Japan to help his successor. Bishop Williams was also a dear friend of Bishop Schereschewsky (see October 15), who succeeded him as bishop in China; and he did much to foster the scholarly work of Bishop Schereschewsky to the great benefit of the whole Christian enterprise in the Orient.

4. CLEMENT OF ALEXANDRIA, Priest, ca. 210

Clement was converted to Christianity by Pantaenus, founder of the Catechetical School at Alexandria, and succeeded his teacher as head of the School about 180. For over twenty years he labored effectively as an apologist for the faith and catechist of the faithful. His speculative theology helped to establish the good reputation of Christianity in the world of learning and prepare the way for his pupil, Origen, the most eminent theologian of Greek Christianity. Clement was a gentleman and a scholar, a man of unusual refinement of manners and cheerful disposition. He is accounted a saint of the Eastern Church, and his name appears on most of the modern Anglican Calendars. His influence has been very notable upon modern Anglican theology.

6. NICHOLAS, *Bishop of Myra in Lycia, ca. 342*

Very little is known of the life of St. Nicholas; the traditions that have come to surround his name as the patron of children and of sailors have largely overshadowed the few facts of his career that can be ascertained. He was certainly no mythical figure (as, for example, St. George), having been a confessor in the persecution of Diocletian. But it cannot be proved that he attended the Council of Nicaea, though it is possible that he did so. The Commission recognizes that of all the names proposed for the Calendar, that of St. Nicholas presents the greatest degree of difficulty so far as authentic information is concerned. But it believes that the beautiful associations that have come to surround his cult, especially his devotion to children and poor folk, doubtless have a basis in fact, and represent in any event a quality of saintliness that deserves both recognition and imitation. He is commemorated by both the Eastern and the Western Church; his name is found in the Sarum Calendar and in all Anglican Prayer Books with Black Letter Days.

Appendix 1: Comparative Tables of Anglican Calendars

In the following tables a complete listing is given of the entries in the major Anglican Prayer Books, whether adopted or proposed. By way of comparison, these entries are noted whenever they occur in the Roman or the Sarum Calendars, but no attempt has been made to list in entirety the names in these two Missals.

Editor's Note: In addition to the columns provided in the original PBS IX, I have also added a column entitled "[Frere]". Because of the pivotal influence of Frere's *Some Principles of Liturgical Reform* on early to mid-twentieth century liturgical thought, Frere's picks are in here too.

Furthermore, this table contains errors in some of the other Anglican calendars. These will be corrected and updated in the table published in PBS XVI, vol. 4.

The Calendar 221

JANUARY

Day	Feast	Roman	Sarum	English 1661	[Frere]	English 1928	Canadian 1922	Canadian 1955	Scottish	South African	Indian	American 1928	Proposed
1	CIRCUMCISION	X	X	X	X	X	X	X	X	X	X	X	
	OCTAVE OF CHRISTMAS							X					
	HOLY NAME OF JESUS												X
2													
3													
4	Titus [1]									X		X	
5													
6	THE EPIPHANY	X	X	X	X	X	X	X	X	X	X	X	X
7													
8	Lucian		X	X									
9													
10	William Laud				X			X					X
11	David								X				
12	Benedict Biscop				X					X			
	John Horden							X					
13	Hilary		X	X	X	X	X	X	X	X		X	
14	Hilary	X											X
	Kentigern								X				
15													

JANUARY (continued)

16									
17	Antony	X	X		X		X	X		X
18	Prisca	X	X	X				X		
19	Wulfstan	X		X	X		X	X		
	Henry (of Finland)					X	X			
20	Fabian	X	X		X		X	X	X	
21	Agnes	X	X	X	X	X	X	X	X	X
22	Vincent	X	X	X	X	X	X	X	X	X
23	Phillips Brooks									X
24	Saint Timothy [1]	X			X	X	X	X	X	X
25	THE CONVERSION OF SAINT PAUL THE APOSTLE	X	X	X	X	X	X	X	X	X
26	Polycarp	X		X	X	X	X	X	X	X
27	John Chrysostom	X		X	X	X	X	X	X	X
28										
29										
30	King Charles I [2]		X	X		X				
31										

1. See February 6; Canadian 1955 commemorates with Timothy on the 24th.
2. Not listed in the 1661 Book, but a commemorative service provided until 1859.

The Calendar 223

FEBRUARY

Day	Feast	Roman	Sarum	English 1661	[Frere]	English 1928	Canadian 1922	Canadian 1955	Scottish	South African	Indian	American 1928	Proposed
1	Bride				X				X				
	Ignatius [1]	X	X			X						X	X
2	PURIFICATION	X	X	X	X	X	X	X	X	X	X	X	X
3	Blasius [2]	X	X	X								X	X
	Ansgarius					X		X		X		X	X
4	Cornelius											X	X
	Gilbert of Sempringham				X								
5	Agatha	X	X	X						X			
6	Saint Titus [3]	X							X	X	X		X
7													
8													
9													
10													
11	Caedmon							X					
	Finnian								X				
12													
13													
14	Valentine	X	X	X			X	X		X			

FEBRUARY (continued)

15 Thomas Bray								X
16								
17 Finan					X			
18 Colman					X			
19								
20 African Missionaries and Martyrs						X		
21								
22								
23								
24 SAINT MATTHIAS THE APOSTLE	X	X	X	X	X	X	X	X
25 Charles Inglis				X				X
26								
27 George Herbert				X		X		X
28								
29								

1. See December 17.
2. The American 1928 Proposed list placed him on the 11th.
3. See January 4.

MARCH

Day	Feast	Roman	Sarum	English 1661	[Frere]	English 1928	Canadian 1922	Canadian 1955	Scottish	South African	Indian	American 1928	Proposed
1	David		X	X	X	X	X	X	X	X	X	X	X
2	Chad		X	X	X	X	X	X	X	X			
3	John and Charles Wesley							X					
4													
5													
6	Baldred								X				
7	Perpetua and Felicitas	X	X	X	X	X	X	X	X	X	X		X
8	Thomas Aquinas	X							X	X	X		X
9													
10	Kessog								X				
11													
12	Gregory the Great	X	X	X	X	X	X	X	X	X	X	X	X
13													
14													
15													
16													
17	Patrick	X	X	X	X	X	X	X	X	X	X	X	X

MARCH (continued)

Day	Name	1	2	3	4	5	6	7	8	9	10
18	King Edward						X				
	Cyril of Jerusalem	X	X	X						X	
19	Saint Joseph	X		X	X	X	X	X	X	X	X
	Thomas Ken					X		X			
20	Thomas Ken										X
			X		X						
	Cuthbert		X			X	X	X		X	
21	Benedict [1]	X	X	X	X	X	X	X	X	X	
	Thomas Cranmer [2]						X				
22											
23	Gregory the Illuminator										X
24											
25	THE ANNUNCIATION OF THE BLESSED VIRGIN MARY	X	X	X	X	X	X	X	X	X	X
26											
27											
28											
29	John Keble					X		X	X		
30											
31											

1. See July 11.
2. See June 9.

APRIL

Day	Feast	Roman	Sarum	English 1661	[Frere]	English 1928	Canadian 1922	Canadian 1955	Scottish	South African	Indian	American 1928	Proposed
1	Gilbert								X				
	John Frederick Denison Maurice												X
2													
3	Richard		X	X	X	X	X	X	X	X			
4	Ambrose [1]		X	X	X	X	X	X	X	X	X	X	X
5													
6	William Law									X			X
7													
8	William Augustus Muhlenberg												X
9													
10													
11	Leo the Great [2]	X				X		X	X	X	X		X
12	George Augustus Selwyn [3]									X			X
13													
14	Justin Martyr [4]	X			X				X	X	X		X
15													
16	Magnus								X				
17	Donnan								X				

APRIL (continued)

18											
19	Alphege		X	X	X	X	X	X	X		
20	Serf						X				
21	Anselm	X		X	X	X	X	X	X	X	X
22	Maelrubha					X					
23	George	X	X	X	X	X	X	X	X	X	
24	Wilfrid							X			
25	SAINT MARK THE EVANGELIST	X	X	X	X	X	X	X	X	X	X
26											
27											
28											
29											
30	Catherine of Siena	X		X		X	X	X	X	X	
	David Livingstone				X						

1. Roman lists on December 7.
2. Sarum lists on June 28.
3. South African places on the 11th.
4. Scottish observes on the 13th; Canadian on June 1; Frere on October 23.

The Calendar 229

MAY

Day	Feast	Roman	Sarum	English 1661	[Frere]	English 1928	Canadian 1922	Canadian 1955	Scottish	South African	Indian	American 1928	Proposed
1	SAINT PHILIP AND SAINT JAMES	X	X	X	X	X	X	X	X	X	X	X	X
2	Athanasius	X			X	X	X	X	X	X	X	X	X
3	Invention of Cross	X	X	X									
4	Monnica	X			X	X		X	X	X	X	X	X
5													
6	St. John at Latin Gate	X	X	X		X	X	X	X	X	X		
7	John of Damascus [1]												X
8													
9	Gregory of Nazianzus	X					X	X	X	X			X
10								X					
11	Cyril and Methodius											X	X
12										X			
13	Martyrs of Uganda												
14													
15													
16													

MAY (continued)

17									
18									
19	Dunstan	X	X	X	X	X	X		X
20	Alcuin								X
21									
22									
23									
24	Jackson Kemper								X
25	Aldhelm	X	X	X		X			
26	Augustine of Canterbury [2]	X	X	X	X	X	X	X	X
27	Venerable Bede	X	X	X	X	X	X	X	
28									
29									
30	Joan of Arc				X	X			
31									

1. Roman observes on March 27.
2. Roman lists on the 28th.

The Calendar 231

JUNE

Day	Feast	Roman	Sarum	English 1661	[Frere]	English 1928	Canadian 1922	Canadian 1955	Scottish	South African	Indian	American 1928	Proposed
1	Nicomede		X	X									
	Justin Martyr [1]						X	X		X			X
2	The Martyrs of Lyons				X								
	The Martyrs of China											X	
3													
4													
5	Boniface	X	X	X	X	X	X	X	X	X	X	X	X
6													
7													
8													
9	The First Book of Common Prayer												X
	Columba				X	X	X	X	X	X	X	X	
10	Columba												X
	Margaret				X			X	X	X			
11	SAINT BARNABAS THE APOSTLE	X	X	X		X	X	X	X	X	X	X	X
12	Ternan								X				
13													
14	Basil of Caesarea	X	X		X	X	X	X	X	X	X		X
15													

JUNE (continued)

16	Joseph Butler					X			X
17	Botolf							X	
18	Ephrem of Edessa				X				X
19	Bernard Mizeki								
20	Trans. King Edward	X	X						
21	Fillan					X			
22	Alban [2]	X	X	X	X	X	X	X	X
23									
24	THE NATIVITY OF SAINT JOHN BAPTIST	X	X	X	X	X	X	X	X
25	Moluag					X			
26									
27									
28	Irenaeus [3]	X		X	X	X	X	X	X
29	SAINT PETER		X	X	X	X		X	
	SAINT PETER AND SAINT PAUL	X		X	X		X		X
30									

1. See April 14.
2. The 1661 Book observes on the 17th.
3. Sarum commemorates Leo on this day.

JULY

Day	Feast	Roman	Sarum	English 1661	[Frere]	English 1928	Canadian 1922	Canadian 1955	Scottish	South African	Indian	American 1928	Proposed
1	Dominion Day							X					
2	The Visitation of the Blessed Virgin Mary	X	X	X	X	X	X	X	X	X	X		X
3													
4	Trans. of Martin		X	X									
	INDEPENDENCE DAY											X	X
5													
6	Octave Peter and Paul	X	X					X					
	Thomas More							X					
	Palladius								X				
7													
8													
9	Stephen Langton							X					
10													
11	Benedict of Nursia [1]												
12													
13	Silas									X			
14										X			
15	Swithun		X	X	X	X	X	X	X				

JULY (continued)

16										
17	Osmund	X								
18	William White								X	
19										
20	Margaret	X	X	X	X	X	X		X	
21										
22	Saint Mary Magdalene	X	X	X	X	X	X	X	X	X
23										
24										
25	SAINT JAMES THE APOSTLE	X	X	X	X	X	X	X	X	X
26	Anne	X	X	X	X	X	X	X	X	
	Thomas a Kempis									X
27	William Reed Huntington								X	X
28										
29	Olaf				X	X	X			
	William Wilberforce				X		X			X
30	Mary and Martha [2]	X					X	X		
31	Germanus and Lupus		X	X			X	X		
	Ignatius Loyola	X						X		

1. See March 21.
2. Roman and Indian observe Martha only, on the 29th.

AUGUST

Day	Feast	Roman	Sarum	English 1661	[Frere]	English 1928	Canadian 1922	Canadian 1955	Scottish	South African	Indian	American 1928	Proposed
1	Lammas			X									
	St. Peter's Chains	X	X										
2													
3													
4	Dominic	X			X								X
5	Oswald		X		X	X							
6	THE TRANSFIGURATION OF OUR LORD JESUS CHRIST	X	X	X	X	X	X	X	X	X	X	X	X
7	Name of Jesus		X	X	X	X	X	X	X	X	X		
8													
9													
10	Laurence	X	X	X	X	X	X	X	X	X	X	X	X
11													
12													
13	Hippolytus	X	X					X					X
	Jeremy Taylor							X					
14	Jeremy Taylor												X
15	Repose of Blessed Virgin Mary	X	X		X			X	X	X	X		X
16													

AUGUST (continued)

17										
18										
19										
20	Bernard of Clairvaux	X				X	X	X		X
21										
22										
23										
24	SAINT BARTHOLOMEW THE APOSTLE	X	X	X	X	X	X	X	X	X
25	Louis	X								X
	Ebba						X			X
26										
27										
28	Augustine of Hippo	X	X	X	X	X	X	X	X	X
29	Beheading of John the Baptist	X	X	X	X	X	X	X		
30				X	X	X				
31	Aidan of Lindisfarne			X	X	X	X	X	X	X

The Calendar 237

SEPTEMBER

Day	Feast	Roman	Sarum	English 1661	[Frere]	English 1928	Canadian 1922	Canadian 1955	Scottish	South African	Indian	American 1928	Proposed
1	Giles	X	X	X	X	X	X	X	X	X	X		
2	Robert Gray									X			
3													
4	Trans. Cuthbert				X								
5													
6													
7	Evurtius			X									
8	Nativity of Blessed Virgin Mary	X	X	X	X	X	X	X	X	X	X	X	
9	Boisil; Kiaran								X				
10	E. J. Peck							X					
11													
12	John Henry Hobart												X
13	Cyprian of Carthage [1]	X	X		X	X		X	X	X	X	X	X
14	The Exaltation of the Holy Cross	X	X	X		X	X	X	X	X	X	X	X
15													
16	Ninian				X	X	X	X	X	X	X		
17	Latimer and Ridley [2]							X					
	Lambert		X	X						X			

SEPTEMBER (continued)

18										
19	Theodore of Tarsus			X	X	X	X	X		X	X
20	John Coleridge Patteson			X		X		X			X
21	SAINT MATTHEW	X	X	X	X	X	X	X	X	X	X
22											
23	Adamnan					X					
24											
25	Sergius										X
	Finnbar							X			
	Lancelot Andrewes					X					X
26	Lancelot Andrewes										
27											
28											
29	SAINT MICHAEL AND ALL ANGELS	X	X	X	X	X	X	X	X	X	X
30	Jerome	X	X	X	X	X	X	X	X	X	X

1. Sarum and American 1928 place on the 14th, Roman on the 16th (with Cornelius); also observed on the 26th in Sarum, English 1661, and Canadian 1922 lists.
2. See October 16.

OCTOBER

Day	Feast	Roman	Sarum	English 1661	[Frere]	English 1928	Canadian 1922	Canadian 1955	Scottish	South African	Indian	American 1928	Proposed
1	Remigius	X	X	X	X	X	X	X	X	X			
2													
3													
4	Francis of Assisi	X			X	X		X	X	X	X	X	X
5													
6	Faith		X	X	X	X				X			
	William Tyndale							X					X
	Thomas of India										X		
7													
8													
9	Denys	X	X	X	X	X	X	X	X	X		X	
	Grosseteste							X					
10	Paulinus						X	X		X			
11	Kenneth								X				
	Philip the Deacon							X		X			
12													
13	Edward the Confessor	X	X	X	X	X	X	X	X	X		X	
	Congan								X				
14													
15	Teresa	X										X	

The Calendar 239

				OCTOBER (continued)						
16	Samuel Isaac Joseph Scherescewsky									X
	Martyn						X			X
17	Latimer and Ridley [1]									X
	Etheldreda	X	X	X	X	X	X			
18	SAINT LUKE THE EVANGELIST	X	X	X	X	X	X	X	X	X
19	Frideswide	X				X				
20										
21										
22										
23	James						X			
24										
25	Crispin and Crispinian	X	X		X	X	X			
26	King Alfred the Great			X	X					X
	Cedd				X	X	X			
27										
28	SAINT SIMON AND SAINT JUDE	X	X	X	X	X	X	X	X	X
29	James Hannington and his Companions [2]					X	X			X
30										
31										

1. Canadian 1955 observes on September 17.
2. Canadian 1955 observes on the 21st.

The Calendar

NOVEMBER

Day	Feast	Roman	Sarum	English 1661	[Frere]	English 1928	Canadian 1922	Canadian 1955	Scottish	South African	Indian	American 1928	Proposed
1	ALL SAINTS	X	X	X	X	X	X	X	X	X	X	X	X
2	All Souls	X	X			X		X	X	X	X	X	
3	Richard Hooker							X					
4													
5	Elizabeth											X	
6	Leonard		X	X	X	X			X	X			
7	Willibrord				X					X			
8	Saints of the Anglican Communion					X		X	X	X	X		
	Gervadius								X				
9													
10													
11	Martin of Tours	X	X	X	X	X	X	X	X	X	X	X	X
12	Machar								X				
	Charles Simeon							X		X			X
13	Britius		X	X									
	Devenic								X				
14	Consecration of Samuel Seabury												X
15	Machutus		X	X									

		NOVEMBER (continued)									
16	Fergus										
	Margaret						X				X
	Edmund	X									
17	Hugh [1]	X	X	X	X	X	X	X			
	Hilda	X		X	X	X	X		X		X
18	Hilda				X		X	X	X		
19	Elizabeth	X							X		X
20	King Edmund	X	X	X	X	X	X	X			
21	Columban		X								
22	Cecilia	X	X	X	X	X	X	X	X		
23	Clement of Rome	X	X	X	X	X	X	X	X		X
24											
25	Catherine	X	X	X	X	X	X				
26											
27											
28											
29											
30	SAINT ANDREW THE APOSTLE	X	X	X	X	X	X	X	X		X

1. Canadian 1922 observes on the 16th.

The Calendar 243

DECEMBER

Day	Feast	Roman	Sarum	English 1661	[Frere]	English 1928	Canadian 1922	Canadian 1955	Scottish	South African	Indian	American 1928	Proposed
1	Nicholas Ferrar									X			
2	Channing More Williams												X
3	Birinus												
	Francis Xavier	X									X		X
4	Clement of Alexandria					X					X	X	X
5													
6	Nicholas of Myra	X	X	X	X	X	X	X	X	X	X	X	X
7													
8	Conception of Blessed Virgin Mary	X	X	X		X	X	X	X	X	X		
9	Pantaenus										X		
10													
11													
12													
13	Lucy	X	X	X						X			
14	Drostan								X				
15													
16	O Sapientia		X	X		X	X	X	X	X			
17	Ignatius of Antioch [1]				X	X		X	X	X	X		

244 PRAYER BOOK STUDIES IX

Day		DECEMBER (continued)									
18											
19											
20											
21	SAINT THOMAS THE APOSTLE	X	X	X	X		X	X	X	X	X
22											
23											
24											
25	THE NATIVITY OF OUR LORD JESUS CHRIST	X	X	X	X	X	X	X	X	X	X
26	SAINT STEPHEN	X	X	X	X	X	X	X	X	X	X
27	SAINT JOHN	X	X	X	X	X	X	X	X	X	X
28	THE HOLY INNOCENTS	X	X	X	X	X	X	X	X	X	X
29	Thomas Becket	X	X		X	X	X	X			
	John Wycliffe										
30											
31	Silvester	X	X	X							
	John West					X					

1. February 1.

Appendix 2: The Proposed Calendar in Chronological and Topical Order

Inasmuch as the Calendar can be a valuable instrument for teaching the history of the Church, it may be of some value to list the commemorations in an order and arrangement that may be more readily seen from this perspective. *We do not propose that such a table as this be included in the Prayer Book.* The purpose of this appendix is chiefly an effort to illustrate the way in which the proposed Calendar covers all periods of Church History, and includes a wide variety of saintly "types" who have served their Lord in manifold ways.

The Life of Christ

Annunciation	Mar. 25
Visitation	Jul. 2
Nativity of John the Baptist	Jun. 24
Joseph	Mar. 19
Christmas Day	Dec. 25
Holy Name	Jan. 1
Epiphany	Jan. 6
Holy Innocents	Dec. 28
Baptism of Jesus	Epiphany II
Temptation of Jesus	Lent I
Apostles' Days	
Mary Magdalene	Jul. 22
Transfiguration	Aug. 6
Holy Week	
Holy Cross	Sep. 14
Easter	
Ascension	
Evangelists' Days	

The Apostolic Church

Pentecost	
Apostles' Days	
Virgin Mary	Aug. 15
Barnabas	Jun. 11
Stephen	Dec. 26
Conversion of St. Paul	Jan. 25
Cornelius	Feb. 4
Timothy	Jan. 24
Titus	Feb. 6
Evangelists' Days	

The Ante-Nicene Church

Bishops	Theologians	Martyrs	Date
Clement of Rome	Clement	Clement	Nov. 23
Ignatius of Antioch	Ignatius	Ignatius	Feb. 1
Polycarp of Smyrna		Polycarp	Jan. 26
	Justin	Justin	Apr. 14
		Martyrs of Lyons	Jun. 2
Irenaeus of Lyons	Irenaeus		Jun. 28
	Clement of Alexandria		Dec. 4
		Perpetua and Companions	Mar. 7
Hippolytus of Rome	Hippolytus	Hippolytus	Aug. 13
		Laurence	Aug. 10
Cyprian of Carthage	Cyprian	Cyprian	Sep. 13
		Agnes	Jan. 21
		Vincent	Jan. 22
		Alban	Jun. 22
Gregory the Illuminator			Mar. 23

The Age of the Ecumenical Councils

Bishops	Theologians	Monks	Date
	Holy Cross		Sep. 14
	Monnica		May 4
Nicolas of Myra			Dec. 6
Athanasius of Alexandria	Athanasius		May 2
		Antony	Jan. 17
Basil of Caesarea	Basil	Basil	Jun. 14
Gregory Nazianzen	Gregory Naz.		May 9
	Ephrem		Jun. 18
Hilary of Poitiers	Hilary		Jan. 14
Ambrose of Milan	Ambrose		Apr. 4
John Chrysostom	John Chrysostom		Jan. 27
Martin of Tours		Martin	Nov. 11
	Jerome	Jerome	Sep. 30
Augustine of Hippo	Augustine		Aug. 28
Leo the Great	Leo		Apr. 11
		Benedict	Jul. 11
Gregory the Great	Gregory	Gregory	Mar. 12
	John of Damascus		May 6

The Conversion of the British Isles

Missionary Bishops	Monks	Scholars	Martyrs	Date
Patrick (Ireland)				Mar. 17
David (Wales)	David	David		Mar. 1
Columba (Scotland) — a Priest	Columba	Columba		Jun. 10
Gregory the Great				Mar. 12
Augustine of Canterbury	Augustine			May 26
Aidan (Northern England)	Aidan	Aidan		Aug. 31
	Hilda			Nov. 17
Theodore of Tarsus (England)		Theodore		Sep. 19
Boniface (Germany)	Boniface	Boniface	Boniface	Jun. 5
Willibrord (Netherlands)	Willibrord	Willibrord		Nov. 7
	Alcuin	Alcuin		May 20

The Middle Ages

Bishops	Missionaries	Monks and Friars	Scholars	Royalty	Date
Cyril and Methodius	Cyril and Methodius		Cyril and Methodius		May 11
Ansgarius	Ansgarius	Ansgarius			Feb. 3
				Alfred	Oct. 26
Dunstan		Dunstan	Dunstan		May 19
				Margaret	Nov. 16
Anselm		Anselm	Anselm		Apr. 21
		Bernard			Aug. 20
	Francis	Francis			Oct. 4
	Dominic	Dominic	Dominic		Aug. 4
		Aquinas	Aquinas		Mar. 8
				Louis	Aug. 25
				Elizabeth	Nov. 19
		Sergius			Sep. 25
		a Kempis			Jul. 26

The Reformation

First Prayer Book	Jun. 9
Tyndale	Oct. 6
Latimer and Ridley	Oct. 16

The Church of England

Bishops	Priests	Theologians	Philanthropists	Date
Andrewes		Andrewes		Sep. 26
	Herbert			Feb. 27
Laud		Laud		Jan. 10
Jeremy Taylor		Jeremy Taylor		Aug. 14
Ken				Mar. 20
	Bray		Bray	Feb. 15
Butler		Butler		Jun. 16
	Law	Law		Apr. 6

Bishops	Priests	Theologians	Philanthropists	Date
			Wilberforce	Jun. 16
	Simeon			Nov. 12
	Keble			Mar. 29
	Maurice	Maurice		Apr. 1

Bishops-Missionaries	Martyrs	Date
Patteson	Patteson	Sep. 20
Selwyn		Apr. 12
Hannington	Hannington	Oct. 29

The Church in America

Colonial	
Bray	Feb. 15

National			
Bishops	Priests	Missionary-Bishops	Date
Consecration S. Seabury			Nov. 14
White			Jul. 17
Hobart			Sep. 12
Kemper		Kemper	May 24
	Muhlenberg		Apr. 8
Williams		Williams	Dec. 2
Schereschewsky		Schereschewsky	Oct. 15
Brooks			Jan. 23
	Huntington		Jul. 27

Other types of classification can be made than those appearing in the above schedule. A few examples are suggested as follows:

APOLOGISTS: Justin; Athanasius; Augustine of Hippo; Aquinas; Butler.

PREACHERS: Gregory of Nazianzus; Ambrose; John Chrysostom; Augustine of Hippo; Leo the Great; Bernard; Dominic; Latimer; Andrewes; Brooks.

HUMANITARIANS: Bray; Law; Wilberforce; Maurice; Muhlenberg; Elizabeth of Hungary.

TRANSLATORS OF THE BIBLE: Jerome; Bede; Tyndale; Schereschewsky.

DEVOTIONAL WRITERS: Augustine of Hippo; Gregory the Great; Bernard; a Kempis; Jeremy Taylor; Law.

HYMNODISTS AND POETS: Ephrem; Hilary; Ambrose; John of Damascus; Aquinas; Herbert; Ken; Keble; Brooks.

LITURGISTS: Hippolytus; Ambrose; Leo the Great; Gregory the Great; Alcuin; Muhlenberg; Huntington.

Appendix 3: Notes on Certain Rejected Commemorations

The Calendars of the other Anglican Prayer Books contain a number of names from the early history of Christianity in the British Isles. We know a great deal about many of these saints, thanks to the excellent historical records of Bede and other writers of that early period. Devotion to these men and women has been constant in both the English and Scottish traditions, and their offshoots, and many churches bear their names in dedication. Several of them have found their way increasingly in American church dedications also. It is very tempting to include them in our proposed Calendar for the American Church, for they are part of our heritage also, and their lives are replete with holy example. The Commission believes, however, that the inclusion of so many worthies from this single tradition would be disproportionate in the total scheme and balance of the Calendar herewith proposed. The memory of these saints may well be considered, in parishes and missions that desire some memorial of them, under the Common Propers for Bishops, Confessors, Martyrs, etc. A list of some of the most popular of these saints would include:

January 19	Wulfstan, Bishop of Worcester, 1095
March 2	Chad, Bishop of Lichfield, 672
March 20	Cuthbert, Bishop of Lindisfarne, 687
April 3	Richard, Bishop of Chichester, 1253
April 19	Alphege, Archbishop of Canterbury and Martyr, 1012
May 25	Aldhelm, Bishop of Sherborne, 709
July 15	Swithun, Bishop of Winchester, ca. 862
August 5	Oswald, King of Northumbria and Martyr, 642
October 13	Edward, King and Confessor, 1066
October 17	Etheldreda, Queen and Abbess of Ely, 679
November 20	Edmund, King of East Anglia and Martyr, 870

There are other worthies whose names appear in Anglican Calendars that the Commission does not believe the American Church should adopt. Yet the appearance of our Calendar without these names will doubtless raise objections in some quarters. Our reasons for excluding them should therefore be stated, at least in brief:

Valentine (Feb. 14) is listed in the Sarum, English 1661, Canadian and South African Calendars. It is not clear whether this name represents a bishop of Umbria or a priest of Rome. According to legend both of these men of the same name suffered martyrdom about the year 270. There are no trustworthy historical records of either of them. The day has ceased to have much religious significance. For Americans, St. Valentine's day is secularized, and associated with the exchange of greetings by lovers.

George (Apr. 23), the "Patron" of England appears in all Anglican Calendars, and was proposed in the American list for the 1928 Book. His popularity is exceeded only by his total obscurity. In the Eastern Church his feast is a major holy day, and the territory of Georgia in Asia Minor is named for him. The tale of his conflict with the dragon is pure mythology, a re-working of the myth of Theseus. Though his martyrdom is attributed to the year 304, it cannot be certified from any historical record that he ever lived. The widespread cultus of St. George throughout the Church cannot be accepted as proof of his historicity. The Commission does not believe that we should commemorate so legendary a person a kind of allegorical figure of the Christian soldier.

St. John the Evangelist before the Latin Gate (May 6) is listed in all the Anglican Calendars. The basis of this feast is an apocryphal story of the Evangelist's survival of an ordeal of being plunged in boiling oil before the Latin Gate in the city of Rome. This story is as old as Tertullian (early third century), but it does not have the slightest claim to historicity. The date marks the dedication of a basilica in Rome to commemorate the legend.

Anne (July 26), listed in all Anglican Calendars and also included in the list proposed for the American Book of 1928, is known as the name of the mother of our Lord's mother only from apocryphal and utterly legendary sources. Of course, our Lord's mother had a mother, too, and she was doubtless a good woman. But the fact is that we know nothing about her at all, and cannot be certain of the authenticity of her name. The fact that many churches and religious guilds and societies are named for her does not create a history out of a vacuum.

Beheading of St. John Baptist (Aug. 29), a major feast of the Western Church, appears as early as the Gelasian Sacramentary. It is included in all the Anglican Calendars. Of this festival, there is certainly an historical basis, both in the Gospels and in the Jewish historian Josephus. The Commission questions its appropriateness in a Christian Calendar, however, since there is no evidence that the Baptist's martyrdom was due to his faith in Christ. The only feast of the Baptist that is relevant to the Christian faith is that of his Nativity on June 24.

Nativity of the Blessed Virgin Mary (Sept. 8), a major festival of both the Eastern and Western Churches, finds a place in all the Anglican Calendars. The story upon which the feast is based is purely apocryphal. The New Testament ignores the Virgin's birth altogether. The Commission believes that the mother of our Lord is best commemorated, as are other Christian saints, on the day of her death.

Cecilia (Nov. 22), a virgin and martyr of Rome, has become in tradition the Patroness of Musicians. All the Anglican Calendars and the American proposed Calendar of 1928 include her name. Unfortunately, there is no trustworthy history of her life or death, and even the date of her martyrdom is much disputed. The problems surrounding her tomb in the catacomb of Callistus at Rome are as yet unsolved, and many competent archaeologists and historians have considerable doubt of her historicity.

Catherine (Nov. 25), another virgin and martyr, appears in all the Anglican Calendars except the Indian. She is said to have been martyred in Alexandria, Egypt, ca. 307. Despite the fame of her cultus and the popularity of her name in church, school, and guild dedications, there is not one shred of authentic history that has come down to us about this worthy.

Conception of the Blessed Virgin Mary (Dec. 8), though of ancient commemoration in England, and listed in all the Anglican Calendars, rests upon no authentic history. This feast stands or falls with the festival of the Virgin's Nativity. In addition, however, the modern Roman dogma of the Immaculate Conception of the Blessed Virgin is so repugnant to most Anglicans, that it is difficult to see how this feast would be acceptable in the American Church.

Appendix 4: General Bibliography

Bradshaw, Henry, "Calendar," *A Dictionary of Christian Antiquities*, edited by William Smith and Samuel Cheetham. Hartford, 1880, Vol. I, pp. 256-58.

Cabrol, Fernand, "Fetes Chretiennes," *Dictionnaire d'archéologie chrétienne et de liturgie*, edited by F. Cabrol and H. Leclercq, Vol. V, pp. 1403-52.

Clarke, W. K. Lowther, "The Calendar," *Liturgy and Worship, A Companion to the Prayer Books of the Anglican Communion*, edited by W. K. Lowther Clarke and Charles Harris. London: S.P.C.K., 1932, pp. 201-44.

Delehaye, Hippolyte, *Sanctus, Essai sur le culte des saints dans l'antiquite.* Bruxelles: Société des Bollandistes, 1927.

———, *Les origines du culte des martyrs.* 2d ed. Bruxelles: Société des Bollandistes, 1933.

Dix, Gregory, *The Shape of the Liturgy.* Westminster: Dacre Press, 1945, pp. 333-85.
Dowden, John, *The Church Year and Kalendar.* Cambridge: University Press, 1910.
Frere, W. H., *Some Principles of Liturgical Reform, A Contribution Towards the Revision of the Book of Common Prayer.* London: John Murray, 1911, pp. 16-69.
———, *Studies in Early Roman Liturgy: I. The Kalendar.* Alcuin Club Collections. No. XXVIII. Oxford University Press, 1930.
Kemp, Eric Waldram, *Canonization and Authority in the Western Church.* Oxford University Press, 1948.
MacLean, A. J., "Festival," *The Prayer Book Dictionary,* edited by George Harford and Morley Stevenson. New York: Long-mans, 1912, pp. 337-48.
Proctor, F., and Dewick, E. S., *The Martiloge.* Edited with Introduction and Notes. The Henry Bradshaw Society, Vol. III. London, 1893.
Rodgers, Edith Cooperrider, *Discussion of Holidays in the Later Middle Ages.* New York: Columbia University Press, 1940.
Simpson, W. J. Sparrow, *The Minor Festivals of the Anglican Calendar.* New York: E. P. Dutton and Co., 1901.
Staley, Vernon, *The Liturgical Year,* An Explanation of the Origin, History and Significance of the Festival Days and Fasting Days of the English Church. London: Mowbray, 1907
———, "Black-Letter Days," *The Prayer Book Dictionary,* edited by George Harford and Morley Stevenson. New York: Longmans, 1912, pp. 103-05.
Wordsworth, John, *The Ministry of Grace,* Studies in Early Church History with Reference to Present Problems. 2d ed. rev. London: Longmans, 1903, pp. 392-438.
Wormald, Francis, *English Kalendars before A.D. 1100.* The Henry Bradshaw Society, Vol. LXXII. London, 1935.
———, *English Benedictine Kalendars after A.D. 1100.* The Henry Bradshaw Society, Vols. LXXVII, LXXXI. London, 1939, 1946.

Appendix 5: Alphabetical Index of Commemorations, with Special Bibliographies

The listing in this appendix will serve both as an alphabetical index to the fixed holy days proposed in the present study, and as a guide to further reading with respect to each of the new entries. For those who have neither the time nor the resources to explore the varied volumes here recommended, a few general listings of encyclopedias, dictionaries, and biographical collections may be of use. Almost all of the saints here proposed have biographical notices in the *Encyclopaedia Britannica,* and other similar reference works. Attention is called, however, to the following series:

> *A Dictionary of Christian Biography,* edited by William Smith and Henry Wace. 4 vols. London: John Murray, 1877-87.
> An old but generally reliable work, containing thorough accounts of all the worthies of the ancient and early medieval periods.

Dictionary of National Biography, edited by Leslie Stephen and Sidney Lee. 63 vols. London, 1885-1900. Various supplementary volumes, indices, etc.

A standard reference for all periods of English history.

A Dictionary of English Church History, edited by S. L. Ollard, Gordon Crosse, and M. F. Bond. New Edition. London: Mowbray, 1948.

Dictionary of American Biography, edited by Allen Johnson and Dumas Malone. 20 vols. New York: Scribners, 1928-37.

The Catholic Encyclopedia, edited by C. G. Herbermann and others, 16 vols. and Supplement. New York, 1907-14, 1922.

Contains all the entries up to the Reformation. Articles are trustworthy, though uneven in quality and length.

Baring-Gould, S., *The Lives of the Saints*. 16 vols. New and Revised edition. Edinburgh: John Grant, 1914.

Butler, Alban, *Lives of the Fathers, Martyrs and Other Principal Saints*. Revised and Supplemented by H. Thurston and D. Attwater, 12 vols.

AGNES, January 21.

Ambrose, *Concerning Virginity* (Nicene and Post-Nicene Fathers, Second Series, Vol. X, page 364.)

Kirsch, J. P., in *The Catholic Encyclopedia*, I, 214.

AIDAN, August 31.

Bede, *Ecclesiastical History*, Book III.

Howorth, H. H., *The Golden Days of the Early English Church*, (New York: Dutton, 1917) Vol. I, Chapter I.

Bright, William, *Chapters in Early English Church History*, 3d ed. (Oxford, 1897), Chapter V.

ALBAN, June 22.

Bede, *Ecclesiastical History*, Book I, c. 7.

Williams, Hugh, *Christianity in Early Britain* (Oxford, 1912), Chapter V.

ALCUIN, May 20.

Browne, G. F., *Alcuin of York* (London: S.P.C.K., 1908).

Duckett, E. S., *Alcuin, Friend of Charlemagne* (New York: Macmillan, 1951) (With full bibliography).

Laistner, M. L. W., *Thought and Letters in Western Europe A.D. 500 to 900* (New York: Dial, 1931), Part III.

ALFRED THE GREAT, KING, October 26.

    Asser, *Life of King Alfred* (The King's Classics; London: Chatto and Windus, 1908); ed. by W. H. Stevenson (Oxford, 1904).

    Plummer, Charles, *The Life and Times of Alfred the Great* (Ford Lectures, 1901; Oxford, 1902).

    Browne, G. F., *King Alfred's Books* (London: S.P.C.K., 1920).

    Stenton, F. M., *Anglo-Saxon England* (Oxford, 1943), Chapter VIII.

    Duckett, E. S., *Alfred the Great* (University of Chicago Press, 1956).

ALL SAINTS, November I.
AMBROSE, April 4.

    Select works translated in *Nicene and Post-Nicene Fathers*, Second Series, Vol. X.

    Paulinus the Deacon, "The Life of St. Ambrose," *The Western Fathers*, translated and edited by F. R. Hoare (New York: Sheed and Ward, 1954), pp. 145-88.

    deLabriolle, P., *The Life and Times of St. Ambrose*, trans. by H. Wilson (St. Louis: Herder, 1928).

    Dudden, F. Homes, *The Life and Times of St. Ambrose*, 2 Vols. (Oxford, 1935) (With full bibliography).

    Rand, E. K., *Founders of the Middle Ages* (Lowell Lectures; Cambridge: Harvard University Press, 1929), pp. 69-101.

ANDREW, SAINT, the Apostle, November 30.
ANDREWS, LANCELOT, September 26.

    Works, in Library of Anglo-Catholic Theology (Memoir by H. Isaacson).

    Preces Privatae (A Manual of the Private Prayers and Meditations). Editions by A. Whyte (with a biography; New York: James Pott, 1896); by F. E. Brightman (London: Methuen, 1903); and others.

    Overton, J. H., in *Dictionary of National Biography*, I, 401-05.

    Ottley, R. L., *Lancelot Andrewes* (Boston: Houghton Mifflin, 1894).

    Higham, Florence, *Lancelot Andrewes* (New York: Morehouse-Gorham, 1952).

    Reidy, M. F., *Bishop Lancelot Andrewes*, Jacobean Court Preacher (Chicago: Loyola University Press, 1955).

ANNUNCIATION OF THE BLESSED VIRGIN MARY, THE, March 25.
ANSELM, April 21.

    Deane, S. N., *St. Anselm* . . . Translated from the Latin (Philosophical Classics, Religion of Science Library, 54; Chicago: Open Court Publishing Co., 1903).

Church, R. W., *Saint Anselm* (New ed.; London: Macmillan, 1888).

Welch, A. C., *Anselm and His Work* (New York: Scribners, 1901).

Brooke, Z. N., *The English Church and the Papacy from the Conquest to the Reign of John* (Cambridge, 1931).

ANSGARIUS, February 3.

Robinson, C. H., *Anskar, the Apostle of the North, 801-865* (London: S.P.G., 1921). Translation of "Life" by Rimbert, the successor of Ansgarius.

Wordsworth, John, *The National Church of Sweden* (Hale Lectures; London: Mowbray, 1911), Chapter II.

Latourette, K. S., *The Thousand Years of Uncertainty, A.D. 500-A.D. 1500* (New York: Harpers, 1938), pp. 106-43.

Addison, J. T., *The Medieval Missionary*, A Study of the Conversion of Northern Europe, A.D. 500-1300 (New York: International Missionary Council, 1936), pp. 17-10.

ANTONY, January 17.

St. Athanasius, *The Life of Saint Antony*, Newly Translated and Annotated by Robert T. Meyer (Ancient Christian Writers, No. 10; Westminster, Md.: Newman Press, 1950).

Mackean, W. H., *Christian Monasticism in Egypt to the Close of the Fourth Century* (London: S.P.C.K., 1920).

Waddell, Helen, *The Desert Fathers*. Translations from the Latin. (New York: Henry Holt, 1936).

ATHANASIUS, May 2.

Select Works translated in Nicene and Post-Nicene Fathers, Second Series, Vol. IV (by A. Robertson).

Gregory Nazianzen, "On the Great Athanasius," *ibid.*, VII, pp. 269-80.

Bright, William, "Athanasius," *A Dictionary of Christian Biography*, ed. by W. Smith and H. Wace, Vol. I, pp. 179-203.

Duchesne, Louis, *Early History of the Christian Church* (London: John Murray, 1912), Vol. II.

AUGUSTINE, OF CANTERBURY, May 26.

Bede, *Ecclesiastical History*, Books I and II.

Mason, A. J., *The Mission of St. Augustine to England according to the Original Documents* (Cambridge, 1897).

Browne, G. F., *Augustine and His Companions* (London: S.P.C.K., 1895).

Howorth, H. H., *Saint Augustine of Canterbury* (New York: Dutton, 1913).

AUGUSTINE, OF HIPPO, August 28.

Works, selected and translated in *Nicene and Post-Nicene Fathers*, First Series, Vols. I-VIII.

Confessions. Numerous translations.

St. Possidius, "The Life of St. Augustine," *The Western Fathers* (New York: Sheed and Ward, 1954), pp. 189-244.

Adam, Karl, *Saint Augustine, The Odyssey Of His Soul* (New York: Macmillan, 1932).

Pope, Hugh, *Saint Augustine of Hippo* (Westminster, Md.: Newman Press, 1949).

Bourke, V. J., *Augustine's Quest of Wisdom* (Milwaukee: Bruce Publishing Co., 1944).

Battenhouse, R. W., *A Companion to the Study of St. Augustine* (New York: Oxford University Press, 1954).

BARNABAS, SAINT, the Apostle, June 11.
BARTHOLOMEW, SAINT, the Apostle, August 24.
BASIL THE GREAT, June 14.

Select works, translated in *Nicene and Post-Nicene Fathers*, Second Series, Vol. VIII.

The Ascetic Works of Saint Basil, translated by W. K. Lowther Clarke (London: S.P.C.K., 1952).

Gregory Nazianzen, "On St. Basil the Great," *Funeral Orations*, translated by L. P. McCauley and others (Fathers of the Church; New York, 1953).

Morison, E. F., *St. Basil and His Rule, A Study in Early Monasticism* (Oxford, 1912).

Clarke, W. K. Lowther, *St. Basil the Great, A Study in Monasticism* (Cambridge, 1913).

BEDE, THE VENERABLE, May 27.

Historical writings, translated in Everyman Library, and the Loeb Classical Library.

Browne, G. F., *The Venerable Bede, His Life and Writings*, (London: S.P.C.K., 1919).

Thompson, A. H. (ed.), *Bede, His Life, Times, and Writings*, Essays in Commemoration of the Twelfth Centenary of His Death (Oxford, 1935).

Chambers, R. W., *Bede* (Oxford, 1936).

Duckett, E. S., *Anglo-Saxon Saints and Scholars* (New York: Macmillan, 1947), Chapter III.

BENEDICT OF NURSIA, July 11.

Gregory the Great, *Dialogues*, Book II: "Of the Life and Miracles of St. Benedict" (translation by E. G. Gardner; London: Medici Society, 1911; also by O. J. Zimmermann and B. R. Avery; Collegeville, Minn.: St. John's Abbey Press, 1949).

The Rule of St. Benedict, ed. and trans. by J. McCann (Westminster, Md.: Newman Press, 1952).

Cabrol, Fernand, *Saint Benedict* (London: Burns, Oates and Washbourne, Ltd., 1934).

McCann, Justin, *Saint Benedict* (New York: Sheed and Ward, 1937).

Lindsay, T. F., *Saint Benedict, His Life and Work* (London: Burns, Oates and Washbourne, Ltd., 1949).

BERNARD, August 20.

The Complete Works . . . translated by S. J. Eales, 5 vols. London, 1889-96.

Storrs, Richard S., *Bernard of Clairvaux*, The Times, the Man, and His Work (New York: Scribners, 1893).

Williams, Watkin, *Saint Bernard of Clairvaux* (Manchester University Press, 1935)

Gilson, E., *The Mystical Theology of Saint Bernard*, trans. by A. H. C. Downes (New York: Sheed and Ward, 1940).

Taylor, H. O., *The Mediaeval Mind* (London: Macmillan, 1911), Vol. I, Chapter XVII.

BONIFACE, June 5.

Willibald, "The Life of St. Boniface," *The Anglo-Saxon Missionaries in Germany*, trans. and ed. by C. H. Talbot (New York: Sheed and Ward, 1954), pp. 23-62.

Emerton, E., *The Letters of Saint Boniface*, Translated with an Introduction (New York: Columbia University Press, 1940).

Browne, G. F., *Boniface of Crediton and His Companions* (London: S.P.C.K., 1910).

Crawford, S. J., *Anglo-Saxon Influence on Western Christendom 600-800* (Oxford, 1933).

Duckett, E. S., *Anglo-Saxon Saints and Scholars* (New York: Macmillan, 1947), Chapter IV.

BOOK OF COMMON PRAYER, FIRST, June 9.

The First and Second Prayer Books of Edward VI (Everyman Library).

Ratcliff, E. C., *The Booke of Common Prayer, Its Making and Revisions 1549-1661* (Alcuin Club Collections: XXXVII; London: S.P.C.K., 1949).

Morison, Stanley, *English Prayer Books* (3d ed.; Cambridge, 1949)

BRAY, THOMAS, February 15.

Overton, J. H., in *Dictionary of National Biography*, II, '147-49.

Pennington, E. L., *The Reverend Thomas Bray* (Church Historical Society Publication, No. VII; Philadelphia, 1934).

Lydekker, J. W., *Thomas Bray*, 1658-1730, Founder of Missionary Enterprise (Church Historical Society Publication, No. 14; Philadelphia, 1943).

Cropper, M., *Sparks among the Stubble* (New York: Long-mans, 1955), pp. 33-59.

Thompson, H. P., *Thomas Bray* (London: S.P.C.K., 1954).

BROOKS, PHILLIPS, January 23.

Allen, A. V. G., *Life and Letters of Phillips Brooks* (New York: Dutton, 1900).

Lawrence, William, *Life of Phillips Brooks* (New York: Harpers, 1930).

Chorley, E. C., *Men and Movements in the American Episcopal Church* (Hale Lectures; New York: Scribners, 1946).

Addison, J. T., *The Episcopal Church in the United States, 1789-1931* (New York: Scribners, 1951), pp. 262-70.

BUTLER, JOSEPH, June 16.

Works, editions by W. E. Gladstone (Oxford, 1896), 2 vols.; and by J. H. Bernard (London, 1900).

Church, R. W., *Pascal and Other Sermons* (London: Macmillan, 1896), Sermon II: "Bishop Butler."

Mossner, E. C., *Bishop Butler and the Age of Reason*, A Study in the History of Thought (New York: Macmillan, 1936). (Contains a full bibliography.)

Stephen, L., in *Dictionary of National Biography*, III, 519-24.

CHRISTMAS DAY, December 25.
CIRCUMCISION OF CHRIST, THE, see HOLY NAME
CLEMENT OF ALEXANDRIA, December 4.

Works, translated in Ante-Nicene Fathers, Vol. II.

Oulton, J. E. L., and Chadwick, H., *Alexandrian Christianity* (The Library of Christian Classics; Vol. II; Philadelphia: Westminster Press, 1954).

Bigg, C., *The Christian Platonists of Alexandria* (Oxford, 1886).

Westcott, B. F., in *Dictionary of Christian Biography*, I, 559-67.

Tollinton, R. B., *Clement of Alexandria*, A Study in Christian Liberalism (London: Williams and Norgate, 1914), 2 vols.

CLEMENT OF ROME

Clarke, W. K. Lowther, *The First Epistle of Clement to the Corinthians* (Translations of Early Documents; London: S.P.C.K., 1937).

Kleist, J. A., *The Epistles of St. Clement of Rome and St. Ignatius of Antioch* (Ancient Christian Writers, No. I; Westminster, Md.: Newman Press, 1946).

Lightfoot, J. B., *The Apostolic Fathers*. Part I: *S. Clement of Rome* (rev. ed.; London: Macmillan, 1890), 2 vols.

Bardy, G., *The Church at the End of the First Century*, trans. by P. W. Singleton (London: Sands and Co., 1938).

COLUMBA, June 10.

St. Adamnan, *Prophecies, Miracles and Visions of St. Columba*, A New Translation, by J. T. Fowler (London: Henry Froude, 1895).

Menzies, Lucy, *Saint Columba of Iona*, A Study of His Life, His Times, and His Influence (London: Dent, 1920).

Duke, John A., *The Columban Church* (Oxford, 1932).

Pochin Mould, D. D. C., *Scotland of the Saints* (London: Batsford, 1952).

CORNELIUS THE CENTURION, February 4.
CYPRIAN, September 13.

Works, translated in Ante-Nicene Fathers, Vol. V.

Benson, E. W., *Cyprian, His Life, His Times, His Work* (London: Macmillan, 1897).

Gregg, J. A. F., *The Decian Persecution* (Edinburgh: Blackwood, 1897).

Lietzmann, Hans, *The Founding of the Church Universal* (A History of the Early Church, Vol. II; New York: Scribners, 1950), pp. 2 16-5 7.

Greenslade, S. L., *Early Latin Theology* (The Library of Christian Classics, Vol. V; Philadelphia: Westminster Press, 1956).

CYRIL AND METHODIUS, May 11.

Jagie, V., in *Cambridge Mediaeval History*, IV, 215-29.

Latourette, K. S., *The Thousand Years of Uncertainty, A.D. 500–A.D. 1500* (New York: Harpers, 1938), pp. 155-70.

Spinka, M., *A History of Christianity in the Balkans* (Studies in Church History, Vol. I; Chicago: The American Society of Church History, 1933), pp. 17-36.

Potoček, C. J., *Saints Cyril and Methodus, Apostles of the Slavs* (New York: P. J. Kenedy and Sons, 1941).

DAVID, March 1.

Wade-Evans, A. W., *Life of St. David* (Translations of Christian Literature Series: Lives of the Celtic Saints: London: S.P.C.K., 1923).

Williams, Hugh, *Christianity in Early Britain* (Oxford, 1912).

Lloyd, J. E., *A History of Wales from the Earliest Times to the Edwardian Conquest* (London: Longmans, 1911), I, 124-61.

Williams, A. H., *An Introduction to the History of Wales* (Cardiff: University of Wales Press Board, 1941), I, 83-146.

DOMINIC, August 4.

Lives of the Brethren of the Order of Preachers, 1206-1259, translated by Placid Conway; edited by Bede Jarrett (London: Burns, Oates and Washbourne, Ltd., 1924).

Jarrett, Bede, *Life of St. Dominic (1170-1221)* (New York: Benziger Bros., 1924).

Bennett, R. F., *The Early Dominicans*, Studies in Thirteenth Century Dominican History (Cambridge, 1937).

Mandonnet, Pierre, *St. Dominic and His Work*, trans. by M. B. Larkin (St. Louis: Herder, 1944). Full bibliography.

DUNSTAN, May 19.

Symons, Thomas, *Regularis Concordia*, The Monastic Agreement of the Monks and Nuns of the English Nation, Translated with Introduction and Notes (Medieval Classics; London: Thos. Nelson, 1953).

Robinson, J. A., *The Times of Saint Dunstan* (Ford Lectures, 1922; Oxford, 1923).

Knowles, David, *The Monastic Order in England* (Cambridge, 1949), pp. 31-56.

Duckett, E. S., *Saint Dunstan of Canterbury*, A Study of Monastic Reform in the Tenth Century (New York: W. W. Norton, 1955).

ELIZABETH OF HUNGARY, November 19.

Jacobus de Voragine, *The Golden Legend*, translated by G. Ryan and H. Kipperger (New York: Longmans, 1941), II, 675-89.

Bihl, M., in *The Catholic Encyclopedia*, V, 389-91.

Schmidt-Pauli, E. von, *Saint Elizabeth, Sister of Saint Francis* (New York: Holt), 1932.

Seesholtz, Anne, *Saint Elizabeth* (New York: Philosophical Library, 1948).

EPHREM OF EDESSA, June 18.

Works, translated in *Nicene and Post-Nicene Fathers*, Second Series, Vol. XIII.

Smith, R. P., in *Dictionary of Christian Biography*, II, 137-44.

Burkitt, F. C., *Early Eastern Christianity* (St. Margaret's Lectures, 1904, On the Syriac-Speaking Church; London: John Murray, 1904), Chapter III.

EPIPHANY OF OUR LORD JESUS CHRIST, THE, January 6.
FRANCIS OF ASSISI, October 4.

Robinson, P., *The Writings of Saint Francis of Assisi*, Translated with Introduction and Notes (Philadelphia: Dolphin Press, 1906).

Thomas of Celano, *The Lives of S. Francis of Assisi*, Translated by A. G. F. Howell (New York: Dutton, 1908).

The Little Flowers of St. Francis, The Mirror of Perfection, The Life of St. Francis (by St. Bonaventura). Everyman Library.

Sabatier, Paul, *Life of St. Francis of Assisi*, trans. by L. S. Houghton (New York: Scribners, 1894).

Salvatorelli, L., *The Life of St. Francis of Assisi*, trans. by E. Sutton (New York: Knopf, 1928).

Petry, R. C., *Francis of Assisi, Apostle of Poverty* (Durham: Duke University Press, 1941).

Moorman, John R. H., *Saint Francis of Assisi* (London: SCM Press, 1950).

GREGORY THE GREAT, March 12.

Works, translated in *Nicene and Post-Nicene Fathers*, Second Series, Vols. XII, XIII.

Gasquet, F. A., *A Life of Pope St. Gregory the Great*, written by a Monk of the Monastery of Whitby (Westminster: Art and Book Co., 1904).

Barmby, J., in *Dictionary of Christian Biography*, II, 779-91.

Hutton, W. H., in *Cambridge Medieval History*, II, 236-62.

Dudden, F. Homes, *Gregory the Great*, His Place in History and Thought (London: Longmans, 1905), 2 vols.

Batiffol, P., *Saint Gregory the Great*, trans. by J. L. Stoddard (London: Burns, Oates and Washbourne, Ltd., 1929).

GREGORY THE ILLUMINATOR, March 23.

Davidson, L., in *Dictionary of Christian Biography*, II, 737-39

Attwater, D., *The Golden Book of Eastern Saints* (Milwaukee: Bruce Publishing Co., 1938), pp. 17-25.

Arpee, Leon, *A History of Armenian Christianity* (New York: The Armenian Missionary Association of America, 1946), pp. 15-23.

GREGORY OF NAZIANZUS, May 9.

Works, translated in *Nicene and Post-Nicene Fathers*, Second Series, Vol. VII.

Hardy, E. R., *Christology of the Later Fathers* (The Library of Christian Classics, Vol. III; Philadelphia: Westminster Press, 1954), pp. 111-232.

Watkins, H. W., in *Dictionary of Christian Biography*, II, 741-61.

Brooke, Dorothy, *Pilgrims Were They All*, Stories of Religious Adventure in the Fourth Century of Our Era (London: Faber and Faber, 1943), Chapter IV.

HANNINGTON, JAMES, AND HIS COMPANIONS, October 29.

Dawson, E. C. (ed.), *The Last Journals of James Hannington* (London: Seeley and Co., 1888).

———, *James Hannington, A History of His Life and Work 1847-1885* (New York: Anson D. F. Randolph and Co.).

Berry, W. G., *Bishop Hannington and the Story of the Uganda Mission* (London: Fleming H. Revell Co., n.d.).

HERBERT, GEORGE, February 27.

The Temple, and A Priest to the Temple. Introduction by Edward Thomas. Everyman Library.

Walton, Isaak, *Life of George Herbert* (1670). Reprinted by S. B. Carter, *Walton's Lives* (London: Falcon Educational Books, 1951), pp. 197-258.

Palmer, G. H. (ed.), *The English Works of George Herbert* (Boston: Houghton Mifflin, 1905).

Hyde, A. G., *George Herbert and His Times* (London, 1907).

Cropper, M., *Flame Touches Flame* (New York: Longmans, 1949), pp. 1-28.

HILARY, January 14.

Works, translated in *Nicene and Post-Nicene Fathers*, Second Series, Vol. IX.

Cazenove, J. G., in *Dictionary of Christian Biography*, III, 54-66.

Duchesne, Louis, *Early History of the Christian Church* (London: John Murray, 1912), Vol. II, passim.

HILDA, November 17.

Bede, *Ecclesiastical History*, Book IV, c. 23.

Howorth, H. H., *The Golden Days of the Early English Church* (New York: Dutton, 1917), Vol. III, pp. 175-95.

Browne, G. F., *The Importance of Women in Anglo-Saxon Times* (London: S.P.C.K., 1919).

Eckenstein, L., *Women under Monasticism*, Chapters on Saint lore and Convent Life, 500-1500 (Cambridge, 1896).

HIPPOLYTUS, August 13.

Works, translated in *Ante-Nicene Fathers*, Vol. V.

The Apostolic Tradition. Trans. and ed. by B. S. Easton (Cambridge, 1934); and by G. Dix (London: S.P.C.K, 1937).

Bonwetsch, N., in *The New Schaff-Herzog Encyclopedia of Religious Knowledge*, V, 291-95.

Duchesne, L., *Early History of the Christian Church* (London: John Murray, 909), Vol. I, pp. 212-236.

Quasten, J., *Patrology*, Vol. II (Westminster, Md.: Newman Press, 1953), pp. 163-207. Full bibliography.

HOBART, JOHN HENRY, September 12.

Lowndes, A. (ed.), *The Correspondence of John Henry Hobart* (Archives of the General Convention; New York, 1911-12), 6 vols.

Schroeder, J. F., *Memorial of Bishop Hobart*, A Collection of Sermons . . . with a Memoir of His Life and Writings (New York, 1831).

Chorley, E. C., *Men and Movements in the American Episcopal Church* (Hale Lectures; New York: Scribners, 1946). Full bibliography.

Addison, J. T., *The Episcopal Church in the United States 1789-1931* (New York: Scribners, 1951), pp. 96-102.

HOLY CROSS, THE EXALTATION OF THE, September 14.

Eusebius, "The Life of Constantine," Nicene and Post-Nicene Fathers, Second Series, Vol. I, pp. 526-30 (III. 25-40).

Crowfoot, J. W., *Early Churches in Palestine* (The Schweich Lectures; London: British Academy, 1941), pp. 9-21.

Harvey, W., *Church of the Holy Sepulchre Jerusalem* (Structural Survey, Final Report; Oxford, 1935).

Black, M., "The Festival of Encaenia Ecclesiae in the Ancient Church with special reference to Palestine and Syria," *The Journal of Ecclesiastical History* V (1954), 78-85.

HOLY INNOCENTS, THE, December 28.
HOLY NAME OF OUR LORD JESUS CHRIST, THE, January 1.
HUNTINGTON, WILLIAM REED, July 27.

Huntington, W. R., *The Church-Idea, An Essay towards Unity* (New York, 1870; 5th ed., Boston: Houghton Mifflin, 1928).

———, *A Short History of the Book of Common Prayer*: With a Study of the Te Deum (New York: Thomas Whitaker, 1893).

Suter, J. W., *Life and Letters of William Reed Huntington*, A Champion of Unity (New York: Century, 1925).

IGNATIUS, February 1.

Kleist, J. A., *The Epistles of St. Clement of Rome and St. Ignatius of Antioch* (Ancient Christian Writers, No. I; Westminster, Md.: Newman Press, 1946).

Richardson, C. C., *Early Christian Fathers* (The Library of Christian Classics, Vol. I; Philadelphia: Westminster Press, 1953), pp. 74-120. Full bibliography.

Lightfoot, J. B., *The Apostolic Fathers*, Part II: *St. Ignatius, St. Polycarp* (rev. ed.; London: Macmillan, 1889), 3 vols.

Richardson, C. C., *The Christianity of Ignatius of Antioch* (New York: Columbia University Press, 1935).

Schilling, F. A., *The Mysticism of Ignatius of Antioch* (Philadelphia: University of Pennsylvania Press, 1932).

INDEPENDENCE DAY, July 4.
IRENAEUS, June 28.

The *Against Heresies*, translated in Ante-Nicene Fathers, Vol. I.

The *Demonstration of the Apostolic Preaching*, trans. by J. A. Robinson (Translations of Christian Literature Series IV: Oriental Texts; London: S.P.C.K., 1920); and by J. P. Smith (Ancient Christian Writers, No. 16; Westminster, Md.: Newman Press, 1952).

Hitchcock, F. R. M., *Irenaeus of Lugdunum*, A Study of His Teaching, Foreword by H. B. Swete (Cambridge, 1914). McGiffert, A. C., A History of Christian Thought (New York: Scribners, 1931), Vol. I, pp. 132-48.

Lietzmann, Hans, *The Founding of the Church Universal* (A History of the Early Church, Vol. II; New York: Scribners, 1950), Chapter Nine.

Quasten, J., *Patrology*, Vol. I (Westminster, Md.: Newman Press, 1950), pp. 287-313. Full bibliography.

JAMES, SAINT, the Apostle, July 25.
JAMES, SAINT, Apostle (with Philip), May 1.
JEROME, September 30.

Select Works, translated in *Nicene and Post-Nicene Fathers*, Second Series, Vols. III and VI.

Fremantle, W. H., "Hieronymus," *Dictionary of Christian Biography*, III, 29-50.

Monceaux, P., *St. Jerome, The Early Years*, trans. by F. J. Sheed (New York: Sheed and Ward, 1937).

Murphy, F. X. (ed.), *A Monument to Saint Jerome*, Essays on Some Aspects of His Life, Works and Influence (New York: Sheed and Ward, 1952).

Rand, E. K., *Founders of the Middle Ages* (Lowell Lectures; Cambridge, Mass.: Harvard University Press, 1929), Chapter IV.

JOHN, SAINT, Apostle and Evangelist, December 27.
JOHN BAPTIST, THE NATIVITY OF SAINT, June 24.
JOHN CHRYSOSTOM, January 27.

Works, translated in *Nicene and Post-Nicene Fathers*, First Series, Vols. IX-XIV.

Moxon, T. A., *St. Chrysostom On the Priesthood* (Translations of Christian Literature Series I: Greek Texts; London: S.P.C.K., 1907).

Venables, E., in *Dictionary of Christian Biography*, I, 518-35.

Attwater, D., *St. John Chrysostom, the Voice of Gold* (Milwaukee: Bruce Publishing Co., 1939).

Stephens, W. R. W., *St. John Chrysostom, His Life and Times* (3d ed.; London, 1883).

Duchesne, L., *Early History of the Christian Church* (London: John Murray, 1924), Vol. III, pp. 49-75.

JOHN OF DAMASCUS, May 6.

Selected works, translated in *Nicene and Post-Nicene Fathers*, Second Series, Vol. IX.

Lupton, J. H., in *Dictionary of Christian Biography*, III, 409-23.

Martin, E. J., *A History of the Iconoclastic Controversy* (London: S.P.C.K., 1930).

Harnack, A., *History of Dogma*, trans. by N. Buchanan (Boston: Little, Brown and Co., 1898), III, 241-315; IV, 264-67, 304-30.

JOSEPH, SAINT, March 19.
JUDE, SAINT, Apostle (with Simon), October 28.
JUSTIN MARTYR, April 14.

Works, translated in *Ante-Nicene Fathers*, Vol. I; also in *Fathers of the Church*, trans. by T. B. Falls (New York: Christian Heritage, Inc., 1948).

"The Martyrdom of Justin and his Companions," trans. in B. J. Kidd, *Documents Illustrative of the History of the Church*, Vol. I, to A.D. 313 (Translations of Christian Literature, Series VI: Select Passages; London: S.P.C.K., 1920).

Quasten, J., *Patrology*, Vol. I (Westminster, Md.: Newman Press, 1950), pp. 196-219. Full bibliography.

Richardson, C. C., *Early Christian Fathers* (The Library of Christian Classics, Vol. I; Philadelphia: Westminster Press, 1953), pp. 225-89.

Carrington, P., *Christian Apologetics of the Second Century in their Relation to Modern Thought* (London: S.P.C.K., 1921).

Little, V. A. Spence, *The Christology of the Apologists* (New York: Scribners, 1935), pp. 90-176.

KEBLE, JOHN, March 29.

Coleridge, J. T., *Memoir of John Keble* (London, 1869). Lock, W., John Keble (London: Methuen, 1895).

Donaldson, A. B., *Five Great Oxford Leaders* (London: Rivingtons, 1902), pp. 1-67.

Church, R. W., T*he Oxford Movement: Twelve Years, 1833-1845* (London: Macmillan, 1891), Chapter II.

Overton, J. H., in J. Julian, *A Dictionary of Hymnology* (New York: Scribners, 1892), pp. 610-13.

KEMPER, JACKSON, May 24.

Historical Magazine of the Protestant Episcopal Church, Vol. IV (1935). Special issue devoted to Kemper, with bibliography.

White, G., *An Apostle of the Western Church*. Memoir of the Rt. Rev. Jackson Kemper . . . (New York: Thomas Whitaker, 1911).

Addison, J. T., *The Episcopal Church in the United States 1789-1931* (New York: Scribners, 1951), pp. 140-44.

KEN, THOMAS, March 20.

Anderdon, J. L., *The Life of Thomas Ken, Bishop of Bath and Wells, by a Layman* (London, 1851).

Pumptre, E. H., *Life of Thomas Ken* (rev. ed.; London, 1890), 2 vols.

Bennett, H. L., and Crawford, G. A., in J. Julian, *A Dictionary of Hymnology* (New York: Scribners, 1892), pp. 616-22.

Cropper, M., *Flame Touches Flame* (New York: Longmans, 1949), pp. 182-225.

Overton, J. H., *The Non-Jurors* (London: Smith, 1902).

LATIMER, HUGH, October 16.

Sermons (Parker Society, 1844); *Remains* (Parker Society, 1845), ed. by G. E. Corrie.

Darby, H. S., *Hugh Latimer* (London: Epworth Press, 1953)

Chester, A. G., *Hugh Latimer, Apostle to the English* (Philadelphia: University of Pennsylvania Press, 1954).

Gairdner, James, *The English Church in the Sixteenth Century from the Accession of Henry VIII to the Death of Mary* (London: Macmillan, 1902).

LAUD, WILLIAM, January 10.

Works, in *Library of Anglo-Catholic Theology*.

Hutton, W. H., *William Laud* (London: Methuen, 1895).

Benson, A. C., *William Laud*, Sometime Archbishop of Canterbury, A Study (new ed.; London: Kegan Paul, Trench, Truebner and Co., 1897).

Duncan-Jones, A. S., *Archbishop Laud* (London: Macmillan, no date).

Bourne, E. C. E., *The Anglicanism of William Laud* (London: S.P.C.K., 1947).

Gardiner, S. R., in *Dictionary of National Biography*, XI, 626-35.

LAURENCE, August 10.

Cyprian, *Epistle* lxxx (or lxxxi), trans. in *Ante-Nicene Fathers*, Vol. V, p. 408.

Healy, P. J., T*he Valerian Persecution*: A Study of the Relations between Church and State in the Third Century A.D. (Boston: Houghton Mifflin, 1905).

LAW, WILLIAM, April 6.

A Serious Call to a Devout and Holy Life, with an Introduction by J. V. Moldenhawer (Philadelphia: Westminster Press, 1948). Also in Everyman Library.

Works, ed. by G. H. Morgan (G. Moreton; Privately Printed, 1892-93).

Overton, J. H., *William Law, Nonjuror and Mystic*, A Sketch of his Life, Character, and Opinions (London: Longmans, 1881).

Hopkinson, A. W., *About William Law*, A Running Commentary on his Works, with a Foreword by E. G. Selwyn (London: S.P.C.K., 1948).

Cropper, M., *Sparks among the Stubble* (New York: Longmans, 1955), pp. 60-97.

LEO THE GREAT, April 11.

Works, translated in *Nicene and Post-Nicene Fathers*, Second Series, Vol. XII; the *Tome*, in Vol. XIV, pp. 254-58.

Gore, C., in *Dictionary of Christian Biography*, III, 652-73.

Jalland, Trevor, *The Life and Times of St. Leo the Great* (London: S.P.C.K., 1941). Full bibliography.

Sellers, R. V., *The Council of Chalcedon*, A Historical and Doctrinal Survey (London: S.P.C.K., 1953).

Duchesne, Louis, *Early History of the Christian Church*, Vol. III (London: John Murray, 1924), Chapters XI, XV.

LOUIS, August 25.

St. Louis of France, trans. and ed. by R. Hague (The Makers of Christendom Series; New York: Sheed and Ward, 1955).

Perry, F., *Saint Louis, the Most Christian King* (New York: G. P. Putnam's, 1901).

Runciman, S., *A History of the Crusades*, Vol. III (Cambridge, 1954), pp. 255-92.

Munro, D. C., and Sellery, G. C., *Medieval Civilization* (New York: Century, 1904), pp. 491-523 (trans. from Langlois in Lavisse, *Histoire de France*, III).

LUKE, SAINT, the Evangelist, October 18.
MARGARET, November 16.

> Anderson, A. O., *Early Sources of Scottish History A.D. 500 to 1286* (Edinburgh: Oliver and Boyd, 1922), II, ,1-88.
>
> Dowden, John, *The Celtic Church in Scotland* (London: S.P.C.K., 1894).
>
> Barnett, T. R., *Margaret of Scotland, Queen and Saint*, Her Influence on the Early Church of Scotland (Edinburgh: Oliver and Boyd, 1926).
>
> Menzies, Lucy, *St. Margaret, Queen of Scotland* (London: Dent, 1925).

MARK, SAINT, the Evangelist, April 25.
MARTIN, November 11.

> Sulpicius Severus, "The Life of St. Martin of Tours," *The Western Fathers*, trans. and ed. by F. R. Hoare (New York: Sheed and Ward, 1954), pp. 1-60.
>
> Holmes, T. S., *The Origin and Development of the Christian Church in Gaul during the First Six Centuries of the Christian Era* (Birkbeck Lectures, 1907-08; London: Macmillan, 1911).
>
> Cazenove, J. G., in *Dictionary of Christian Biography*, III, 838-45.

MARTYRS OF LYONS, THE, June 2.

> Eusebius, *Ecclesiastical History*, Book V, c. 1-4.
>
> Workman, H. B., *Persecution in the Early Church*, A Chapter in the History of Renunciation (2d ed.; Cincinnati: Jennings and Graham, 1906).
>
> Canfield, L. H., *The Early Persecutions of the Christians* (New York: Longmans, 1913).
>
> Holmes, T. S., *The Origin and Development of the Christian Church in Gaul during the First Six Centuries of the Christian Era* (Birkbeck Lectures, 1907-08; London: Macmillan, 1911).

MARY, SAINT, Mother of our Lord Jesus Christ, August 15.
MARY MAGDALENE, SAINT, July 22.
MATTHEW, SAINT, Apostle and Evangelist, September 21.
MATTHIAS, SAINT, the Apostle, February 24.
MAURICE, JOHN FREDERICK DENISON, April 1.

> Maurice, F., *The Life of Frederick Denison Maurice*, Chiefly Told in His Own Letters (New York: Scribners, 1884), 2 vols.
>
> Reckitt, M. B., *Maurice to Temple*, A Century of the Social Movement in the Church of England (Scott Holland Memorial Lectures, 1946; London: Faber and Faber, 1947).

Vidler, A. R., *Witness to the Light*, F. D. Maurice's Message for To-day (Hale Lectures; New York: Scribners, 1948).

Wood, H. G., *Frederick Denison Maurice* (Cambridge, 1950).

METHODIUS, May 11.

For Bibliography, see under CYRIL AND METHODIUS.

MICHAEL, SAINT, AND ALL ANGELS, September 29.
MONNICA, May 4.

St. Augustine, *Confessions*.

Simpson, W. J. Sparrow, *St. Augustine's Conversion*, An Outline of His Development to the Time of His Ordination (New York: Macmillan, 1930).

O'Meara, John J., *The Young Augustine*, The Growth of St. Augustine's Mind up to His Conversion (New York: Longmans, 1954).

MUHLENBERG, WILLIAM AUGUSTUS, April 8.

Ayres, Anne, *The Life and Work of William Augustus Muhlenberg* (New York: Harpers, 1881).

——— (ed.), *Evangelical Catholic Papers*, A Collection of Essays, Letters, and Tractates from Writings of Rev. William Augustus Muhlenberg (New York: Thomas Whitaker, 1875).

Potter, Alonzo, *Memorial Papers* . . . (Philadelphia: Butler, 1857).

Wallace, P. A. W., *The Muhlenbergs of Pennsylvania* (Philadelphia: University of Pennsylvania Press, 1950).

Chorley, E. C., *Men and Movements in the American Episcopal Church* (Hale Lectures; New York: Scribners, 1946).

NATIVITY OF OUR LORD JESUS CHRIST, THE, December 25.
NATIVITY OF SAINT JOHN BAPTIST, THE, June 24.
NICHOLAS, December 6.

Stokes, G. T., in *Dictionary of Christian Biography*, IV, 41-42.

M. Ott, in *The Catholic Encyclopedia*, XI, 63-64.

PATRICK, March 17.

The Works of St. Patrick . . . trans. and annotated by L. Bieler (Ancient Christian Writers, No. 17; Westminster, Md.: Newman Press, 1953).

Bury, J. B., *The Life of St. Patrick and his Place in History* (London: Macmillan, 1905).

MacNeill, Eoin, *St. Patrick, Apostle of Ireland* (London: Sheed and Ward, 1934).

Bieler, L., *The Life and Legend of St. Patrick*, Problems of Modern Scholarship (Dublin: Clonmore and Reynolds, 1949).

Pochin Mould, D. D. C., *Ireland of the Saints* (London: Batsford, 1953).

PATTESON, JOHN COLERIDGE, September 20.

Yonge, C. M., *Life of John Coleridge Patteson*, Missionary Bishop of the Melanesian Islands (London: Macmillan, 1888).

Paton, F. H. L., *Patteson of Melanesia*, A Brief Life . . . (London: S.P.C.K., 1930).

Montgomery, H. H., *The Light of Melanesia*, A Record of Fifty Years' Mission Work in the South Seas, written after a Personal Visitation (London: S.P.C.K., 1896).

Armstrong, E. S., *The History of the Melanesian Mission* (New York: Dutton, 1900).

PAUL, SAINT, the Apostle (with Saint Peter), June 29.
PAUL, THE CONVERSION OF SAINT, the Apostle, January 25.
PERPETUA AND HER COMPANIONS, March 7.

"The Passion of the Holy Martyrs Perpetua and Felicitas," *Ante-Nicene Fathers*, Vol. III, pp. 699-706.

Workman, H. B., *Persecution in the Early Church*, A Chapter in the History of Renunciation (2d ed.; Cincinnati: Jennings and Graham, 1906).

Donaldson, S. A., *Church Life and Thought in North Africa A.D. 200* (Cambridge, 1909).

Frend, W. H. C., *The Donatist Church*, A Movement of Protest in Roman North Africa (Oxford, 1952), Chapter IX.

PETER AND PAUL, SAINTS, Apostles, June 29.

Cullmann, O., *Peter, Disciple, Apostle, Martyr*, trans. by F. V. Filson (Philadelphia: Westminster Press, 1953).

Toynbee, J., and Perkins, J. W., *The Shrine of St. Peter and the Vatican Excavations* (New York: Longmans, 1956).

PHILIP, SAINT, the Apostle (with James), May 1.
POLYCARP, January 26.

Letter to the Philippians, and Martyrdom, trans. in all collections of the Apostolic Fathers. See also, with full bibliography: Richardson, C. C., *Early*

Christian Fathers (The Library of Christian Classics, Vol. I; Philadelphia: Westminster Press, 1953), pp. 121-58.

Lightfoot, J. B., *The Apostolic Fathers*, Part II: *St. Ignatius, St. Polycarp* (rev. ed.; London: Macmillan, 1890).

Harrison, P. N., *Polycarp's Two Epistles to the Philippians* (Cambridge, 1936).

Cadoux, C. J., *Ancient Smyrna*, A History of the City from the Earliest Times to 324 A.D. (Oxford: Blackwell, 1938), pp. 303-67.

PRESENTATION OF CHRIST IN THE TEMPLE, THE, February 2.
PURIFICATION OF SAINT MARY THE VIRGIN, THE, February 2.
RIDLEY, NICHOLAS, October 16.

Works (Parker Society, 1841); ed. by H. Christmas.

A Brief Declaration of the Lord's Supper (with a memoir by Bishop Moule, Parker Society, 1895).

Ridley, G., *Life of Bishop Ridley* (London, 1763).

Gairdner, James, *The English Church in the Sixteenth Century from the Accession of Henry VIII to the Death of Mary* (London: Macmillan, 1902).

SCHERESCHEWSKY, SAMUEL ISAAC JOSEPH, October 15.

Muller, J. A., *Apostle of China*, Samuel Isaac Joseph Schereschewsky, 1831-1906 (New York: Morehouse, 1937).

SEABURY, CONSECRATION OF SAMUEL, November 14.

Historical Magazine of the Protestant Episcopal Church, Vol. III, September, 1934. Bishop Seabury Sesqui-Centennial Number.

Beardsley, E. E., *Life and Correspondence of the Right Reverend Samuel Seabury, D.D.* . . . (Boston: Houghton Mifflin, 1881).

Manross, W. W., *A History of the American Episcopal Church* (2d ed.; New York: Morehouse-Gorham, 1950), Chapters IX-X.

SELWYN, GEORGE AUGUSTUS, April 12.

Tucker, H. W., *Memoir of the Life and Episcopate of George Augustus Selwyn* (London: W. W. Gardner, 1877), 2 vols.

Curteis, G. H., *Bishop Selwyn of New Zealand and of Lichfield* (London: Kegan Paul, Trench and Co., 1889).

Creighton, Louise, *G. A. Selwyn, D.D., Bishop of New Zealand and Lichfield* (London: Longmans, 1923).

SERGIUS, September 25.

Zernov, N., *St. Sergius, Builder of Russia*. Translated by Adeline Delafeld (London: S.P.C.K., 1939).

―――, *The Russians and Their Church* (London: S.P.C.K., 1945). pp. 38-43.

SIMEON, CHARLES, November 12.

Moule, H. C. G., *Charles Simeon* (London: Methuen, 1892).

Smyth, Charles, *Simeon and Church Order*, A Study of the Origins of the Evangelical Revival in Cambridge in the Eighteenth Century (Birkbeck Lectures for 1937-38; Cambridge, 1940).

Overton, J. H., *The English Church in the Nineteenth Century (1800-1833)* (London: Longmans, 1894), Chapter III.

Elliott-Binns, L. E., *The Early Evangelicals*, A Religious and Social Study (London: Lutterworth Press, 1953).

SIMON, SAINT, the Apostle, October 28.
STEPHEN, SAINT, DEACON AND MARTYR, December 26.
TAYLOR, JEREMY, August 14.

Works, in *Library of Anglo-Catholic Theology*. Many editions of *Holy Living and Holy Dying*. Especially edition of works by R. Heber, rev. by C. P. Eden (London, 1847-54).

Gosse, E., *Jeremy Taylor* ("English Men of Letters" : New York: Macmillan, 1904).

Stranks, C. J., *The Life and Writings of Jeremy Taylor* (London: S.P.C.K., 1952).

Cropper, M., *Flame Touches Flame* (New York: Longmans, 1949), pp. 103-54.

Tulloch, John, *Rational Theology and Christian Philosophy in England in the Seventeenth Century* (Edinburgh: Blackwood, 1872), Vol. I, pp. 344-410.

Williamson, H. R., *Jeremy Taylor* (London: Dennis Dobson, 1952).

THEODORE OF TARSUS, September 19.

Bede, *Ecclesiastical History*, Book IV.

Browne, G. F., *Theodore and Wilfrith* (London: S.P.C.K., 1897).

Howorth, H. H., *The Golden Days of the Early English Church* (London: John Murray, 1917), 3 vols.

Reany, W., *St. Theodore of Canterbury* (St. Louis: Herder, 1944).

Duckett, E. S., *Anglo-Saxon Saints and Scholars* (New York: Macmillan, 1947).

THOMAS, SAINT, the Apostle, December 21.
THOMAS A KEMPIS, July 26.

> *The Imitation of Christ.* Many editions; especially, ed. with an introduction by E. J. Klein (New York: Harpers, 1941). Also in Everyman Library.
>
> Hyma, A., *The Brethren of the Common Life* (Grand Rapids: Eerdmans, 1950).
>
> Sperry, W. L., *Strangers and Pilgrims* (Boston: Little, Brown and Co., 1939), pp. 61-85.
>
> Jones, Rufus M., *Studies in Mystical Religion* (London: Macmillan, 1909), pp. 298-332.

THOMAS AQUINAS, March 8.

> Pegis, A. C. (ed.), *The Basic Writings of Thomas Aquinas* (New York: Random House, 1945); also Selected Writings, ed. M. C. D'Arcy, in Everyman Library.
>
> Grabmann, M., *Thomas Aquinas, His Personality and Thought*, trans. by V. Michel (New York: Longmans, 1928).
>
> Vann, G., *Saint Thomas Aquinas* (London: Hague and Gill, 1940).
>
> D'Arcy, M. C., *Thomas Aquinas* (Westminster, Md.: Newman Press, 1944).

TIMOTHY, SAINT, January 24.
TITUS, SAINT, February 6.
TRANSFIGURATION OF OUR LORD JESUS CHRIST, THE, August 6.
TYNDALE, WILLIAM, October 6.

> *Works* (Parker Society, 1848).
>
> Mozley, J. F., *William Tyndale* (New York: Macmillan, 1937).
>
> Smith, H. M., *Henry VIII and the Reformation* (London: Macmillan, 1948), pp. 276-321.
>
> Pollard, A. W., *Records of the English Bible* (London: Frowde, 1911).

VINCENT, January 22.

> Mershman, F., in *Catholic Encyclopedia*, XV, 434.
>
> Mason, A. J., *The Persecution of Diocletian* (Cambridge: Deighton Bell and Co., 1876).

VISITATION OF THE BLESSED VIRGIN MARY, THE, July 2.
WHITE, WILLIAM, July 17.

> White, W., *Memoirs of the Protestant Episcopal Church* . . (New York: Dutton, 1880).

Wilson, Bird, *Memoir of the Life of the Rt. Rev. William White* (Philadelphia, 1839).

Stowe, W. H. (ed.), *The Life and Letters of Bishop William White* (Church Historical Society Publication, No. 9; New York: Morehouse, 1937).

Temple, S. A., *The Common Sense Theology of Bishop White* (New York: King's Crown Press, 1946).

WILBERFORCE, WILLIAM, July 29.

Stephen, L., in *Dictionary of National Biography*, XXI, 208-17.

Cropper, M., *Sparks among the Stubble* (New York: Longmans, 1955), pp. 181-221.

Coupland, R., *Wilberforce* (Oxford, 1923).

Howse, E. M., *Saints in Politics*, The "Clapham Sect" and the Growth of Freedom (University of Toronto Press, 1952). Full bibliography.

Buxton, T., *William Wilberforce, The Story of a Great Crusade* (London, 1904).

WILLIAMS, CHANNING MOORE, December 2.

Tucker, H. St.G., *The History of the Episcopal Church in Japan* (New York: Scribners, 1938).

Cary, Otis, *A History of Christianity in Japan: Protestant Missions* (New York: Fleming H. Revell Co., 1909), Chapter IV.

WILLIBRORD, November 7.

Alcuin, "The Life of St. Willibrord," *The Anglo-Saxon Missionaries in Germany*, trans. and ed. by C. H. Talbot (New York: Sheed and Ward, 1954), pp. 1-22. Also trans. by A. Grieve (London: S.P.C.K., 1923).

Crawford, S. J., *Anglo-Saxon Influence on Western Christendom 600-800* (Oxford, 1933).

Levison, W., *England and the Continent in the Eighth Century* (Ford Lectures, 1943; Oxford, 1946), Chapter III.

www.ingramcontent.com/pod-product-compliance
Lightning Source LLC
Chambersburg PA
CBHW061345300426
44116CB00011B/2001